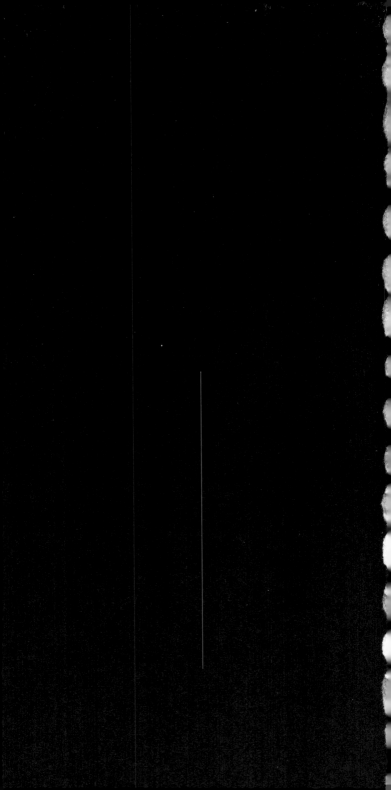

Taylor's Guides to Gardening

Roger Holmes and
Rita Buchanan, Editors

Frances Tenenbaum, Series Editor

HOUGHTON MIFFLIN COMPANY
Boston · New York · London 1992

Taylor's Guide to Gardening in the Southwest

Copyright © 1992 by Houghton Mifflin Company

For information about permission to reproduce selections from
this book, write to Permissions, Houghton Mifflin Company,
215 Park Avenue South, New York, New York 10003.

Based on *Taylor's Encyclopedia of Gardening,* Fourth Edition,
copyright © 1961. *Taylor's Guide* is a registered trademark
of Houghton Mifflin Company.

Library of Congress Cataloging-in-Publication Data

Taylor's guide to gardening in the Southwest / Roger Holmes, editor.
    p.   cm. — (Taylor's guides to gardening)
  "Based on Taylor's encyclopedia of gardening, fourth edition,
  copyright 1961" — T.p. verso.
  Includes index.
  ISBN 0-395-59680-7
  1. Landscape gardening — Southwest, New. 2. Plants, Ornamental —
Southwest, New. I. Holmes, Roger. II. Taylor's encyclopedia of
gardening. III. Series.
SB473.T39 1992 91-32310
712'.6'0979 — dc20   CIP

Printed in Japan

DNP 10 9 8 7 6 5 4 3 2 1

Drawings by Steve Buchanan

Contents

Contributors

Rita Buchanan, a general editor for this book, was trained in both botany and horticulture. She has worked and gardened in Texas, Colorado, Virginia, Connecticut, England, and Costa Rica. A founding editor of *Fine Gardening* magazine, she now writes and edits for *The Herb Companion* and other publications. She especially enjoys growing herbs and other fragrant plants and flowers for cutting.

Roger Holmes, a general editor for this book, was the founding editor of *Fine Gardening* magazine and editorial consultant for *Taylor's Guide to Gardening Techniques*. Trained as a cabinetmaker in England, Holmes builds furniture in addition to working as a freelance writer and editor. He gardens for pleasure at his home in Woodbury, Connecticut.

Steve Buchanan, the illustrator of this book, specializes in natural history subjects, doing black-and-white drawings and color paintings of plants, gardens, birds, insects, and outdoor scenes. His work has appeared in *Horticulture, Garden Design, Fine Gardening, Scientific American, Organic Gardening,* the *New York Times, The Herb Companion,* and several books.

Kevin Connelly, author of the essay on native plants, received a master's degree in psychology but decided to become a professional landscape gardener in the mid-1970s. A specialist in California native plants and drought-tolerant gardens, he has established wildflower plantings for private and public gardens, including the Theodore Payne Foundation in Sun Valley, Earthside Nature in Pasadena, and the El Alisal Garden at the Lummis Home Historical Monument in Los Angeles. Kevin is a regular contributor to the *Los Angeles Times* and *Pacific Horticulture* and is the author of a book on the wildflowers of southern California. He lives in Arcadia, California.

John R. (Dick) Dunmire, author of the essay on lawns, was a senior editor in the gardening department of *Sunset* magazine at his retirement in 1990. During his twenty-seven years with

Sunset, Dunmire edited three editions of the *Western Garden Book.* Prior to joining *Sunset* he taught English literature and composition at the University of Kansas, then worked for a California nursery. Dunmire, who lives in Los Altos and Inverness, California, was founding director and twice president of the Western Horticultural Society. He is a past president of the California Horticultural Society and a board member of several other horticultural organizations in the region.

Eric Johnson, author of the essay "Old Standbys and Regional Favorites," has been active in Southwestern horticulture for more than fifty years. A 1935 graduate of the University of California at Davis in horticulture and landscape design, Johnson has worked for nurseries, operated his own landscaping company, conducted research, and been involved in numerous landscape design projects. He is a former editor of *Sunset* and has written several books.

Mike MacCaskey, author of the essay on garden design, is the Southern California garden editor for *Sunset.* A 1976 graduate of California Polytechnic with a degree in ornamental horticulture, MacCaskey has worked as a landscape designer and contractor and has written several books. He is an avid grower of roses and exotic fruits at his Burbank home.

Scott Millard, author of the essay on the gardening year, has been involved in regional gardening as an editor, author, and photographer since the late 1970s. Raised on a Missouri farm, Millard has lived and gardened in California and the Southwest for thirty years and is now experimenting with low-water-use plants at his home in Tucson. He recently started his own publishing company, Ironwood Press, specializing in gardening books for the arid west.

Joseph F. Williamson, author of the book's introductory essay, retired in 1990 after forty-two years at *Sunset.* During that time he did just about everything at the magazine, including stints as garden editor and managing editor. He was editorial director of the *Western Garden Book* from 1967 to 1990. Williamson continues to write about gardening and horticulture and is currently president of the board of the Pacific Horticulture Foundation.

Preface

Gardening in Southern California and the Southwest can be wonderfully rewarding. The region's long gardening history provides ample inspiration, and its varied climates and terrain supply a wealth of opportunities. Spared the frigid winters of more northerly states, gardeners in most of the region can enjoy their favorite pastime year-round.

The range of plants that can be grown in the region is breathtaking. Some come from the far corners of the world, ranging from towering Australian eucalyptus trees to diminutive South African gladioluses, their finely wrought flowers blazing with intense color. Others — the giant saguaro cactus, the cheerful California poppy — were known to Native Americans centuries before the arrival of the missionaries and conquistadors. In the mountains, gardeners grow plants, such as creeping juniper, that can survive bitter cold and wind. On the coast, striking tropical species like bougainvillea thrive. Desert gardeners delight in nature's adaptations to searing heat and scant water, as in the ocotillo, whose showy clusters of red flowers burst from seemingly barren stems after a summer rain.

This is a land of immigrants, and each wave of newcomers has contributed distinctive landscaping styles and gardening expertise as well as favorite plants. Today the region's gardeners can draw on the traditions of eighteenth-century Spanish missionaries and twentieth-century English cottage gardeners, pre-Columbian Indians and recent Asian immigrants, to name just a few.

All of these wonderful possibilities are tempered by the conditions set by nature. Gardeners on the coast must contend with fog and salt air. The region's alkaline soils are inhospitable to many introduced plants, as is the intense heat of a desert summer.

But of all the natural challenges faced by Southwestern gardeners, none is more insistent than that posed by water. This is an arid region; without a dependable supply of water neither the courtyard gardens of the Spanish missions or the backyard borders of the modern suburbs would have been possible.

For most of this century, the gardener's solution to the water problem was as close to hand as the garden hose. Water from wells, rivers or reservoirs, some located hundreds of miles away, was cheap and abundant. In recent years, however, the hose has threatened to run dry, and gardeners have begun to explore ways of growing plants without large quantities of imported water. These gardens, although not abundantly leafy, turfy, or dense, can be just as interesting and rewarding as traditional gardens.

What plants to grow, how to design and cultivate your garden, and what to do about water — these and other topics of concern to gardeners in the Southwest are discussed in the pages that follow. Whether you are a longtime regional resident and gardener or a newcomer, we hope this guide will help you enjoy the many pleasures of gardening in Southern California and the Southwest.

How to
Use This Guide

For a lifetime of interest and satisfaction, gardening asks very little of us — a few seeds, a bit of earth and some patience. Yet, as with many seemingly simple things, there is a great deal to learn about gardening, more than any shelf of books can contain. We hope the information, observations, and encouragement in this book will help beginners make a good start and enhance the pleasures of gardening for those with more experience.

Why a Regional Guide?

Ours is a vast country, and in recent years gardeners have come to appreciate the limitations of books that purport to address every gardener everywhere. It is the premise of this book that gardeners in Southern California, Arizona, New Mexico, and west Texas have much more in common with each other than they do with those in Connecticut, Iowa, or England.

There are, to be sure, significant differences within the region itself. Some are as obvious as the contrast between a mild summer's day in San Diego and a scorcher in Lubbock. Others, having to do with soil type, seasonal winds, or rainfall, are less obvious but are of great importance to gardeners. Regional differences as well as similarities are pointed out throughout the book. Knowing how your garden site relates to others in the region will help you select plants wisely and grow them well.

How This Guide Is Organized

This book is divided into three main parts. The six introductory essays discuss important aspects of gardening in the

Southwest. In the second part, a number of the region's best garden and landscape plants are highlighted in a section of color plates. The third part, the encyclopedia, describes the plants shown in the plates and gives information on their uses and cultivation.

The Essays

The introduction presents an overview of the region, its climates and terrain, water problems and solutions, and some of its distinctive plants. The essay "Old Standbys and Regional Favorites" highlights those plants that have been the mainstays of gardeners from the early mission period to today. "Native Plants" introduces the region's indigenous species, plants increasingly sought for gardens because they are adapted to local conditions and evoke the natural landscape.

Recent droughts have prompted many homeowners to reconsider their attachment to a water-guzzling greensward. The essay on lawns explores a full range of options. "Designing Your Garden" covers plants, lawns, and garden structures in light of family needs. You will learn what factors to consider as well as how to incorporate the features you want into a handsome, functional landscape. The final essay walks you through a Southwestern gardening year, identifying what needs to be done in each season.

The Plants

There are many, many excellent plants for the region's gardens. We have selected some 275 of the best, emphasizing those that are likely to be readily available from major local nurseries or established mail-order suppliers. Whenever possible, we have chosen plants with more than one noteworthy characteristic (attractive foliage as well as flowers, for example) and those that contribute something to the garden in more than one season (such as flowers in summer, foliage in fall). We looked for plants that require little maintenance, tolerate heat and drought, resist fungus diseases, and are relatively free of insect problems. Finally, we tried to select plants that can be grown in a large part of the region.

Color plates

It's difficult to choose plants if you don't know what they look like. The color plates will give you a good idea of a plant's foliage, flowers, and, in some cases, its growth habit. The plates are arranged by plant type: trees, shrubs, perennials, ground covers, and vines. A short description accompanies each plate, including the plant's botanical and common names, its height or spread, the time of bloom (if appropriate), a comment on its uses or culture, its hardiness zone rating, and the page on which you'll find its encyclopedia entry.

The plant encyclopedia

If you're captivated by the color plate of a plant that is new to you or need some basic information on a familiar plant, you will find it in this section. The encyclopedia contains descriptions of each plant shown in the plates as well as a number of additional cultivars or related species. The entries are arranged alphabetically by genus. (If you don't know the botanical name, consult the index, where botanical and common names are cross-referenced.)

The encyclopedia entries. Under each genus, you'll find a general description of the plants within the genus and comments on how to grow them. Selected species and cultivars are then listed, with descriptions of foliage and flowers, landscape and garden uses and, in some cases, additional information on growing the plant. Rounding out the species descriptions are the plant's place of origin and its hardiness zone rating. (Many species entries are accompanied by a sketch highlighting a noteworthy characteristic.)

Zones. Plants vary considerably in their ability to withstand cold temperatures. Those native to high-elevation northern regions, for instance, can survive bitter cold, many degrees below zero, while some tropical plants may die when touched by the slightest frost.

In the early years of this century, horticulturists began to correlate the cold-hardiness of plants with gradients of temperature as plotted on a map. The zone map on pp. xiv–xv is based on the U.S. Department of Agriculture's recently revised map, representing the ten temperature zones of North America. The zone rating given for each plant indicates the lowest temperatures at which the plant can usually be expected to survive. A plant rated zone 5, for instance, should survive minimum temperatures between -10 and -20 degrees Fahrenheit. If you live in zone 5 or higher, cold should not kill that plant in your garden.

When selecting plants, remember that zone ratings indicate cold-hardiness *only*. Many other factors — drought, heat, wind, soil alkalinity, to name a few — are at least as important for gardeners in the Southwest. These factors are mentioned in the plant descriptions; if you are in doubt about a plant's suitability for your location, ask a knowledgeable person at a local nursery.

Appendices

Gardeners aren't the only ones who enjoy the plants they grow. A host of creeping, crawling, and flying critters depend on plants for sustenance and shelter. Your garden can live with many of these; some are even beneficial. But on occasion, your needs and those of the wildlife will be at odds. The appendix "Pests and Diseases" gives an overview of insects, other pests, and plant diseases. A chart summarizes the controls that can be used for some of the problems.

The other appendices introduce some of the many excellent resources for gardeners in the region. "Sources of Seeds and Plants" lists a variety of regional suppliers. There is no better way to learn about plants and approaches to landscaping and gardening than to see them in person. The appendix "Public Gardens" lists a selection of noteworthy examples you can visit. For a library of helpful books, see "References."

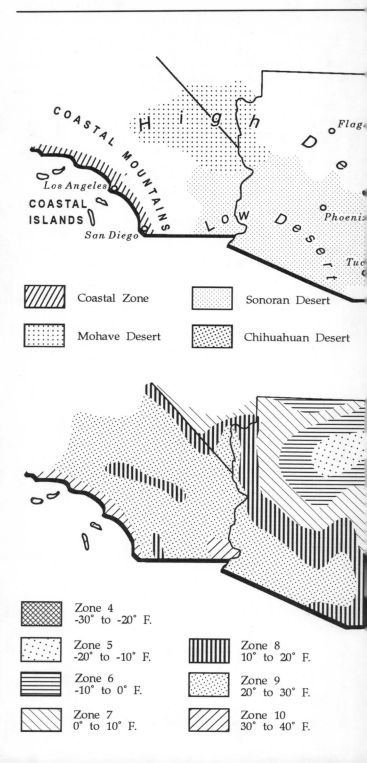

Coastal Zone

Mohave Desert

Sonoran Desert

Chihuahuan Desert

Zone 4
-30° to -20° F.

Zone 5
-20° to -10° F.

Zone 6
-10° to 0° F.

Zone 7
0° to 10° F.

Zone 8
10° to 20° F.

Zone 9
20° to 30° F.

Zone 10
30° to 40° F.

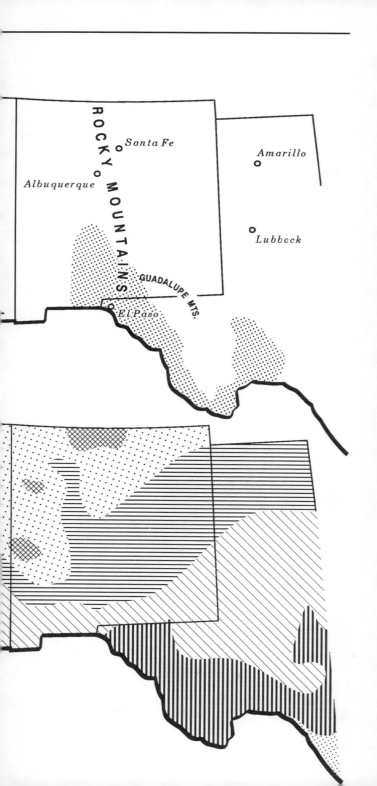

Introduction

Some of the kindest environments in all of North America for gardening are found in our region. Close enough to the equator to avoid fierce snowy winters, we're just far enough away to enjoy some of the seasonal change that supplies the glorious, slow and steady pulse of gardening.

But our geographical good fortune comes with a price, for the Southwestern United States gets less water than other areas of the country. In an average year, we can expect just 3 to 14 inches of rainfall, while the rest of the country typically receives from 15 to 60 inches. The Garden of Eden did not flourish on the kind of rainfall you get from Santa Barbara and San Diego to Lubbock and Laredo.

Between the blessings of magnificent temperatures and the bane of aridity, there is a wide world of gardening in the region. For most of us, it's a world of year-round gardening, where snow shovels, mittens, garden boots, and months of mud are unknown and flowers, vegetables, and fruit can be grown and harvested in every season. Here we'll take a look at this world and the influences on it.

The Climates of the Southwest

The region's terrain and weather create three quite distinct climates — ocean-influenced, desert, and mountain — and a variety of subclimates within them. The climate where you live greatly affects the style of your garden and the kinds of plants you can grow.

Ocean-influenced climates

The lowlands sandwiched between the Pacific beaches and a series of mountain ranges roughly 40 to 70 miles inland make up, with their counterparts in northern California, one of the earth's six "Mediterranean" climate areas. (These mountain ranges, from north to south, include the Tehachapis, San Gabriels, San Bernardinos, San Jacintos, Santa Rosas, and Cuyamacas.) Most of the people in Southern California live in this narrow strip.

Mediterranean climates are lovely for gardening. The winters are not very cold — temperatures seldom drop below 30 degrees, and maybe once or twice a century below 17 degrees. The summers are comparatively cool, but the coolness is in direct proportion to how close a place is to the ocean and to how many hills or mountain ranges stand between it and the ocean. The farther inland you go, the hotter the summers and the cooler the winters. The summers are also very dry, with little or no rainfall between late April and late November. Summer showers are so scarce, coming only once or twice every 2 or 3 years, that they make the local papers and highlight neighborhood conversations.

The many hills, mountains, plains, and river valleys in this area create several distinct subclimates.

The coastal strip. The coastal strip, from Point Conception in Santa Barbara County south to Imperial Beach in San Diego County, is as close as the Western United States gets to tropical. Winter temperatures occasionally drop below freezing, but most of the time they range from the 30s up into the 60s. It is so mild that the most tropical of the lawn grasses — kikuyu grass — runs rampant in places, actually shouldering out Bermuda grass.

Oddly, the mild winters pose the only real gardening problem — some plants don't get enough winter chill. Apples, many of which need to accumulate a certain amount of chill to set fruit, are the most common example. (You can, however, buy low-winter-chill varieties bred for the climate.) The coastal strip is also known for its high morning fogs, notably in May and June. They are both a blessing and a curse for gardeners. They cool the days and lessen the water stress on plants, but make it more difficult to grow plants like tomatoes and melons, which thrive in hotter weather.

You can grow almost anything on the coast, and plants that don't tolerate much heat, cold, or dryness thrive there. Some of the top examples — coastal specialties that no other climate can grow as well — are fuchsias, pride of Madeira (*Echium fastuosum*), the succulent shrub called elephant bush (*Portulacaria afra*), and the big beach impatiens (*Impatiens oliveri*).

Coastal flats and hills. This, the best climate zone in Southern California, includes Beverly Hills, downtown Los Angeles, Corona, Santa Ana, Vista, and Escondido. Hotter in summer and colder in winter than the coastal strip, it still enjoys the mild ocean air. The extra heat makes many garden plants grow stronger, bigger, more floriferous, and more fruitful than those on the coastal strip. The hills are a few degrees warmer in winter than the flats, making them safer for some subtropicals; California's commercial avocado belt is in these hills.

The interior valleys. The next zone inland is the harshest of the Mediterranean climates, hotter in summer and colder in winter than those nearer the ocean. This area includes the San Fernando Valley, Pomona, Ontario, San Bernardino, and Riverside. Here, winter brings frost, with lows in the 20s and occasionally the high teens. Still, winter is mild enough to pose little threat to citrus, the area's grand crop, and the heat of the other seasons makes the fruit tasty and sweet. Many deciduous plants do better here than on the coast, including apple, flowering and fruiting crabapple, crape myrtle, hosta, peegee and oakleaf hydrangeas, lilacs, mayten, pears, peonies, skimmias, spiraea, tulip tree, and walnut.

Desert climates

Beyond the mountains bordering the Mediterranean climate zone come the Southwest's deserts. Although desert rain is scarce throughout the year, ranging from next to nothing to 8 inches, imported water has made the gardens and farms rich and abundant. The deserts are generally cold in winter and hot in summer. Temperatures, however, vary considerably according to the elevation.

Low deserts. For a century, vacationers have flocked to the low desert cities of Palm Springs, Indio, Yuma, Phoenix, Scottsdale, and Tempe to escape cold, damp winters at home. Low deserts (from below sea level to about 1,200 feet) have extremely hot summers and coolish but mild winters. The heat is ideal for the sweetest kinds of citrus and many other heat-loving plants. It is also a splendid climate for roses, and there are many commercial rose growers in the area.

Gardeners new to the low desert soon accustom themselves

to a calendar turned upside down. Fall and winter are very active times, with most of the planting done in September and October. Spring brings harvests and flowers. Summer is so hot that people do their garden chores in the early morning or in the evening and stay inside with air conditioning during the day.

Intermediate and high deserts. High deserts (represented by the communities of Ridgecrest, Mojave, Lancaster, Kingman, Douglas, and Albuquerque) have much colder winters than low deserts. Summers are hot, but not as furnace-hot as in the low deserts. As you'd expect, temperatures in intermediate deserts, like that around Tucson, fall between the other two in both winter and summer.

Tucson, at 2,437 feet, enjoys a considerably balmier climate than many other desert communities at about the same elevation (or even a bit lower). Mild enough for citrus and many other mild-winter specialties, Tucson gets many more frosty nights than do Phoenix and the rest of the low desert, and summers are slightly cooler. As in low desert areas, big, booming thunderstorms occur almost daily in July and August, but they don't put enough water into the ground to reduce the need for irrigation. Most flowers and vegetables are planted in the fall.

The high and intermediate deserts to the west of the Colorado River and Lake Mead are cooler and windier in all seasons than the low desert and the Tucson desert. (Wind is a major part of life in this climate.) Here, you plant in spring for harvest in late spring, summer, and early fall.

The eastern high desert (land at 3,000- to 5,000-foot elevations east of the Colorado River) possesses the most severe of the Southwest desert climates — colder winters, cooler summers, shorter growing seasons. This climate is the last frontier for broadleafed evergreen trees and shrubs.

The mountain climate

Rising above the lowlands and deserts are the mountains and high plateaus, where snow falls and stays on the ground every winter. Such climate zones appear from the Tehachapis and San Gabriels of Southern California to the Guadalupe Mountains in Texas — with dozens of snowy-winter ranges and plateaus in between.

Gardening life here is very different from that below 5,000 feet, for these climates lack the continuity of other Western climates. Everything stops when winter comes. Then, 4 to 6 months later, gardeners work quickly to crowd in what vegetable and flower growth they can between frosts. The number of frost-free days is crucial for mountain gardeners; they know the number of days as well as their social security card numbers. The number of frost-free days varies mostly by elevation: in general, the higher the elevation the fewer the days.

Gardeners in these climates have one seldom-recognized advantage over those in the lowlands. Because they share the same growing season and thus grow the same plants as Easterners, they can use the many "national" garden books that are published in the East. Viburnum, lilacs, phlox, and showplace bluegrass lawns — all grown in the East — also flourish in the Southwest's snowy-winter climates and essentially nowhere else in the region.

Water and the Settlement of the Southwest

Water is probably the single most important factor affecting gardening in the region. In fact, it can be said that water has been one of the most important factors affecting the region's life in general. Where there was water, or where water could be supplied, people settled.

The early Spanish settlers in the Southwest were accustomed to drought and understood the need to conserve water. (If all your water had to be carried from a nearby stream, well, or spring, you'd use it sparingly.) The Spanish also knew how to bring water from the mountains or streams to the fields through irrigation ditches. They also observed the careful water husbandry of the Native Americans in parts of Arizona and New Mexico.

The mission and hacienda gardens of the 18th and 19th centuries resembled the utilitarian gardens of Spain, with citrus, grapes, and olives prominent in the landscape. A well or fountain in a courtyard or patio was a social center as well as a source of water. The few ornamental plants were familiar ones from the Mediterranean, chiefly oleanders and roses.

Around the middle of the last century, immigration from the Eastern United States and from the rest of the world increased. At first the effect on the water supply was not severe. The transplanted Easterners used their technical ability to collect and move water with dams, aqueducts, and pumps. The resulting year-round supply of water, coupled with the favorable climate, created an agricultural system of unparalleled efficiency — and unparalleled thirst.

The urban population in the Southwest began to increase rapidly around 1900 (and hasn't stopped yet). Here, the cities have grown out rather than up (as in the East), with each family occupying a house and lot of its own. Wealthier newcomers built estates based on those of the East or England, with extensive lawns, shrubbery, and flower beds, and the less wealthy emulated them. As a result, vast suburbs spread from horizon to horizon, each household with thirsty shrubs, trees, flowers, and lawn.

To meet the growing demand for water from residential, agricultural, and industrial users, water districts reached farther and farther, sometimes tapping streams and watersheds hundreds of miles away. The supply was abundant and inexpensive, and many people believed it would always be that way.

The 1980s, however, brought a series of dry years, and millions suffered the personal inconvenience of water rationing. People downstream from dams discovered that their dwindling supplies were also increasingly polluted, while upstream users began to demand a larger share of the water from their mountains and forests. Shaken from their complacency, people began to get serious about water conservation.

Gardens for the Water-Conscious Southwest

Spurred by the need to conserve water and inspired by the beauty of the native plants and terrain, many gardeners and landscapers today have rethought their approach to gardening. They're rediscovering old methods and trying new designs, plants, and irrigation techniques as they make gardens that truly work with — and speak for — Southwestern climates.

Most of what you see along suburban streets in the Southwest represents an approach to gardening borrowed from other places and times. A big front lawn displaying three birch trees in a broad area of mowed grass, for instance, copies a scene from somewhere in the Eastern United States or northern Europe. Every wave of newcomers brought similar cherished plants and visions of their old landscape, many completely unsuited for our arid conditions.

There's nothing wrong with nostalgia or borrowing, of course. But it makes more sense to emulate the gardens of Spain and Italy, which share our climates, than those of the East, the British Isles, or northern Europe, which don't. A visit to the carefully reconstructed gardens around the old missions, haciendas, and other 18th- and 19th-century sites will show you how gardeners used to landscape in harmony with our climate and terrain.

Today's gardeners are increasingly using ground covers and various types of paving in place of lawns. They select trees to create shade and summertime coolness, and perhaps to cool the houses by shading the roofs. They construct water-graded zones so that plants needing more water can be irrigated without wasting any on drought-tolerant plants. Walls 4 to 6 feet high create outdoor rooms and cut down on the evaporation caused by wind.

Getting water to the garden

Thoughtful gardeners have also begun to realize that some of the watering methods they've taken for granted are downright prodigal. Topping the wasteful list — the least efficient way of watering — is running a sprinkler system or a hose-end sprinkler in broad daylight. In second place is flooding. Both lose great quantities of water to nature's main evaporators, wind and sun, and deliver water to soil where no cultivated plants grow. Sprinkling at night (by installing a clock or timer to turn the valves on at 3 or 4 A.M.) cuts down on evaporation but still puts water into ground that contains no roots.

In the 1970s a new watering device — drip irrigation — came to the rescue of the concerned Southwestern gardener. Introduced in Israel to water row crops, drip systems use flexible plastic hoses fitted with low-pressure emitters to deliver water only where it is wanted. Gradually, landscape architects and inventive home gardeners have shown that drip irrigation can also do a beautiful job of sustaining a mixed landscape of flowers, shrubs, trees, vines, and what-have-you while substantially lowering water use.

Plant selection

Gardeners have also reconsidered the kinds of plants they grow. Some display a few favorites from rainy climates but plant the great bulk of the landscape with plants that come from arid climates. (See "Native Plants" and "Old Standbys and Regional Favorites" for more on these plants.) Many people have gone further, planting only native or drought-resistant shrubs and trees, perennials, and annuals, which result in extremely attractive gardens.

A small group of much-cherished, water-loving plants will probably continue as part of the Southwestern gardener's palette. Like temperamental but charming guests, they demand special treatment but have become an emotionally significant part of our lives. In the garden, they express the concept of oasis, supplying beauty and lushness while withstanding our heat, aridity, and wind. Among these plants are artichokes, avocados, azaleas, bamboos, bougainvilleas, camellias, citrus, clivia, fatshedera, ferns, kniphofia, ophiopogon, and philodendrons.

Trees and shrubs. Interestingly, the Southwest was mostly treeless to begin with. Only in the highest elevations and in the live oak regions of Southern California's lowlands did developers move into forests to build streets and houses. Elsewhere, new houses generally stood on bare lots, so most of the trees and shrubs you see today were planted — even in the oldest neighborhoods.

The landscaping emblem or symbol of the highly populated, nonmountainous areas of the Southwest could well be the broadleafed evergreens. Retaining their leaves and color throughout the winter, these trees and shrubs provide lush greenery in the Southwest at a time when much of the country must shake the snow off needle-leaved conifers to see some green. Many of the most beloved plants in the West — palms, eucalyptus, camellias, citrus — are broadleafed evergreens.

Western gardeners also value coniferous and deciduous trees and shrubs. Two favorites in Western landscaping are the redwood, originally from the world-famous groves in northern California and southern Oregon, and a huge, graceful tree called the deodar cedar. Each has a distinct, beautiful form and needs a lot of space. The redwood takes well only to the areas of Southern California that aren't desert, but the deodar grows just about everywhere.

The mild conditions that favor broadleafed evergreens also allow many deciduous plants to flourish. A list of the Southwest's favorite deciduous trees, shrubs, and vines would include figs (both edible and ornamental), fuchsia, ginkgo (especially in Southern California, where it's one of the few deciduous trees with colorful autumn foliage), grape, jacaranda (with beautiful flowers), persimmon (with spectacular fruit), and wisteria.

Roses. No plant in the region is more popular than roses, which grow and bloom exceedingly well here. (Most of the roses sold in the United States are grown in Texas, Arizona, and California.) The mounding, hard pruning, and other efforts required in some parts of the country to get many forms of roses through cold winters are unnecessary in many parts of the Southwest. In return for regular feeding and watering, gardeners in low elevations can expect at least three periods of bloom from hybrid teas — one in May and June, another in July and August, and a third in September and October.

Furthermore, the rose has become especially valuable to water-conscious gardeners. Most roses are only moderately thirsty, and certain kinds, notably the old-fashioned roses, seem to get along on very little irrigation or (in some climates) none at all.

The Soils of the Southwest

Everywhere, it seems, gardeners claim that they have the worst possible soil or the hardest possible soil to work with. It's the nature of this wonderful material to challenge the person who cultivates it, conditions it, digs planting holes in it, waters it, and tries to bring plants to maturity in it.

Something is always happening in the soil. We soon learn how to handle the routine events: when it gets too dry, we water it; when it gets too wet, we leave it alone until the atmosphere dries it out; when it gets too weedy, we cultivate it.

Soils in the Southwest pose some special challenges that require a little more knowledge and usually some additional action on the part of the gardener. Following is a small cyclopedia of the Southwest's troublesome or worrisome soil conditions and what you can do about them.

Alkalinity

One of the most important measurements of a soil is its pH, which indicates its place on the acidity-alkalinity scale. A pH below 7 means that a soil is acid; one greater than 7 means that it is alkaline; and 7 itself is neutral. In rainy parts of the country, acid soils are commonplace — the rule, in fact. In our arid region, almost all soils are alkaline. This means, chiefly, that you can't easily grow acid-loving plants such as rhododendrons, azaleas, and camellias.

If your heart is set on these plants, you need to provide acidic soil. You can fill containers with a commercially prepared soil mix or you can excavate areas from your natural soil and refill them with prepared soil. The simplest solution, however, is to forgo acid-lovers and choose from among the many plants that thrive in or tolerate alkaline soils.

Caliche

In the Southwestern deserts, some gardeners encounter an especially ornery form of hardpan called caliche. A deposit of calcium carbonate, from a few inches to a few feet beneath the surface, caliche usually won't let water pass through fast enough to allow ordinary plants to grow in the soil above it. Sometimes it's as tight as concrete; sometimes it's loose enough to be dug easily.

If the caliche is hard but only a few inches thick, you can try breaking it up with a shovel, mattock, or even iron bars, removing the material in the area where roots will grow. Or try to drill a drainage hole to the subsoil below. Thick caliche may be impossible to penetrate; if so, plant in well-drained raised beds on top of it.

Chlorosis

Plants grown on alkaline soils (and over or in caliche) are frequently paler or yellower than normal. This condition, called chlorosis, is usually caused by a lack of available iron in the soil. (The iron is often present, but because of the soil's chemical makeup, the plants can't use it.) You can treat chlorosis by applying iron chelate or iron sulfate.

Decomposed granite

In several of Southern California's mountain ranges, people must learn to garden in decomposed granite (commonly called DG). As topsoil, DG has several problems. It is not very rich (you have to fertilize it often to grow showy plants), and its lower layers are typically so dense that they're difficult to dig. Surprisingly, the density of DG doesn't hinder drainage. But if you loosen the granite when starting transplants, the roots will penetrate other layers and make it easier to dig. Gardeners elsewhere in the region may also encounter DG — it's a serviceable material for garden paths.

Salinity

The word refers to various salts being present in the soil to a degree that hinders plant growth. Salinity is never a problem where there's enough rain to wash out the salts. In the Southwest, however, you may have to supply the water yourself. If you suspect that a garden bed is suffering from salinity or salt buildup (plants are stunted, leaves yellow or brown), water that bed as heavily and long as you can to wash the salts from upper soil.

Designing Your Garden

Many people design a garden as they go, one year adding a shade tree, the next some shrubs or a new flower bed, and so on. In comparison, developing an overall plan can seem daunting, and the temptation to avoid it and just start in is strong. But a piecemeal approach can leave you with big headaches in a few years: trees blocking views, a flower bed across the children's favorite short cut to school. Fixing these problems takes time and money; if you plan first, you can avoid as many as possible.

Just because you make an overall plan does not mean that you have to install it at one time. Plan thoroughly, concentrate on the large issues ("Where do we need shade or privacy? Do we want a deck? How much should be lawn?"), but don't specify every detail. Then install the garden gradually, modifying this or that when you've lived with it for a while. One of the pleasures of gardening is changing things around.

If you plan your own garden, you save the cost of design fees, but more important, the garden will be yours in a way that another person's design never can be. If some aspect of the plan bogs you down, however, don't be reluctant to consult a professional. A few hours of a landscaper's time may be all you need. You can also look into classes in landscape design offered by adult education schools, botanic gardens, and other organizations.

Where to Begin

First take stock of what you have (the character of your property and climate), what you need, and what you want. This may take some time. Noting the seasonal changes of shade and wind, for example, can take a full year. If you can't bear to wait, talk with your neighbors or someone at a nearby nursery who is familiar with your area.

As you walk around your property or gaze out the window, be observant and make notes. Here are some important factors to consider.

Sun

The path and the intensity of the sun, through the seasons of the year and the hours of the day, largely determine both the amount of outdoor living space and the kinds of plants you can grow.

For instance, in Santa Monica, where summer days are often foggy, you may appreciate paths, patios, or terraces of concrete, brick, or asphalt which absorb the sun's heat and radiate it in the evening. In Phoenix or El Paso, where the summer is long and the sun intense, you may take the opposite approach, using screens of foliage or structure overhead to provide maximum shade and a minimum of heat-storing paving. Consider the time of day you will use your garden. Pavements that are too hot during the day may be perfectly toasty in the evening.

Water

Water is as important to plants as sunlight, and its increasing scarcity in the region has had a major effect on gardening. In addition to noting the amount and seasonal pattern of the rain, check on the price of water in your area and find out if its use is or will soon be restricted. The cost of water varies dramatically — a given amount can run from $200 to $2,000 a year. And prices are likely to keep rising. If you are moving to an established garden, ask the previous owner to show you a year's water bills. If they are high or if there is a good chance that water will be rationed, plan your garden accordingly.

Water in the garden needn't be restricted to thirsty plants. A small water feature can cool and humidify the air, mask sounds from a nearby street, attract birds, and soothe your nerves after a day on the freeway.

Wind

Whether it is cool or hot, dry or moist, a wind or breeze changes conditions for people and plants alike. With a breeze of 10 to 15 miles an hour, a person on a shady patio may feel chilly even though the thermometer reads a comfortable 75 degrees. The wind speeds evaporation, and it most affects plants by drying them out.

As you check the wind around your house, remember that the house itself is a windbreak. Wind can spill over the roof and drop on the other side, which may be a critical consideration in placing a patio. If you're planning a windbreak, a solid fence is not always best; it offers protection against the wind only to a distance equal to the height of the fence. A fence or planting that slows but allows some wind to pass through affords the most protection.

Topography

Note the features of your land — the high and low spots, the natural drainage channels, the boggy and dry areas. Also note the compass orientation; south-facing slopes are hot and harder to irrigate than north-facing slopes, which are cool.

Seasons

One of the great virtues of living in the Southwest is the opportunity for outdoor living. But despite the popular image of year-round, 78-degree comfort, every part of the region has distinct seasons. Tucson and Phoenix are hot in the summer but receive most of their annual rainfall then. Throughout Southern California, winters are cool and wet, summers hot and dry.

As you design your garden, consider the seasons and what you will be doing outdoors in each one. If you want to be outside in Scottsdale during the summer heat, you'll need a ramada and probably a swimming pool.

If possible, plan different parts to accommodate your being outdoors in different seasons. A terrace warmed by heat reflected off a south-facing wall would be perfect for cool times of the year, whereas a bench under a shade tree would be welcome on a summer afternoon.

Microclimate

Most gardens include several microclimates — areas where the sun, moisture, topography, and/or structures combine to create conditions that differ from those nearby. You'll grow different plants and do different things in a cool, shady space beneath a tree than in a hot, sunny area next to a brick wall.

Not all microclimates are obvious. Look for the warm place where frost never forms, the cool spot where rain evaporates last, or the wet spot where the soil never dries. This way, you'll greatly expand the range of plants you can use and, in the process, bring attention to the unique character of your garden.

Soil and drainage

In most small gardens, you don't need to worry too much about whether the soil is rich or poor, sandy or clay. You can easily improve it by adding organic materials or topsoil or you can feed the plants with fertilizers. But if your soil is shallow with a compacted layer underneath that is impervious to water and roots, or if water does not drain from your lot, you must either correct the situation or plant as if you had no soil — in raised beds or containers.

As you're planning, dig a bit in the places you think you'd like flower beds or trees or shrubs. If you're not certain about the soil, ask an experienced gardener for advice. If one location looks bad, try another; soil conditions may not be uniform throughout your property. If existing plants are growing poorly, you may want to have the soil tested.

In Arizona, New Mexico, Nevada, and Texas, the cooperative extension service tests soil for free or for a small charge. In California, you can find many commercial soil testing laboratories listed in the Yellow Pages.

Fire

Fire is a real threat to many people in the region. Anyone who has lived in Southern California for more than a few years knows the horror and power of brushfires that are out of control. If you live in a chaparral environment, assume that there will be a fire someday. And plan on being your own first line of defense — the fire department or forest service can't possibly guarantee help to all.

Among the protective measures you can take are several involving landscaping: plant low-growing, fire-retardant plants, and clear brush from the surrounding area to reduce potential fire fuel. For more specific suggestions, check with your fire department. Most are happy to inspect your property and offer advice. Also ask for the handy booklet *A Homeowner's Guide to Fire and Watershed Management at the Chaparral/Urban Interface*.

Legal restrictions

Before putting shovel to earth, be sure to check if your city has any restrictions that apply to construction or landscaping on your property. City planning offices, listed in the telephone book, will tell you about any ordinances concerning fence heights or setbacks. Permits may be required for new structures or for buried watering systems.

Personal Considerations

Now think about what you and your family need and want. How do you want your garden to look? How do you expect to live and work in it? Start with the following considerations.

Compost and trash. You'll need a convenient but unobtrusive place for trash bins or barrels. Every gardener should find a place for a compost pile. Most organic refuse — leaves, grass clippings, kitchen waste (excluding meat) — can be composted. The result enriches the garden and reduces the burden on the local landfill.

Food garden. You may want to grow some of your own vegetables, or perhaps you'd like an orchard. Often a garden can provide both vegetables and fruit without sacrificing beauty or play space. Edible landscaping, where fruits and vegetables are grown beside ornamental plants throughout the garden, may be particularly attractive if you don't have much space.

Outdoor storage. Your garden tools, lawn mower, garden cart or wheelbarrow, fertilizers, soil mixes, and similar equipment need a home. A covered shelter or free-standing wall may be enough, or you may need a separate structure.

Outdoor work area. Small children need to build things, teenagers like to tinker with cars, adults fiddle with lawn mowers. If your family is always involved in an outdoor project, set aside an area specifically for such activities to save part of the lawn or a garden bed from repeated trampling. If you are a plant enthusiast, you may want a lathhouse or a greenhouse for your projects.

Patio or deck. Take advantage of our lovely weather. Be it a small square of gravel or an elaborate wooden platform, almost every Southwest garden will be well served by either a patio or a deck.

Play area. Everybody likes to play outdoors. Preschool children want sand and water and tricycle runs. Older kids toss baseballs and footballs. Adults play badminton and croquet or practice chipping golf balls. Remember that a play area will need to change along with your family. In addition to the size and location, consider the surface. Grass is nice, but some varieties are hard to maintain if water is scarce; choose a variety or blend that is well adapted to both your climate and play.

What kind of gardener are you? This is probably the most important question. Do you garden because you must or because you love it? Even if you love to garden, is your time limited? Is money scarce? If so, you may want to limit the garden's size, or you may want to fill a large garden with drifts of inexpensive, easily maintained plants.

What do you want from your garden? Some gardeners have never seen a plant they didn't want to grow. Others are less intrigued by individual plants than by how plants can be combined for an aesthetic effect. The first gardener will go to great lengths to accommodate the needs of each plant. The second will be as happy with an easy plant as a difficult one as long as that plant contributes to the overall effect.

Finding a Style

We expect our landscapes, like our houses and our clothes, to do more than simply serve our needs. A tile-roofed adobe farmhouse and a suburban ranch house both provide shelter. Which one you prefer depends on a great many personal considerations: background, taste, temperament, and so on.

You may already know exactly what sort of landscape and garden you want or you may take years to find a style you like. (Trying different styles is half the fun for some gardeners.) Keeping a file of ideas can be a great help. Clip magazine pictures of attractive landscapes, plant combinations, individual plants, benches, decks, fences, paths, and pools. Scour books. Take photographs of gardens you like. Visit public and private gardens (with permission, of course), arboretums, botanic gardens, and demonstration gardens.

Be aware of the variety of gardening and landscaping styles in the region. The Southwest has a rich gardening tradition, from the Spanish missions to the ranchos and haciendas to the great suburban boom of this century. You can visit lovely examples of historic and contemporary styles throughout the area.

The sustainable landscape

Of all the ideas driving garden design today, one is of particular significance in our region. Typical Southwestern landscapes created over the last 30 years or so depend much more on outside supplies of energy and resources (water, fossil fuel–based pesticides and fertilizers, and electricity) than is desirable.

To address this problem, some landscape designers and gardeners have been exploring the idea of sustainable landscaping. Such landscapes are designed to follow principles of conservation, recycling, and the re-use of resources (particularly energy and water) so that the benefits derived from the landscape equal or exceed the costs. Experts consider a great many factors in constructing this equation, such as the energy costs of manufacturing, transporting, and applying fertilizers and pesticides as well as the benefits of carbon storage and oxygen generation derived from plants. Gardeners, however, can apply sustainable principles without a calculator. Here are some suggestions.

Waterwise gardening. What is a thirsty garden? The answer depends, of course, on where you live, the plants you choose, and how you water them. A study conducted in Irvine, California, found that the city's turf (parks, median strips, and golf courses) received an average of 6 feet of irrigation water a year. That's thirsty. The lower Mississippi floodplain may get that much rainfall, but no place in the Southwest approaches it.

A waterwise garden is, above all, well planned. Big water users are grouped together so they can be watered without waste, and plants requiring less water are placed where irrigation will be minimal or unnecessary. Keep lawn area to a minimum — lawns use more water than anything else in the garden.

Make sure that your watering practices and devices use water as thriftily as possible. Today, there are efficient irrigation systems for every kind of planting: trees, shrubs, ground covers, lawns, vine and bush crops, flowers, and vegetables planted in rows or in masses. A modern belowground irrigation system can cost between one third and one half of the total cost of the landscape. In return, however, a well-planned and properly installed system will save water, time, and money for years to come. Ask about these systems at your nursery, garden center, or cooperative extension office.

Energy-saving gardening. Energy is rapidly becoming an important consideration for landscape design. Residents of single-family homes in hot climates may pay $1,000 and more a year in energy bills, mostly for cooling. And costs are rising. But carefully placed shade trees, shrubs, and vines can reduce such costs significantly. These and other plants not only shade the house, but evaporation and transpiration from their leaves helps cool the surrounding air. Researchers in Phoenix found that three trees shading a typical ranch house reduced the number of air-conditioning hours by 17 percent. Dense shade cast on all surfaces of an energy-efficient home in Tucson can reduce yearly cooling costs from $439 to $204.

In the summer, over half of a home's heat is gained through windows that face east and west. To reduce this gain, place trees so that their shade will cover as large a roof and wall area as possible. Trees with many leaves and branches near the top block more sunlight and provide greater cooling than trees with more open canopies. Remember that deciduous trees lose their leaves in the winter, allowing sunlight to reduce the costs of heating.

Gardening also consumes energy. Reducing the use of water, fertilizers, and pesticides helps, even in a small way, to reduce the energy expended in their production and delivery.

Some landscape designers specialize in energy-efficient designs, and cooperative extension agents or farm advisers often have information on energy-saving measures. You can also contact your power and water companies; many are taking an active role in energy conservation, and some have even installed demonstration gardens.

Natural gardening. Abundant and cheap water coupled with a mild climate produced an extraordinarily wide plant palette for Southern California. As the first two parts of that equation have changed, so has the catalog of plants that are best to grow. Increasingly, gardeners are turning to native plants (those indigenous to the region) or native-like plants (those from other regions with similar climates). Adapted to the often rigorous conditions of the region, these plants usually require minimal irrigation and fertilizing once they are established. (See the next chapter, "Native Plants," for more on this subject.)

Although native plants can be used in traditional garden designs, they can be particularly effective in designs that take their inspiration more directly from nature. Such "natural landscaping" can be very energy and water efficient. All gardens, of course, are to some extent unnatural. Natural landscaping does not seek to recreate nature but to learn from and adapt to it. For instance, a garden in Phoenix integrates a native creosote bush found on the site with a transplanted mesquite tree and nursery-grown barrel cactus. A garden in Southern California combines existing native oaks with nursery-grown native ceanothus and non-native lavender and thyme. The plants are compatible with the site conditions (temperature, exposure, and water), but they are not necessarily native. They are arranged, not as nature does, but as nature might.

Nontoxic gardening. There is a nationwide perception that our lives, though enhanced by comfort and convenience, are increasingly blighted by the toxic by-products of our affluence. In Los Angeles, for example, the booming postwar economy has left the city with intractable smog and groundwater of questionable quality. Confronted by such large and complex problems, it is natural to respond by doing what you can in your own backyard.

The most obvious home garden toxins are the numerous pesticides found in so many nurseries. Although we try to use pesticides ever more prudently, and while we rediscover or invent less toxic kinds, the problem often begins with our design and plant choices. You can go a long way toward reducing your use of pesticides by choosing plants that are adapted to your environment.

Lawns require a great amount of water, fertilizer, and pesticides. You can reduce this consumption by your choice of turf grass and proper maintenance or by reduction (or elimination) of your lawn. (See the chapter "Lawns".)

Making a Plan

With all these considerations rattling around in your mind, it's helpful to put pencil to paper to begin sorting them out.

The base map

Start by making a scale drawing of your property as viewed from directly overhead (called a plan view), showing all the important existing features. Use a large sheet of tracing paper (24 by 36 inches works well) with a grid of ⅛- or ¼-inch squares. For a large property, each square can represent 1 square foot. To make things easier, you may want basic drafting tools such as a triangle, an architect's scale, drafting tape, an eraser, and unruled tracing paper.

Your drawing should show the property's overall dimensions and indicate its orientation to north. Outline the house and indicate rooms, doors, and windows. Note existing trees, shrubs, hedges, and important smaller plants. Include neighboring trees and shrubs that overhang your property, too. Indicate slopes. Add all outdoor structures and storage and work spaces. Show existing paths (and not just formal ones — you want to avoid putting a flower bed across the kids' favorite short cut.) Mark utilities such as water meters, hose bibs, shallowly buried utility lines, and septic fields. Note where setbacks are required by town codes.

A 100-foot tape measure is a great help in precise positioning; if you don't have one, pace off the distances. You can save a lot of time if you can find a deed map, architect's drawings, or other accurate survey. A contour map is useful for hillside sites.

Analysis

Once your plan view is complete, tape a sheet of tracing paper over it and note all the elements that affect plant growth, privacy, outdoor activities, and views. For instance, use a bold marking pen to indicate views you want to block (telephone poles, a neighboring house) and those you want to accent (hills, ocean). Indicate the direction and intensity of the prevailing summer and winter winds, sunny and shady areas, places where the soil is good or poor, areas with drainage problems.

Next, translate all those personal needs cited earlier into landscape elements and make a list. It may include an outdoor cooking area, a place for casual entertaining, flower beds, a vegetable garden, a sandbox, a pool (for swimming or viewing), and a shady area created by trees or trellises.

Preliminary plan

Now you're ready to start creating. Tape another piece of tracing paper over your plan view and analysis and begin to position the different elements. Take into account the analysis you've just done. Think about the sun and wind patterns as you position the deck. Consider the soil and drainage conditions for plantings and the views to be directed or screened for hedges, trees, and shrubs. Keep in mind the intangible things you've identified — the seasons and times of day when you're most often outdoors, the type of gardening you enjoy.

This is the time to be bold and imaginative; don't get bogged down in details. Try different ideas — tracing paper is cheap. Play with shapes. Focus on the major elements first. For instance, try one design where the garden beds and patio have flowing outlines, another with hard edges and geometric forms. Remember that you can remove existing elements as well as add new ones. Keep in mind the less glamorous aspects of gardening, too — irrigation, hauling compost, seasonal cleanup.

When working with a plan view, it's easy to forget that plants and structures have height. Experiment with changes in elevation — raised beds, terraces, mounds, multilevel decks, walls, fences, garden seats, layers of trees, shrubs, and herbaceous plants. Sketch some elevations on tracing paper. Or, if it's easier, you can try working with pictures. Take photographs from various vantage points on the property and have inexpensive 8-by-10-inch prints made. Tape tracing paper over the prints and sketch in your ideas.

If you have trouble imagining how your ideas on paper will translate to life-size, try marking them out in your yard. Use gypsum (available for a few dollars a bag at garden centers) to outline flower beds, groupings of shrubs and trees, sheds, patios, and paths. Small flags on wire stems or stakes of various heights can indicate smaller plants. If you don't like what you see, wash the gypsum away, pull up the stakes, and start over.

The final plan

When you're finally comfortable with the overall design, draw it accurately to scale. Now you're ready to sort out the specifics — plants, irrigation, materials for paths, fences, and structures.

If you're just starting out, the sheer number of plants that can be grown in our region may be overwhelming. The advice of experienced gardeners and trusted nursery personnel is invaluable. Concentrate on the major plants — trees, shrubs, important perennials — and remember that you don't have to put in the entire plan at once. If you get hooked on gardening, you'll spend a lifetime choosing (and changing) plants.

When you mark plants on the plan, draw them in scale at their mature size. (At a scale of ¼ inch to 1 foot, represent a tree with a 35-foot spread by an irregular circle about 8¾ inches in diameter.) Planting so that the garden looks full right away wastes money and creates work for the future. You can fill out a young landscape with annuals or fast-growing perennials that it's easy to take out later. Never place large trees near foundations, where their roots can cause damage.

If you've decided on an irrigation system belowground, lay out the basic piping on the plan. Refer to your file of ideas to choose paving materials for paths and driveways and to work out the details of design and placement for benches, decks, fences, patios, and trellises. It isn't necessary to include detailed renderings of structures or paths on your plan. But note their outlines accurately.

Installation

After all this paperwork, you probably can't wait to get digging, planting, and building. But first call your city's building department to see if you need a building permit for structures, fences, decks, and pools and to check on easements. If your plans include any large construction or grading, it's prudent to consult a professional contractor, even if you intend to do most of the work yourself.

For designs of any size or complexity, an installation plan is helpful. What needs to be done first and what can wait? Here is a typical sequence of events in a basic installation. At each stage, make sure the plants or building materials you need are available, and confirm delivery dates with the suppliers.

The first phase is earth moving, including all rough grading, drainage ditches, holes for fence posts, and holes for large trees. The second phase covers all rough carpentry, such as forms for steps, foundations, and walls and headers for concrete paving, asphalt, rock, gravel, and brick.

Masonry, including concrete or brickwork, comes next. Then plant any large trees or shrubs that must be delivered by truck. After these major features are installed, build your fence. But leave a section open if you expect delivery of bulk materials.

Now you can concentrate on the finish carpentry, including raised beds, seats, ramadas, arbors, and trellises. Install the irrigation system. You can set spray sprinklers in their final position, but don't put in the drip emitters until the plants are in place. Then you're ready to plant small trees and shrubs, vines, ground covers, herbaceous annuals, and perennials. The lawn, if any, comes last. If possible, plant during the cool months. New plants will appreciate the cool air and winter rains and can enter their first growing season partially established.

A few words of advice. It is likely, of course, that your particular installation will not proceed so smoothly and logically. Here are some tips to help you avoid headaches.

After the fence is up, beginners tend to plant the entire backyard in lawn if only to keep the family out of the mud. You may intend to change it later, but once the grass is grown, change takes a lot of courage and tough digging. Make an effort to start with the patio or deck. You'll get a resting spot sooner, and the children will have a better playground.

Second, plant trees right away. New gardeners find it difficult to decide which trees to plant. But don't put it off. When the trees are in place, you'll be grateful you planted sooner rather than later.

Finally, be patient. Work usually takes longer than expected, and occasional snafus happen to even the most experienced designers. Keep in mind that the finished product — a beautiful, unique garden — is an important part of life and well worth the expense, wait, and effort.

Native Plants

Each area of the Southwest provides gardeners with native plants for every landscape use, from trees to annuals. There are shade trees and flowering shrubs, cacti and century plants for accents, and ornamental grasses and wildflowers that provide local character no hybridized garden plants can match. If you have ever seen the desert in full flower after a season of heavy rains or come across a stand of scarlet columbines holding their flowers over a rushing stream, it may surprise you that some people question the value of growing native plants. Their irresistible charm and beauty and their readiness to burst into bloom whenever the West's arid climate provides moisture, even a brief thundershower, would seem to be recommendation enough.

Beauty isn't their only virtue, however. In an age of endangered species and disappearing habitats, a garden of native plants, providing forage and shelter for wildlife as well as foliage and flowers for people, has great appeal. Their flowers may not be as large as those of highly bred garden plants, but for making the house and garden fit into the natural surroundings, native plants are unexcelled.

Finally, drought and dwindling water supplies have made native plants even more attractive to gardeners. Since the Southwest was first inhabited thousands of years ago, the climate has become increasingly arid. Lakes have dried up, woodlands have become deserts, and plants and people have been forced to adapt or perish. Today's Westerners must also adapt, and using drought-tolerant native plants is part of the answer.

What Are Native Plants?

Native plants are the ones the Indians found when they settled the North American continent. The wild vegetation provided their daily necessities — food, medicine, shelter, clothing and tools — as well as pleasure. The poems of the Pueblo Indians reveal their delight in the desert flowers that bloom after the unpredictable rains.

When the European settlers arrived, their admiration for the native flora was immediate. On seeing wild roses blooming in Southern California, one member of an early expedition enthused, "Both sides of our way were lined with rose bushes of Castile, from which I broke one bunch with six roses opened and about twelve in bud." Later, the crews of Spanish ships anchored off Los Angeles could see the great poppy fields on the flanks of the mountains 30 miles away.

Botanists followed the conquistadors, finding thousands of new plant species. California poppies were soon known around the world, and a species of *Clarkia* (named for William Clark of the Lewis and Clark expedition) was being sold in the flower markets of London, Paris, Stockholm, and Moscow within eight years of its discovery.

The natives of the West were appreciated at home as well, and some became such familiar garden plants that their origins were forgotten. How many gardeners know that coral bells is native to the mountains of Arizona? Or that Hollywood is not named for English holly but for toyon, or California holly, whose berries have been a Christmas tradition since Gold Rush days?

Studying wild vegetation is the first step in learning to garden with natives. Westerners are lucky, for their region has much of its wild vegetation intact to educate and inspire. The California Native Plant Society is a good source of information. (Consult the listings beginning on page 374 for botanical, demonstration, and display gardens to visit.)

Landscaping with Natives

Western gardens can be divided into traditional and natural in a simple and practical way. Traditional gardens depend on ample irrigation during dry weather, with lawns a common, even dominant, feature. Natural gardens depend solely on precipitation. Given the unpredictability of rain in the West, only a few brave souls opt for rainfall alone. More choose a middle path of moderate irrigation of naturalistic plantings that evoke wild landscapes and comprise native plants and those from similar climate zones.

Whether inspired by Moorish courtyards or English gardens, the traditional Western garden is an oasis, a verdant refuge in a dry land. Many gardeners are reducing the size of the oasis, making it the area of highest water use in a landscape of plants grouped according to their water needs. Such a garden can accommodate a wide variety of plants and still stay within a modest water budget.

Walled patios and courtyards lend themselves to a formal oasis, with fountains, paved walkways, and geometric planting beds bordered with hedges. The focus of a naturalistic oasis could be a small pond planted with water-loving native perennials.

Native plants from naturally moist habitats are perfect for both formal and naturalistic oases. From the cottonwood, whose presence signifies moisture through much of the Southwest, to small perennials such as cardinal flower and columbines from the cool mountain canyons, the native flora offers a wealth of attractive species that require or prefer consistent moisture.

Outer, drier zones of the landscape can recreate or echo the region's natural landscape. Woodland gardens, whether an open planting of pinyon pines and desert scrub oaks or a dense grove of coast live oaks, can support an understory of flowering, drought-tolerant companions. The Southwest flora is rich in ornamental perennial grasses, and a garden grassland interspersed with wildflowers is possible in summer-rain or summer-dry versions.

In areas of California and Arizona where chaparral prevails, you can create a similar look in the garden with dense, low shrub plantings interrupted by openings for annuals, perennials, and dwarf flowering shrubs. Gardeners in the subtropical Sonoran Desert can create either desertscapes, with large cacti and succulents, or a dry streambed, which with moderate irrigation provides a home for summer-blooming species of the desert washes. In mild coastal areas, the gardening palette expands to include species of the Southwest's harsher climates. Apache plume from the pinyon-juniper woodland and desert lavender from the Sonoran Desert grow well in Southern California and harmonize with the natives.

Choosing Natives for Your Garden

Southern California and the Southwest consist of a mosaic of diverse environments with widely varying climates. (See the Introduction for more about these climates.) Wherever you live, plants native to your area will be best suited to your growing conditions. Let these natives form the framework of your garden; then you can experiment with plants from other regions.

Southern California

Native plants that can be integrated most easily into traditional Southern California gardens come from moderately moist environments — streambanks, canyons, coastal prairies, and the California islands, which enjoy a cool, moist, maritime climate.

Trees. Western sycamore (*Platanus racemosa*), white alder (*Alnus rhombifolia*), and big-leaf maple (*Acer macrophyllum*) are deciduous streambank species that make ideal lawn trees. Western sycamore, fast-growing to 30 feet and eventually up to 80 feet tall, is easily recognized by its white or pastel-mottled bark and very irregular, picturesque branching. Compared to sycamores, white alders and big-leaf maples are markedly straight-trunked and symmetrical in their growth habit, but they, too, are fast-growing and well adapted to traditional gardens.

For evergreen shade, a good choice is California bay laurel (*Umbellularia californica*); its dense crown of lustrous, yellow-green leaves is a familiar sight in the cool canyons of the Coast ranges. Small flowering trees for patios include the deciduous Western redbud (*Cercis occidentalis*), typically a many-trunked specimen from 10 to 15 feet high and of similar spread. Its magenta-pink or reddish-purple pea-like flowers appear from late February through early April in Southern California.

Naturalistic gardens in Southern California are likely to mimic two of the dominant natural landscapes, oak woodland and chaparral. California's evergreen oaks, usually called live oaks, are the signature trees of coastal and valley areas. Decimated in the wild by agriculture and housing, these native oaks are too often killed unwittingly when gardeners plant masses of azaleas, impatiens, and other moisture-loving plants under them.

Coast live oak (*Quercus agrifolia*), a round-crowned evergreen tree that grows to 75 feet tall, is the most common oak in Southern California. If you have a mature specimen, treasure it. If you aren't so lucky, coast live oak grows quickly enough so that you can plant a small tree and expect to see it grow to a good size at a rate of about 2 feet per year. Away from the coast, the highly picturesque Engelmann oak (*Quercus engelmannii*) mingles with coast live oaks or grows in pure stands. It is easily distinguished by its bark, which is rough and furrowed out to the end of its rather sinuous branches.

Perhaps the most colorful underplanting for native oaks is their natural companion, fuchsia-flowered gooseberry (*Ribes speciosum*). In winter, its prickly branches are thickly hung with dark red, inch-long flowers. They are an important food source for resident Anna's hummingbirds. Creeping mahonia (*Mahonia repens*) is another valuable ground cover below oaks; its flowers, berries, and leaves provide color nearly year-round.

Shrubs. Toyon, or California holly (*Heteromeles arbutifolia*), is one of the most cherished and adaptable California natives, at home in an irrigated garden, in a dry woodland garden with oaks, and even on hot, dry hillsides if given occasional soakings. It bears great clusters of tiny white flowers during late spring and early summer and huge trusses of red berries from Thanksgiving through New Year's.

The hybrid wild lilac *Ceanothus* 'Ray Hartman' is a large evergreen shrub, sometimes pruned to form a small tree. It tolerates garden watering and blooms early, often around Christmas in the Los Angeles area. The tiny, fragrant, medium blue flowers are borne in 5-inch clusters, and — a bonus — the blossoms of this "soap bush" can be worked into a pleasing, lightly scented lather.

The showiest of California's flowering shrubs are the flannel bushes, or fremontias. The most widely grown is the hybrid *Fremontodendron* 'California Glory', which grows rapidly into a 20-by-20-foot evergreen shrub covered with large, golden yellow, waxy blossoms in March and April. It makes an unforgettable show when planted with the Santa Barbara wild lilac (*Ceanothus impressus*) or any of its beautiful descendants, which include *Ceanothus* 'Julia Phelps', 'Concha', and 'Dark Star', all drought-tolerant evergreen shrubs with deep blue flowers.

There are ten islands off the coast of Southern California, ranging from mere specks to 96-square-mile Santa Cruz Island. Their many distinctive plant species, as a group, are larger in leaf and flower than their mainland counterparts and have a greater tolerance of summer irrigation. One island native, malva rosa or tree mallow (*Lavatera assurgentiflora*) was introduced to the mainland early in the mission period both for its attractive, 3-inch-wide pink flowers and as a fast-growing windbreak in coastal areas. In gardens, it is useful as a long-blooming 8- to 10-foot-tall specimen shrub or massed as a screen planting especially appealing for its blue-green, maple-shaped leaves with a silvery sheen.

Perennials. At the top of the list of native perennials for summer-irrigated gardens are the Pacific coast hybrid irises. Derived from *Iris douglasiana, I. innominata,* and other wild irises of the West, these hybrids form clumps of grasslike leaves usually under 18 inches tall and bear large flowers in a wide range of colors. They don't need summer watering, although they seem to like it, quickly forming large clumps that bloom from March into early June.

Matilija poppy (*Romneya* spp. and cvs.) is justly one of California's most famous wildflowers and a top perennial for dry, sunny gardens. Once established, it requires no irrigation but plenty of room, for it spreads widely by deep, lateral roots. Beginning in late April or May, its tall wandlike stems are topped with enormous flowers — a ball of golden stamens surrounded by crinkled or pleated white petals, the whole as much as 10 inches across. Suitable companions are blue-flowered showy penstemon (*Penstemon spectabilis*), scarlet bugler (*Penstemon centranthifolius*), and Cleveland sage (*Salvia clevelandii*) or its hybrid offspring, *Salvia* 'Allen Chickering', wonderfully aromatic shrubs with a long season of blue or lavender-blue flowers.

Annuals. On open hillsides too dry to support oaks, chaparral and sage scrub are the dominant plant communities in Southern California. When such hillsides burn, they are followed by spectacular displays of wildflowers. You can get the same effect by selectively thinning the shrub cover to reduce fuel and to make open places for wildflowers and ornamental shrubs.

California's annual wildflowers may be the best part of the native flora, but they are neglected in cultivation, perhaps because gardeners are not accustomed to growing flowers from broadcast seed. Still, no sunny hillside should be without its springtime show of California poppies (*Eschscholzia californica*), lupines (*Lupinus succulentus, L. benthamii, L. nanus*), gilias (*Gilia tricolor, G. capitata*), and tidy-tips (*Layia platyglossa*). Sow them around colonies of the glaucous, spine-tipped rosettes of yucca (*Yucca whipplei*) and among drifts of California's state grass, purple needlegrass (*Stipa pulchra*), which produces its graceful inflorescences along with the wildflowers. You will have created a garden scene that is a piece of the real California.

The Sonoran Desert

On the Sonoran Desert, you can forget about imitating the gardens of any other place on earth. Your own backyard is a botanical wonderland where plants of tropical origin have adapted to an increasingly hot, arid environment. The result is a fascinating flora in which the succulent and drought-deciduous habits are conspicuous.

Oasis plants. The California fan palm (*Washingtonia filifera*) is the monarch of the Sonoran Desert oases and, if there is room, a popular tree for the home oasis, too. Much planted in Southern California's intermediate and interior valleys, this heat-loving, stout-trunked palm grows rapidly to 60 feet. Where a smaller tree is desired, the Mexican blue fan palm (*Brahea armata*) is an excellent choice.

The understory of the garden oasis, like its wild counterpart, holds moisture-loving wildflowers. In the desert, yerba mansa (*Anemopsis californica*) is outstanding for its tolerance of alkalinity and its spring and summer floral display, in which showy white bracts subtend cone-shaped clusters of tiny flowers. Its 6-inch-long, aromatic leaves take on red and purple tones as they become dormant in the fall.

Plants of the open desert. The oasis, with its shade and moisture, is a respite from the burning sun, but it is in open, dry areas with full sun that the Sonoran Desert flora is most colorful. With two rainy seasons, winter and summer, this desert supports an unusual variety of trees and large cacti. The trees generally have small leaves, often divided into tiny leaflets, that can be shed in extreme drought to conserve moisture.

Ironwood (*Olneya tesota*) is the signature tree of the Sonoran Desert. It is sometimes compared to an olive tree for its handsome habit and gray-green leaves, but it is quite distinctive in May and June, when it bursts into a haze of rose-purple bloom. Ironwood grows slowly in the wild, but as a specimen tree in an irrigated garden, its growth rate improves.

For quick results in the desert garden, palo verdes are most useful — fast-growing if watered but very drought-tolerant and undemanding once established. Blue palo verde (*Cercidium floridum*), so called for its bluish twigs, and Mexican palo verde (*Parkinsonia aculeata*) both bear bright yellow flowers in spring and have crowns with sparse foliage that cast an airy, light shade.

Desert willow (*Chilopsis linearis*) is another fast-growing species, but it requires more moisture than the palo verdes — it usually grows in washes, where it benefits from the runoff from summer thundershowers. Called willow for its long, narrow leaves, this plant has trumpet-shaped flowers and grows as a shrub or a tree up to 25 feet tall. It occurs on all of the Southwestern deserts and makes a handsome garden specimen in mild Palm Springs as well as in Albuquerque, which has cold winters.

A few members of the mostly tropical acanthus family have adapted to the rigorous climate of the Sonoran Desert and make fine flowering shrubs for the garden. Desert honeysuckle (*Anisacanthus thurberi*) grows from 3 to 8 feet tall and bears orange-red tubular flowers in spring and summer. Chuparosa (*Justicia californica,* sometimes listed as *Beloperone californica*) forms a 3- to 6-foot-tall dense mass of twiggy, nearly leafless stems. Its narrow, tubular, brilliant red flowers appear in winter and spring and are very attractive to hummingbirds.

Cacti are the water misers of the plant kingdom, saving every drop of scanty rain they can, but on Arizona's upland desert cacti become giants. Saguaros (*Carnegiea gigantea,* also called *Cereus giganteus*) can live to be 200 years old, reaching 50 feet in height and 30 inches in diameter. Cactus rustlers have looted many fine saguaros in recent years, but properly tagged, legally salable specimens are available for landscape use.

Should your garden need even more dramatic plants, there is no more striking horticultural accent than ocotillo (*Fouquieria splendens*). Unlike the corpulent cacti, its stems, as tall as 20 feet, are slender, whiplike, and studded with woody spines. After winter or summer rains they are topped with clusters of bright red tubular flowers from which the Indians made a refreshing drink. In cultivation, it requires good drainage and sparing or no irrigation.

The Mojave Desert

The Mojave is the land of the Joshua tree (*Yucca brevifolia*), which grows to 30 feet tall and as much as 3½ feet in diameter. Looking something like a mutant, many-branched palm, the Joshua tree, not the California fan palm, accounts for Palmdale's name.

Mesquite (*Prosopis glandulosa*) is a common deciduous shrub of desert washes and, where moisture is sufficient, can attain treelike heights of up to 35 feet. In gardens it is useful pruned as a many-trunked patio tree whose broad crown of bright green, compound leaves casts a pleasant filtered shade. It produces a heavy crop of greenish-yellow flowers on slender spikes in spring, with scattered bloom throughout the summer. Grown as a shrub, mesquite is a valuable windbreak.

The leaves of the brittlebush (*Encelia farinosa*) are covered with a dense fuzz of short white hairs, which gives it a silvery appearance and protects the leaves from the sun even in the Mojave's famous Death Valley. Following a winter so dry that no annual wildflowers appear, brittlebush faithfully produces a springtime show of long-stemmed clusters of yellow daisies that shoot up well above the foliage.

Mojave gardeners are well advised to hike in their mountains to see some of the many penstemons native to the desert's scrublands, the Joshua tree woodland, and the pinyon-juniper woodland that covers its higher elevations. Palmer's penstemon, or pink wild snapdragon (*Penstemon palmeri*), is notable both for the towering height (up to 6 feet) of its stalks of pouchy, pale pink flowers and for their sweet fragrance, a rarity among penstemons. Palmer's penstemon may bloom the first summer from seeds planted in the fall. Rather than using water to grow hybridized bedding plants on the desert, get to know the beautiful flowers that grow naturally in your area.

The Chihuahuan Desert

The Chihuahuan Desert's vegetation must struggle to live on 8 to 10 inches of precipitation a year, yet more than a thousand species grow wild here and nowhere else. Since two thirds of the rainfall comes in late spring and summer, area gardeners should consider planting a summer-blooming meadow of drought-tolerant native grasses and wildflowers.

A desert meadow. A choice bunchgrass for the meadow, Indian ricegrass (*Oryzopis hymenoides*) combines a graceful non-weedy habit with extreme drought-tolerance. Its round, hard seeds are produced on airy 2-foot-tall spikes and are a favorite food of mourning doves. Several vigorous seed strains are available commercially.

A short list of perennial wildflowers for the meadow would include blue flax (*Linum lewisii*), indispensable for the clear blue of its five-petaled flowers, and gayfeather (*Liatris punctata*), which produces spikes of feathery rose-purple or white flowers from August through October. More typical daisy-like flowers for the meadow are desert zinnia (*Zinnia grandiflora*), with orange-centered yellow flowers, the white-flowered blackfoot daisy (*Melampodium leucanthum*), and blanket flowers (*Gaillardia* spp. and hybrids) in shades of red, orange, yellow, and maroon, with many bicolor combinations.

Yuccas and shrubs. The Chihuahuan Desert cannot compete with the Sonoran for quantity and variety of cacti, but it does have a staggering profusion of century plants (*Agave* spp.), yuccas, and related plants. Gardeners, especially those with limestone-derived soils, should look closely at the Chihuahuan Desert scrub to see what it offers.

Palmilla, or soap tree (*Yucca elata*), is a striking accent plant admired and grown far from its home on the Southwestern deserts. Mescal bean, or Texas mountain laurel (*Sophora secundiflora*), is an excellent small flowering tree, attractive in all seasons thanks to its glossy evergreen foliage.

Flowering shrubs for this area include ceniza, or Texas ranger (*Leucophyllum frutescens*), with lavender-pink flowers that show well against the silver-gray leaves. It grows slowly to 12 feet tall in the wild, but several cultivars with more compact growth are available. Autumn sage (*Salvia greggii*) is a small evergreen shrub that produces tubular flowers much of the year in mild climates, though it can die to the ground in winter in colder areas. West Texas offers a hardy variety of yellow bells (*Tecoma stans*), an erect deciduous shrub that grows to 3 feet tall and bears bright yellow trumpet-shaped flowers.

Pinyon-juniper country

The cold-adapted pinyon-juniper woodlands cover a vast expanse of the Southwest between 4,500 and 7,500 feet in elevation. The more rigidly drought-tolerant junipers are usually more prevalent than pines, but the latter always seem to get top billing, perhaps because of their tasty nuts. Much of this region suffers 150 nights of freezing temperatures a year, so subtropical plants of the warmer deserts are mostly unsuited, although desert willow (*Chilopsis linearis*) can be grown.

Notable trees and shrubs. An oasis planting in Santa Fe or Winslow is likely to be anchored by a cottonwood rather than palms. Eventually a 100-foot-tall giant, cottonwood (*Populus fremontii*) is not for small spaces, but it is the region's finest shade tree and a brilliant spectacle in fall, when the leaves turn bright yellow.

Rose locust (*Robinia neomexicana*) is an attractive flowering tree that is something of a paradox for gardeners. It grows wild in the moist soil of streambanks, and, if given ample moisture in the garden, it grows rapidly but also suckers aggressively. Kept on the dry side, it is better behaved but is slow to develop beyond the size of a shrub. Still, if you can strike the correct balance between too much and too little water, this locust's pendant clusters of rose-pink flowers are decorative during late spring and early summer.

Golden currant (*Ribes aureum*), a 3- to 8-foot-tall deciduous shrub, is widespread in the West. In the pinyon-juniper country, water promotes good bloom; the yellow flowers have a spicy fragrance and the leaves color beautifully in the fall.

Apache plume (*Fallugia paradoxa*), a dense shrub usually 4 to 6 feet tall with a similar spread, is showy in a subtle way. Its 1-inch-wide, five-petaled white flowers are plentiful but rather plain. In seed, however, it earns its reputation as one of the region's best ornamental shrubs. The feathery pink seedheads are both colorful and full of motion, so delicate in appearance that they always seem about to be shattered by the wind.

There's nothing subtle about the show chamisa, or rabbitbrush (*Chrysothamnus nauseosus*), puts on in the early fall.

A fast-growing rounded shrub to 5 feet, chamisa's golden yellow blooms brighten vast stretches of grassland — one of the Southwest's finest spectacles, and one that has inspired some memorable mass plantings in the Santa Fe area.

Growing Native Plants

Native plants are easy to grow if you choose appropriate species for your area, plant them in the correct season, and water wisely. Adapted by thousands of years of evolution to the Southwest's soils and climates, natives make rewarding garden plants that can do without most of the soil preparation, fertilizing, staking, and spraying that many traditional plants require.

"Close to home" natives are the most likely to succeed, especially for desert gardeners, for whom coastal and mountain plants are risky. Southern Californians have more leeway: they can use natives of the local chaparral and oak woodlands along with a wide range of plants from the pinyon-juniper woodland, the Southwestern deserts, and the cooler habitats of northern California. In the very mildest coastal areas, lack of winter chilling and cooler summers may cause problems for some natives.

Timing and soil. The time you plant natives, especially those expected to survive on little or no irrigation, is critical. Fall is the season to plant nearly all natives, with the exception of some subtropical desert species and summer annuals. In fall, the soil is still warm enough to encourage the development of strong roots that will sustain the plants when hot, dry weather returns.

Native plants have adapted to the West's typically alkaline and humus-deficient soils and thrive in all but the worst soils. Amending the soil is usually unnecessary and may actually inhibit root growth. It's better to spread an organic mulch on the surface (winds permitting) to conserve moisture.

Water and maintenance. When you water native plants, keep in mind their natural habitat. Species native to moist environments need consistent moisture as much as any traditional garden plant. Drought-tolerant species, properly planted in the fall, require moderate irrigation through their first summer in the ground. By the second summer they should be thoroughly established and able to live on infrequent dry-season irrigation or, if need be, on natural precipitation alone.

Some California chaparral natives are so unused to summer moisture that, once established, they should never be watered. The hybrid flannel bush *Fremontodendron* 'California Glory' and certain species of wild lilac (*Ceanothus*) sometimes perish from disease brought on by well-intentioned summer watering.

Do native plants make for a low-maintenance garden? Certainly, a well-planned grouping of natives requires less work than a rosebed. Still, the beautiful sycamores native to California and Arizona (*Platanus racemosa, P. wrightii*) drop all of their leaves in fall and winter, burying the plants below if they are not raked up. Lemonade berry (*Rhus integrifolia*) makes a handsome formal hedge, but it needs to be sheared like any hedge. Annual wildflowers grow without the fertilizing and staking given bedding plants, but they do need to be kept free of competing weeds. The allure of native plants is not a maintenance-free garden but one that captures the character of the land and its vegetation.

Finding Native Plants

Part of the fun of gardening with natives is visiting the nurseries devoted to them. Many popular natives are grown by large wholesalers, but to find local natives, you will probably seek out small, specialty nurseries. They are run by people who have a deep and abiding love for the native flora of their region and will go to great effort to provide the genuine article. Plant sales at botanic gardens and native plant societies are also an important source for species that are hard to find and new cultivars developed from wild plants.

Container-grown nursery stock has a much better chance of survival than plants, even small ones, transplanted from the wild. Be aware that each state has laws protecting wild plants, limiting or prohibiting their removal. In recent years, illegal traffic in specimen-sized saguaros and other large cacti has become a serious problem. Before you buy material collected in the field, ranging from mature pinyon pines to mariposa lily bulbs, make sure the seller has the proper state permits. If you wish to collect plants or seeds for your own use, check first with your state government. Your state's native plant society can also provide helpful guidelines for collecting that minimizes harm to wild plant populations.

Old Standbys and Regional Favorites

Blessed with a long season, gardeners in Southern California and the Southwest grow an astounding range of plants. Some of them would have greeted Sir Francis Drake when he planted the English flag on the shores of California in 1579. Many are more recent arrivals. Early settlers from the Old World brought useful and beloved plants. Later newcomers from the East Coast and Midwest added their favorites. Plant explorers introduced a wide range of flora from China, Australia, the Far East, and Africa. Dedicated hybridizers, nursery owners, landscape architects, and designers have all left their mark, as have numerous fads and fashions. From early mission to hacienda to suburb, changes in the way people live have been reflected in the plants they grow.

The Missions

In 1769, the Franciscan padre Junípero Serra, accompanied by fellow missionaries and a soldier, Gasper de Portola, made a trek from the Baja Peninsula into California and established its first mission, at San Diego. Among their provisions, Junípero Serra took care to include seeds and cuttings of fruits, flowers, and vegetables from both the Old and New worlds.

Once missions were established and settlements developed, gardens began to flourish where water was available. In many areas, miles of primitive canals were built to transport water. On other sites, Native Americans walked long distances to bring water to thirsty fruit and shade trees, roses, perennials, favorite shrubs, and vegetable gardens. Because water was scarce, moisture-loving plants were placed next to buildings or in courtyards. Plants needing less water were set around the perimeter. This siting of plants according to their need for water is becoming popular today as water conservation is increasingly important.

Nestled in the Purisima Valley, just north of Santa Barbara outside Lompoc, the Mission La Purísima Concepción of California continues to remind us of mission life and gardens two centuries ago. More than eighty plant species collected from the original plantings at other California missions are part of the landscaping. The famous rose of Castile, introduced from Spain, continues to flourish. Wine grapes and fruit trees, including almonds, figs, olives, peaches, pears, plum, and pomegranate, were other important introductions.

The Haciendas

In the late 1700s, land grants created cattle ranches consisting of thousands of acres. With their red tile roofs and adobe walls, courtyards and ramadas, and an emphasis on friendly, outdoor living, the rancho haciendas introduced a more intimate style of gardening than the simple, functional one of the missions. In addition to roses, herbs, annuals, and perennials, the hacienda gardens included flowering plants grown for bouquets and fragrance. Landscaped gardens, walls, and ramadas were covered with vines such as the native clematis, called virgin's bower (*C. lasiantha* and *C. jackmanii*), honeysuckle (*Lonicera japonica* 'Halliana'), and passion vine (*Passiflora alatocaerulea*). The climbing musk rose (*Rosea* 'Cluticote') and a white Cherokee rose were also introduced.

Bulbs, often selected for easy transportation, were grown in perennial flower borders and included cannas, bearded iris, lilies (*Lilium candidum*) and callas (*Zantedeschia aethiopica*).

Ships sailing around the horn of South America brought plants from Europe and the eastern United States to the hacienda gardens.

The 19th Century

In the 1800s, the large ranchos began to break up, a portent of Southern California's future development. Similar trends occurred in West Texas, New Mexico, and Arizona, as the Spanish hold on the Southwest Territory weakened. The Gold Rush of 1848, California's statehood in 1850, and the arrival of the railroads marked the beginning of tremendous growth and change.

The expanding population meant new homes and a demand for plants to serve and adorn them. Many settlers from the East brought their favorite shade trees, bulbs, and perennials, but the hot, dry summers were too severe for them. Nurseries were soon growing shade trees, flowering shrubs, vines, roses, and perennials (not always adapted to the Southwest) for the newcomers. Growers who had been supplying fruit trees and grapevines to orchardists became enamored of the new ornamental plants introduced by explorers from China, Australia, the Far East, and Africa. Plants that survived intense testing by government agencies and nurseries were introduced in residential areas, on estates, in parks, and along streets and highways by landscape architects, city planners, and members of horticulture societies. These plants stimulated vigorous new landscape themes that changed the face of the Southwest.

Plants were introduced for practical as well as ornamental purposes. To protect fruit trees in the Los Angeles, Orange County, and Ventura areas from the desiccating winds called Santa Anas, orchardists planted thousands of Australian giant blue gum trees (*Eucalyptus globulus*). Growing to heights of 100 to 200 feet, the blue gum develops strong heavy branches and dense foliage that softens the 40- to 60-mile winds. Rows of windbreaks established during this period can still be seen in windy passes and lowland farms. In the low desert areas of the Coachella Valley from Palm Springs to the Salton Sea, tamarisk trees (*Tamarix aphylla*) protected date and citrus groves and vegetable farms from hot, dry winds and blowing sand.

The Golden Age

The period from 1900 through the 1930s is known in the region as the golden age. As Southern California became the fastest growing region in the United States, nurseries were hardly able to keep up with the demand. Growers from around the world introduced new plants, many of which are still available in local nurseries. Landscape architects combined the new plants and old favorites to create some of the most beautiful gardens in America.

A transplanted Italian, Dr. Francesco Francheschi, personifies the energy of the time. A lawyer turned horticulturist, Francheschi established the Southern California Acclimatizing Association in Santa Barbara "to introduce plants from other countries having climate similar to ours, and through appropriate culture, make them thrive and bear." He introduced 90 palms and cycads, 24 bamboos, 130 ornamental trees, more than 100 fruit-bearing and economic trees, as well as countless ornamental shrubs and bulbous and trailing ground covers. The Southwest owes him an immense debt of gratitude.

Trees

Some of the most important introductions to the region have been trees. Nearly permanent features of the landscape, trees can provide structure to a design as well as the pleasure of flowers, fragrance, and leaf color. Used for shade and windbreaks, trees also reduce energy use. Many of the finest introductions were made in the Santa Barbara area, thanks to nurserymen such as Peter Reidel. Here you'll find the red-flowering gum (*Eucalyptus ficifolia*), with its spectacular 1-foot-diameter clusters of flowers. Growing 25 to 40 feet high, it is well adapted to coastal conditions. Weeping acacia (*Acacia pendula*), a 25-foot tree with graceful gray branches, makes a handsome backdrop for close viewing. The widely planted Bailey acacia (*Acacia baileyana*) grows 25 to 40 feet high with fern-leaf silvery, blue-green foliage and offers abundant golden yellow flower clusters in the spring months.

Orchid trees (*Bauhinia variegata* and others), natives of India and China, have a special place in the mild winter gardens of California and Arizona. Although they are partly to entirely deciduous, the flamboyant display of purple to lilac flowers from January to April is spectacular. A recent introduction, the Hong Kong orchid tree (*B. blakeana*) has more compact growth, to 20 feet, and maroon to orchid-pink flowers in the fall and early winter. It is ideal for smaller gardens.

Palms

Palms dominate the skylines of many Southwestern cities and towns and feature prominently in gardens. The mission fathers originally brought the date palm (*Phoenix dactylifera*) from the Middle East and raised the Mexican fan palm (*Wash-*

ingtonia robusta) and the native fan palm (*Washingtonia filifera*) from seeds collected in the deserts.

In the early 1900s, new palm species of a more intimate size were introduced. Adapting well to desert and coastal conditions, they became the basic element in gardens with oasis themes. The graceful queen palm (*Arecastrum romanzoffianum*), with feather fronds, is grown throughout Southern California and even in the Coachella Valley, creating a subtropical feeling, especially around pools. Dwarf Mediterranean fan palm (*Chaemerops humilis*) develops a dramatic 10- to 12-foot-high form with many trunks that can be featured in even the smallest garden. Slow-growing and clean, it is ideal around water features. Other slow-growing favorites include the pindo palm (*Butia capitata*), 10 to 20 feet high with graceful feather fronds, the blue palm (*Brahea armata*), with silvery blue fans, and the Guadalupe palm (*Brahea edulis*), whose light green fans are an ideal accent in smaller gardens.

A Plant Tour Through the Region

From the foggy coast to the sweltering deserts, the varied climates and conditions have a profound impact on which plants thrive in the region. Old standbys and favorites include native plants as well as plants from across the world and across the country. Here we'll look at a number of the most successful and beloved plants in some distinctive areas. (Coastal Southern California figures prominently in the previous discussions, so it isn't included here.) Read about areas other than your own — you'll probably find plants of interest that you may want to try in your garden.

The Mojave Desert

The Mojave stretches from the San Gabriel Mountains, north of the Los Angeles basin, to the Colorado River and Las Vegas in Nevada. It is a land of immense space and four distinct seasons. Given adequate fall rains, the Mojave comes alive in the spring. Immense carpets of wildflowers — including California poppy (*Eschscholzia californica*), blue lupine (*Lupinus odoratus*), owl's clover (*Orthocarpus purpurascens*), California bluebell (*Phalelia campanularia*) — attract thousands of visitors.

The early settlers in this remote land were a rugged lot of prospectors, railroaders, alfalfa ranchers, cattlemen, and sheepherders for whom gardens were not important. In the last 30 years, however, thousands of acres of desert in the Antelope Valley and east to Yucca Valley have been eaten up by housing and development spilling over from the Los Angeles basin, resulting in drastic changes. The tall, many-branched Mojave yucca, or Joshua tree (*Yucca brevifolia*), which once covered large portions of the area, is falling before the bulldozers. The ubiquitous creosote bush (*Larrea tridentata*), whose aromatic foliage is a refreshing delight after a rain, is being grown by Arizona nurseries.

Although the plant palette is relatively limited, there are ample opportunities to enjoy gardening in the Mojave. It is ideal for conifers, deciduous fruit and shade trees, hardy conifers, evergreen and deciduous shrubs, as well as bulbs, annuals, and perennials.

Water is a major concern, and restrictions are likely in the heavily populated Las Vegas area. To explore and encourage the use of water-conserving plants from other dry climates, the University of Las Vegas has a plant testing program and the Las Vegas Water District has established demonstration gardens.

Trees and shrubs. These are important in the Mojave. Summer shade and dense hedges to break the strong winds are essential for both plant and human comfort. Among the most popular and successful deciduous trees are the tree of heaven (*Ailanthus altissima*), Idaho locust (*Robinia ambigua* 'Idahoensis'), mulberry (*Morus alba*), white poplar (*Populus alba*), balm-of-Gilead (*P. balsamifera* 'Mojave Hybrid'), Siberian elm (*Ulmus pumila*), and Russian olive (*Elaeagnus angustifolia*). Purple plum (*Prunus cerasifera* 'Krauter Vesuvius'), Japanese flowering cherry (*Prunus serrulata*), and flowering peaches thrive with the winter cold and provide spring color.

Favorite evergreen trees include the olive (*Olea europaea* 'Swan Hill'), African sumac (*Rhus lancea*), bottle tree (*Brachychiton populneus*), Aleppo pine (*Pinus halepensis*), Afghanistan pine (*Pinus eldarica*), Italian stone pine (*Pinus pinea*), and Arizona cypress (*Cupressus glabra*), which makes a dense windbreak.

Old standbys used successfully by early settlers include the Pfitzer juniper (*Juniperus chinensis* 'Pfitzerana') for large background, tamarix juniper (*J. sabina* 'Tamariscifolia') for use in the foreground, firethorn (*Pyracantha sp.*) for barriers and hedges, and evergreen euonymus (*Euonymus japonica*) for its compact hardy growth. Eastern lilacs (*Syringa vulgaris*), heavenly bamboo (*Nandina domestica*), oleander (*Nerium oleander*), and Fraser photinia (*Photinia fraseri*) are also reliable favorites.

The introduction of Chilean mesquites (*Prosopis chilensis*) and Argentine mesquite (*P. alba*), desert willow (*Chilopsis linearis*), and hardy acacias has increased tree options. New shrub introductions include Texas ranger (*Leucophyllum frutescens*) and desert broom (*Baccharis sarothroides*).

Perennials and ground covers. Mojave gardeners turn to lavender cotton (*Santolina chamaecyparissus* and *S. virens*), clumping gazanias, the mounding hybrid coyote bush (*Baccharis sarothroides* 'Centennial'), daylilies, bearded iris, coreopsis, red salvia (*Salvia greggii*), trailing indigo bush (*Dalea greggii*), St.-John's-wort (*Hypericum calycinum*), and rosemary (*Rosmarinus officinalis* 'Prostrata').

The Coachella Valley

Below the 10,000-foot San Jacinto Mountains, the Coachella Valley stretches from Palm Springs (600 feet above sea level) to the Salton Sea (250 feet below sea level). This low environment is different from any other desert area of the Southwest. Taking advantage of a long growing season and a good supply of water, landscapers and gardeners here have produced a lush, oasis landscape.

A skyline of tall Mexican fan palms, date palms, and native California fan palms sets the stage for gardens. Colorful bougainvillea and hibiscus, oleander hedges, and trees such as California pepper (*Schinus molle*), jacaranda (*Jacaranda mimosifolia*), crape myrtle (*Lagerstroemia indica*), orchid trees, and floss silk tree (*Chorisia speciosa*) enhance the basic garden framework.

Water drawn from wells and aquifers is augmented by supplies piped from the Colorado River. But with an average annual rainfall of only 3.7 inches and summer temperatures from 110 to 120 degrees, Valley residents are water conscious. Conservation efforts have accelerated the use of water-efficient shrubs and ground covers. These include imports from the deserts of Arizona, New Mexico, and Texas — Argentine mesquite (*Prosopis alba*), sweet acacia (*Acacia smallii*) — as well as the local native blue palo verde (*Cercidium floridum*) and the imported Sonoran palo verde (*C. praecox*). Many miles of water-efficient natives and dry climate introductions grace the turfless medians of highways and streets. Increasingly, gardeners are planting naturalistic gardens without large turf areas.

In the spring, colorful annuals (planted in the fall) create a spectacular effect. Sweet alyssum, lobelias, phlox, petunias, pansies, and violas, stocks, and snapdragons are favorites. Perennials help to extend the season and are equally showy: *Euryops pectinatus* and *E. p.* 'Virides', with their yellow marguerite flowers, red sage, mealy-cup blue sage (*Salvia farinacea*), and coreopsis (*Coreopsis grandiflora*). When the heat arrives in the middle of May, many people let their gardens rest, yet the bougainvillea, hibiscus, lantana, daylilies, iris, gazanias, and subtropicals carry on with brilliance until late fall.

Phoenix: Arizona's Valley of the Sun

The open areas surrounding Phoenix developed a productive agriculture in the 1800s with extensive groves of citrus, date, and pecans as well as cotton and alfalfa farms. Canals through the area brought water from distant rivers and dams. With the arrival of the railroads in 1891 came more Easterners, attracted by the climate or looking for new frontiers.

To meet the landscaping needs of the new residents, guest ranches, and tourist spas, nurseries imported plants from California — eucalyptus, tall fan palms, and aleppo pines as well as hardy and subtropical accent plants such as bougainvillea and oleanders. The maples and birches brought by nostalgic Easterners succumbed to the extreme heat and sparse rainfall, giving way to more acclimated plants such as junipers, arborvitae, and pyracantha.

After World War II, Phoenix and the valley boomed with industry and high technology. The proliferation of bedroom communities increased the need for landscape companies to install well-designed plantings and nurseries to supply reliable plants adapted to the environment.

But by the 1970s, increased population and development were straining the water supplies. From 1970 to 1990, comprehensive plans were made to bring water 300 miles, through canals and pumping stations, from the Colorado River to Phoenix and Tucson. In addition, conservation measures were begun. Landscaping guidelines recommended water-efficient plants and the reduction of turf areas.

Gardeners and landscape architects have responded to the need. In many areas where native plants thrive, they attempt to maintain existing grades and growth. Elsewhere, they've made greater use of dryland natives from Texas, New Mexico, California, Australia, South America, and the Mediterranean. Increasingly they have employed the mini-oasis concept, where choice subtropical or succulent plants are confined to entranceways and courtyards. Large areas of turf around homes are being retrofitted with less demanding landscaping, including drainage-swale mounding, boulder groupings, accent plants such as yuccas and cacti, and ground covers. Native trees, such as mesquites, acacias, and palo verde, shelter walls from the summer heat.

Gardeners in Phoenix can draw inspiration from a number of sources. The Desert Botanic Garden in Phoenix and Boyce Thompson Arboretum in Superior have experimented with water-efficient plants. The work of talented landscape architects also provides examples, as do the new plant introductions seen along the freeways, on slopes, and in street medians.

Tucson: A special sense of place

Settled in the 1600s by Jesuit priests, who established three missions in the area, Tucson has a rich heritage that includes some of the oldest favorite plants of the Sonoran Desert. At an altitude of 2,200 feet in the heart of the desert, the area features abundant natural growth and an average annual rainfall of 12 inches, equally spread between summer and winter. It is often cooler than Phoenix in both summer and winter.

Tucson is spectacularly situated against the 9,175-foot Mount Lemmon in the Santa Catalina mountain range and other mountain islands to the west and south. Its rich native flora provides a greater sense of place than any other populated desert area in the Southwest. The giant saguaro (*Carnegiea gigantea*), with its many vertical arms, grows abundantly and accents the skyline in the foothills. In the spring, wildflowers such as Arizona poppy carpet the higher elevations (when the fall rains have been normal), and the arroyos come alive with blue palo verde, which creates sensational yellow patterns.

Rain produces many pleasant effects. After a summer storm comes the refreshing fragrance of creosote bush and other aromatic plants. Rain induces the tall, thorn-studded stems of the ocotillo, also called buggy whip (*Fouquieria splendens*), to put out green leaves and produce orange-red flower clusters at the tips of each stem. (In ancient times, people built barrier fences with the canes; now they're used as an important vertical element in the garden.) Roadside carpets of desert marigold (*Baileya multiradiata*) are prolific for long periods after the seasonal rainfall rolls off the highway. It grows readily from seed and should be in every natural garden seed mix.

Throughout the city, brick homes with flat roofs, covered porches, and courtyards reflect the Spanish and Mexican influence. Many gardens include water features. Containers and flower beds are filled with annuals and bulbs, including narcissus, sweet alyssum, pansies, snapdragons, and Iceland poppy. Most spring-flowering annuals are planted in October and bloom until the middle of May, when the heat arrives. Favorite perennials and biennials include bearded iris, daylilies, delphinium, dusty miller, foxglove, hollyhock, flowering kale, larkspur, red salvia, ruellia (*Ruellia peninsularis*), scarlet flax (*Linum grandiflorum* 'Rubrum'), wormwood, and yarrow. Grown commercially for its oil, Jojoba (*Simmondsia chinensis*) is favored as a garden shrub for hedges.

As everywhere in the region, water has become a concern. Lawns are small and confined to private rear gardens, replaced in front by more natural landscaping. The University of Arizona and the Boyce Thompson Arboretum have introduced water-efficient ground covers and shrubs for slopes and carpets of green. From Texas, the rapidly growing trailing indigo bush (*Dalea greggii*) spreads silvery-blue fine-textured foliage over large areas. The mounding hybrid coyote bush (*Baccharis s.* 'Centennial'), a relative of the native desert broom (*B. sarothroides*), is a durable, dark green ground cover with a spread of 6 feet and height of 2 to 3 feet.

Chosen for their airy look and yellow flowers, the native blue palo verde and graceful pepper-like honey mesquite (*Prosopis glandulosa torreyana*) are used to reduce the heat on walls and create a patterned shade on patios. Old and new roses also grow most successfully, and Rosa banksiae climbers cover many older garden walls. Native plants such as opuntias, yuccas, and barrel cactus are used extensively for accent among boulders in natural gardens.

In less natural gardens in the higher, warmer foothills, citrus prosper. Eucalyptus trees introduced decades ago make strong vertical elements in the landscape. Aleppo pines, which are succumbing to insects in low desert areas, thrive in Tucson.

New Mexico and West Texas

Geographically and historically, New Mexico and West Texas have close ties with the other Southwestern states. The area differs, however, because of its higher elevation, ranging from 2,000 to 4,000 feet.

As in other parts of the region, the Easterners who settled in the Rio Grande Valley and elsewhere brought their favorite plants. Birch, forsythia, juniper, kolkwitzia, poplar, pyracantha, and perennials such as chrysanthemums, gaillardias, and narcissus survived and are widely used in gardens, but other plants succumbed to the unfamiliar climate, soil, and water resources.

The increasing number of gardeners who are grouping plants according to their moisture requirements have a fascinating range of reliable, water-efficient plants from which to choose. Shade trees include Arizona ash (*Fraxinus velutina*), Arizona sycamore (*Platanus wrightii*), desert olive (*Forestiera neomexicana*), desert willow (*Chilopsis linearis*), honey mesquite (*Prosopis glandulosa torreyana*), Gambel's oak (*Quercus gambelii*), Russian olive (*Elaeagnus angustifolia* 'King Red'), quaking aspen (*Populus tremuloides*), and rose locust (*Robinia neomexicana*).

Understory and shrubby plants include Apache plume (*Fallugia paradoxa*), bird of paradise (*Caesalpenia gilliesii*), broom baccharis (*Baccharis emoryii*), broom dalea (*Dalea scoparia*), rabbitbrush (*Chrysothamnus nauseosus*), creosote bush, fourwing saltbush (*Atriplex canescens*), and little-leaf sumac (*Rhus microplylla*), creeping mahonia (*Mahonia repens*), dwarf coyotebrush (*Baccharis pilularis*), and cultivars of the Rocky Mountain juniper (*Juniperus scopulorum*).

Perennials well adapted to local conditions include Blackfoot daisy (*Melampodium leucanthum*), penstemon species, butterfly weed (*Asclepias tuberosa*), red sage, and lavender cotton.

Lawns

The lawn is under siege in the Southwest and Southern California — and not only from such usual suspects as insects and fungal diseases. The new threat is environmental. There simply isn't enough water to meet the increasing demands of agriculture, industry, and the general public. Some areas no longer permit watering lawns; one municipality even pays a bonus for reducing a lawn's size. Other areas demand that new landscaping meet rigid standards for drought-tolerance, standards that often do not conform to our traditional ideas of a home landscape. The plain fact is that we live in a desert, and there is not enough water to convert it all to an oasis.

While our attitude toward the lawn is changing in large part because of water shortages, smaller lots and shifting architectural styles are also reducing its importance in the total landscape. When a lot is small, private space for relaxation and entertainment may be more important than the lawn — especially a front lawn, which is merely a gift to passersby. Barbecuing and sunbathing are not activities for the front lawn.

A lawn can be a considerable drain on leisure time — time many people would prefer to devote to other plants. Maintaining a lawn also requires a lot of energy. In addition to muscle power, there's the energy expended in the production of fertilizers and pest-control chemicals, which are increasingly considered environmental hazards.

A Little History

The ancestors of our lawns were the close-cropped meadows surrounding English country houses. These pleasant approaches were "mowed" by cattle or sheep, which were kept from the door by fencing or artfully concealed trenches called ha-has. A portion of the lawn may have been more carefully trimmed with a scythe for bowling, archery, or other sports. The lawn mower did not appear until late in the 19th century.

When combined with trees, kitchen and flower gardens, and, if possible, water features, these extensive lawns formed a gentleman's park, the model for 19th-century British and American gardens. On a reduced scale, such gardens are still planted in much of this country, but their most widespread legacy has been the lawn, well trimmed and verdant.

Unfortunately, these lawns are simply not adapted to the climate in the Southwest. In the British Isles, moderate temperatures and heavy rainfall throughout the year produce a lush growth of the pasture grasses from which our popular lawn grasses originate. By contrast, in most of the United States west of the 100th meridian, drought is normal. The average rainless period ranges from 50 to 250 days, and yearly rainfall is only 20 inches or less. Under such conditions the natural vegetation is desert, sparse grassland, or scrub, except in the higher mountains and river valleys.

So in today's water-conscious Southwest, a well-kept front lawn, once considered the jewel in the homeowner's crown, can be an albatross. But people still want lawns — a yard needs a covering, a garden needs a floor. What are the options?

Options

Stay the course

The first option, which many people will choose, is to carry on as always, hoping that improved storage and distribution, desalination, or reclamation of water from sewage and industrial use will solve the problem.

Reclaimed water is currently being delivered by tank trucks in some areas of the Southwest. The water is safe, but storage at the delivery site is not easy to manage. The collection and storage of rainwater in underground tanks or cisterns is nearly as old as history, but it is little practiced in this country, posing problems of engineering (excavation, lining, cleaning) and official permission (local authorities, concerned about safety and the municipal water supply, require engineering and groundwater studies). Increasing the supply from dams and aqueducts is uncertain. The expense is great, the environmental hazards considerable, and the upstream users want their share of the water.

With this option, you'll continue to plant traditional turf grasses (bent grass, Bermuda grass, bluegrass, fescues, ryegrass, St. Augustine grass) or, in mild-winter areas, dichondra, a low-growing, spreading perennial requiring little or no mowing. The rewards of such lawns are well known. But if the water problem proves intractable, you may eventually have to give up your lawn.

No lawn at all

An obvious, if drastic, response is to forgo any attempt at a lawn. The gardens of the Mediterranean region, descendants of those attached to the rural villas of the Romans and the enclosed "paradise" gardens of the Arabic world, did not develop a tradition of lawnmaking. In these dry areas, water was too scarce to lavish on mere grass. Brought from afar in aqueducts or lifted from wells, water irrigated food crops or a few cherished plants grown in pots for their beauty or fragrance. The typical garden in these parts was enclosed to keep out wind and animals. It had trees or vines for shade or fruit; ideally, it contained a fountain or pool to provide an illusion of coolness as well as water for cooking or washing. The ground between plants, around the fountain, and so on, was mulched or left bare.

Gardeners in desert areas with small courtyards or larger enclosed gardens may find this option appealing. Gravel, decomposed granite, tile, flagstone, or brick can replace turf grass, providing color, contrast, and a "floor" for ornamental plantings in beds or containers. Omitting the lawn may not, however, be popular with your children or, if you tear out your front lawn, your neighbors.

Go native

If you live in the Rocky Mountains and high plains of the Southwest, you can make a passable lawn from certain native grasses that tolerate extremes of heat and cold and thrive in the area's low humidity, wind, and capricious rainfall. These grasses lack the lushness of bluegrass and fade to an undistinguished straw color in winter, but they are genuine survivors. Prominent among them are buffalo grass, blue grama, and crested wheatgrass.

Ground covers

These low-growing, spreading herbaceous or woody plants are most useful when clothing areas where grass is impractical — on steep slopes, on areas remote from sprinklers, in soils where grass will not thrive, or in landscapes where maintenance time is limited. Further, many ground covers need little irrigation once established; a few can get by on natural rainfall. They also help prevent erosion and suppress weed growth.

Ground covers are far from being merely utilitarian. They offer a wide range of foliage colors and textures, and many produce brilliant sheets of flowers. At the Lummis Home State Historical Monument in Los Angeles, for example, an expanse of yarrow (*Achillea millefolium*) substitutes for a lawn. The 3-inch-high foliage withstands garden party traffic; when in bloom, the area is awash in flowers on stems about 1½ feet tall. Southern Californians can choose from an enormous number of ground covers of every color and texture; the choice in the desert and mountain regions is more limited.

A combination

The last, and possibly the best, choice is to design your landscape with a combination of turf grass, ground covers, and other plants arranged for efficient water use. Concentrate the turf grass and any plants with high water needs in areas of high visibility near the house. Entry, private entertainment, and lounging areas are prime candidates for this "oasis" treatment. Place plants with smaller water requirements near the perimeter of the garden.

Plan your irrigation system to match your plantings — sprinklers for turf grass, low-pressure sprinklers for extensive ground cover areas, and individual drip emitters for shrubby ground covers or specimen plants. Substitute ground covers or "hardscape" — brick, concrete, flagstone, or wooden decking — for grass where appropriate. The initial cost of the hardscape materials may be high, but their usefulness and low upkeep will reward you in the end. Or try inexpensive alternatives: British country estates have entry courts of gravel. Pea gravel, bark, wood chips, or crushed brick or stone can cover large areas at little cost. These materials are also easy to maintain. Used as a mulch, they keep down weeds, retain soil moisture, and allow water to reach tree and shrub roots.

To give you an idea of the possibilities in this option, here are three imaginative, effective examples of low water use:

• A traditional front lawn in Tucson was converted to a water-thrifty garden by retaining a small, semicircular patch of tall fescue lawn edged by a border of gazanias, verbena, and *Aptenia cordifolia,* an ice plant relative. A sprinkler system waters the small lawn and border while outlying areas, planted with native cactus, ocotillo, and yuccas, make do with rainfall. Native wildflowers, which volunteer on the site, enliven the outlying areas, and pots of pansies, petunias, and stock brighten the entry in winter.

• A New Mexico garden combined greenery and colorful flowers by substituting broad sheets of creeping thyme (*Thymus praecox arcticus*) and goldmoss sedum (*S. acre*) for turf grass. In late spring, the dark green thyme becomes a mass of purplish pink, and the succulent, shiny green sedum covers itself with starry yellow flowers. Both remain a few inches tall, need no mowing, and survive with rainfall. Native perennial penstemons provide height and brilliant flowers at the edge of the planting.

• In a Southern California hillside garden, the available level space is used for a paved driveway and parking area. The surrounding slopes are colored by a mix of flowering shrubs and perennials, including rockrose (*Cistus*), lavender, coreopsis, sea lavender (*Limonium perezii*), and Peruvian verbena. Once established, these plants can survive with monthly irrigation.

Getting Started

A turf grass lawn or ground cover substitute will be most successful if it is planted on a carefully prepared site. The most important considerations are the soil, grade, drainage, and irrigation.

Soil
If the soil is poor, you must improve it by either adding amendments or bringing in new soil. Buying and spreading topsoil is a common practice, but it can cause a long-lasting and serious problem. Where one layer of soil meets another with different characteristics — loam above clay or clay above sand, for instance — water moves with difficulty from the upper layer to the lower. The result is a saturated surface and a parched subsoil.

Careless contractors frequently spread a thin layer of good topsoil over poor subsoil, which has often already been compacted by heavy grading machinery. A lawn will sprout readily under such conditions, but the roots will not penetrate the line between topsoil and subsoil. Irrigation merely soaks the upper layer, depriving the roots of oxygen. During hot weather or water shortages, the grass will fail because it has no reservoir of water in the subsoil to draw on, and its roots are already inadequate.

It is best, therefore, to add topsoil only where necessary to raise the grade or fill in hollows. Spread up to half the amount needed, till it thoroughly into the subsoil, then till in the rest. If the subsoil is seriously compacted, have a landscape contractor break it up with a subsoil plow or chisel before blending in the new soil.

If you do not need to add soil to establish a grade, you are better off amending the original soil. Add enough organic material such as ground bark, decomposed or nitrogen-treated sawdust, or other locally available materials to make a real difference in the soil's capacity to hold air and water. In most situations, 2 to 4 inches of amendment spread evenly on the surface and tilled 9 to 12 inches deep should do.

Grade and drainage

Proper drainage is necessary for any lawn or ground cover. A soil that is constantly wet kills plants, either by depriving the roots of oxygen or by encouraging root-destroying fungi. Amending the soil as described above will help open it and keep water and air moving through. But if the soil is not properly graded, water may stand on the surface or, even worse, stand around the house foundation to seep into the basement or crawl space.

An existing, plainly visible slope away from the house may be graded simply by raking. Where the land is nearly flat, you will have to add or move soil to correct the grade or build drains to carry off excess water. A slope of 3 inches in 10 feet is considered a safe minimum.

Adding topsoil or moving the existing soil to create a proper grade can be expensive if large areas are involved. An alternative is to install drains to carry water to a lower level such as a driveway, street gutter, or storm sewer. You can also dig a dry well — a pit at least 3 feet deep and 4 feet wide filled with coarse gravel or drain rock — and lead water to it.

Irrigation

Once you have established a proper grade, consider an irrigation system; it can vary greatly in complexity and expense. You can design and install a system yourself or hire someone to do it. Irrigation specialists, plumbing supply houses, and many hardware stores sell PVC pipe, sprinklers, and a number of automatic controls and timers, along with advice on planning and installing a system.

Controls are central to the ability of these systems to save water and work. Many electric timers can manage several watering zones and programs. You can incorporate a sophisticated moisture sensor (tensiometer) to determine when your lawn needs water. There are also simple mechanical meters that you screw on a hose bibb.

If you install an oasis or zoned irrigation plan, you will probably need several kinds of water delivery systems. Sprinklers can serve turf grass lawns and any small flower beds around them. Ground covers of widely spaced trailing or spreading shrubs are best served by individual drip emitters or bubblers. Closer-growing herbaceous ground covers can be watered economically by low-pressure sprinklers.

Final preparation

When the soil is amended and graded, the drains in place, and the irrigation system installed, rake the surface of the soil smooth, breaking up any large clods. Irrigate thoroughly to settle the soil, then fill any high or low spots that appear. You are now ready to sow seed, lay sod, or plant ground cover.

Seed or Sod?

If you're planting turf grass, seeding offers a wider choice of grasses and is less expensive than laying sod. On the other hand, you must seed in early spring or early fall to have a reasonable hope of success. Seeding also entails more care at the outset. You'll have to water daily or, during hot, dry weather, several times a day, and the seeded area will not tolerate foot traffic for several weeks.

Sod is much more expensive than seed and offers a narrower choice of grasses, but it can be set down at almost any time of the year. Good sod from a sod farm has practically no weeds and gives an instant effect without the concerns that go with seeding — birds, pet, and human footprints, sudden heat waves or washouts, fungus diseases, and insect pests.

Seeding

Information on a number of turf grasses suitable for the region is given in the chart on pp. 58–59, but before you choose, consult with your county extension agent or a knowledgeable person at your nursery. They will be able to help you pick a grass or blend of grasses that best suits your site, conditions, and expectations.

There are two principal kinds of grass. Cool-season grasses make most of their growth during cool weather and slow down during hot weather. These are most useful near the coast or in cool mountain regions. Warm-season grasses have a tropical origin; they flourish in hot weather but become brown and dormant in winter. In the Southwest, when warm-season grasses begin to brown in the fall, people often sow seed of a cool-season grass to green up the lawn during the winter; this is called overseeding.

Each group includes several species, and strains of many of them have been selected for a particular quality. You can purchase seeds of a single or a blend of strains, a single or blend of species, or a blend of species and strains. Some blends contain both warm- and cool-season grasses. A single strain may produce turf of exceptional beauty, but one subject to greater risk from insects, diseases, or severe weather. Blends are safer.

Sow the seed on a windless day in the early fall or early spring (to avoid extreme cold or heat), crisscrossing the area to ensure even coverage. Rake the seed in very lightly. In dry or windy weather, apply a light, damp mulch of peat moss, rotted sawdust, or weed-free compost to help retain moisture. (Dry mulch will simply blow away.) Then press the seed into the soil with an empty roller (a weighted roller would compact the surface). Water thoroughly and keep damp until the seeds sprout, then gradually lengthen intervals between irrigations. Don't mow until the grass is 3 inches tall. Be sure that the mower blades are sharp and the ground is firm.

Laying sod

Prepare the surface just as you would for seeding. Have the sod delivered early on the day you plan to put it down. Moisten the soil lightly, then position and unroll the sod. Butt the edges firmly together and be sure to stagger the end joints, as in bricklaying. Trim around the sprinkler heads, header boards, or paving with a heavy knife. When the sod is in place, press it into the soil with a roller half full of water. Water thoroughly and keep moist for 6 weeks. Keep foot traffic to an absolute minimum, and delay mowing until the grass is growing strongly.

Plugs and sprigs

Grasses that spread by runners can also be established by planting small sections of sod, called plugs, or by planting unrooted or barely rooted runners, called sprigs. You can buy plugs in trays at the nursery or make them at home by cutting 2- to 3-inch pieces from larger sections of sod. Prepare the soil as for seeding or laying sod. Plant the plugs about 18 inches apart in damp soil, making certain the runners are flush with the soil surface. Water immediately and keep moist until the runners begin to spread.

Sprigs can also be purchased at a nursery or torn carefully from flats or strips of sod. Scatter them on moist soil, cover thinly with soil, and water. Keep moist until they begin to grow.

Ground Covers

If you're planting a ground cover of closely spaced, small to medium-size herbaceous plants, such as ajuga or creeping thyme, you'll probably buy them in "six-packs," small plastic trays containing six cells, each holding a plant, or in flats containing 72 or 100 rooted cuttings. Look for plants that have good color and a well-developed but not matted root ball. Prepare the soil as you would for a lawn, loosening the roots gently as you plant. Firm the soil around each plant and water thoroughly.

Larger perennial or shrubby ground cover plants come in containers up to 5 gallons in size. More mature plants are useful for a quick effect, but younger, less expensive plants will be indistinguishable from the larger ones after a few years. Because these ground covers are spaced more widely, it is usually sufficient to amend the soil in and near the planting hole. Make a shallow but wide hole; the top of the soil ball should be slightly above ground level.

Some ground covers can be grown from seed, but direct sowing is rarely successful, so the process requires several transplantings. A few annuals, notably sweet alyssum, can give a quick, temporary show. Sweet alyssum will reseed in much of Southern California. Easily rooted plants, such as ivy and some ice plants, can be started from rooted cuttings inserted where they are to grow.

Near the coast, plant ground covers in the fall or winter to take advantage of the cool weather and rainfall. In the desert, plant as soon as the weather turns cool in fall. Where frosts come early and late, plant in the spring as soon as the soil can be worked.

Weeds can be a problem in ground covers. They're a nuisance to pull and some herbicides developed for use with turfgrass lawns will kill broadleaf ground covers as well as the weeds. So it pays to eliminate weeds, especially perennial weeds, before planting ground covers. You can water before planting to bring up the weeds, then spray with glyphosate to kill them to the roots. (Spray carefully. Glyphosate will kill any vegetation it covers, but it does not persist in the soil.) Digging up soil exposes new weed seeds, so when you plant, disturb the soil as little as possible. After planting, you can keep weeds down by mulching the ground cover.

Keep It Healthy

Although a daunting array of pests and diseases can plague a lawn, the most common reasons for poor performance are insufficient water at the root zone and invasion by weeds. The best way to provide root-zone water is to prepare the soil properly before planting and to maintain it afterward. The best defense against weeds is a dense, healthy population of grass, which also discourages pests.

Older lawns, even where the soil was initially well prepared, can eventually become compacted by traffic and watering, which suffocates roots and slows water penetration. Penetration is often further slowed by thatch, a tangled mat of stems, roots, and dead grass that accumulates just above soil level. This material sheds water, keeping it from soaking in where it is needed.

A simple test will determine whether water is getting to the roots. Push the blade of a long, stout screwdriver into the soil. If you encounter resistance a few inches down, you can be sure that the soil is dry at that point. To remedy the situation, rake out the thatch with a bladed rake called a Bermuda or self-cleaning rake (a tedious job) or with a mechanical de-thatcher (rented from a garden equipment firm). Then open up the soil by coring or spiking to permit air and water to reach the roots. You can rent a coring machine, which removes small, cylindrical cores of sod and earth, or a spiking device, which punches holes in the turf. To keep the holes from filling and compacting the soil again, sweep sand into them. After this treatment the lawn will look shabby for a brief time, but it will soon grow with renewed vigor.

Gardeners often complain about lawns that have been green through the winter but develop brown patches in the summer. Although insects or fungus may play a part, the chief villain is annual bluegrass (*Poa annua*), a weedy grass that is brilliant green in cool, wet weather but that browns out quickly in hot, dry weather. The best way to combat it is to maintain a dense, healthy turf or to apply a pre-emergent herbicide to prevent it from sprouting.

Watering

Most lawns get more water than they need. Much of it runs off slopes or compacted soil, much blows away in the wind or evaporates in the hot sun, and some just seeps away below the roots. The amount of water your lawn actually needs depends on how much evaporates and how much transpires through the leaves. A measure of this water loss, called the evapo-transpiration rate, is given in inches of water per day or week. Contact your farm adviser or extension agent for the evapo-transpiration rate for your area.

There's a simple way to determine how long to run your

sprinklers to provide a recommended amount of water. Set out a number of coffee cans or similar containers at regular intervals on your lawn. Run the sprinklers for 15 minutes. Compare the amounts in each can to see how even the coverage is. Measure the amount in an average can to determine how long to run the sprinklers. An obvious sign of thirst is wilted grass. When it turns pale, lies flat when stepped on, and fails to recover in the cool of the evening, it needs water.

Applying the right amount of water at the right time is just one way to save water. You can also water during still weather, preferably in the early morning, or during cloudy weather. Watch carefully to see that water does not run off — a problem on heavy clay soils or on slopes. To avoid runoff, apply water frequently but a little at a time. Don't overfertilize the lawn; subsequent fast growth will require more water. Cut down feeding when the grass is not growing actively; remember, cool-season grasses tend to rest during summer heat. Don't waste water trying to keep a lawn alive in deep shade; if it is obviously struggling, replace it with a mulch or a shade-tolerant ground cover.

Fertilizing

Because lawns must replace foliage lost to frequent mowing, they require more feeding than most other types of landscaping. All plants need three major elements — nitrogen, phosphorus, and potassium — along with a number of minor or trace elements to live and thrive. The major elements are designated on fertilizer labels by the letters N, P, and K, followed by numbers that represent the percentage of the element in the product.

Nitrogen is the most important element. Because it is highly soluble, it is most easily lost by leaching through overwatering. The other elements are more stable in the soil and need less frequent replacement. So be sure your fertilizer always contains nitrogen.

How often should you feed your lawn? The grass should help give the answer. If it lacks vigor — has poor color and fails to grow — feed it. Early spring, when growth is most vigorous, is the best time to feed a lawn. Where the growing season is long, warm-season grasses stay green longer with a fall application.

The frequency also depends on the fertilizer formulation. Slow-release fertilizers are slow to begin working but act over a long period. Liquid fertilizers give quick results but require frequent application. Granular fertilizers with a high nitrogen content can cause severe damage if you apply them during hot weather and water them inadequately. Follow the package directions carefully. Manures, often considered useful fertilizers, are generally low in the necessary elements and slow to act; they may also contain weed seeds. Consider manures as soil amendment rather than fertilizer.

Mowing

The type of mower you use is a matter of personal preference. But certain kinds of grass, such as some bent grasses and Bermuda, should be cut very short and require a reel-type rather than a rotary mower. How often you mow should be determined by how the grass grows rather than by a rigid schedule. It will need mowing frequently during its best growing season, less often when it is partly or entirely dormant. A good rule with cool-season grasses is to cut when the blades have grown no more than an inch taller than the recommended mowing height. With warm-season grasses such as Bermuda (and with creeping bent), where the mowing height is much lower, cut when the blades are a third taller than the mowing height. If you let the grass grow much taller, the lower part of the blades will turn yellow.

Keep the mower blades sharp to avoid shredding and browning the grass blades. Don't mow when the grass is wet. Should you rake up the cuttings? One school believes that removing cuttings allows better air, light, and water penetration and avoids thatch buildup. Another believes that there is benefit in allowing the cuttings to filter down and decay, thereby releasing their nutrients and helping to mulch the soil. The latter school is in the ascendancy at the moment.

Weed and Pest Control

Weeds have a hard time getting started in any lawn that is well made, adequately fed, watered, and maintained at the proper height. If you have one of the new, environmentally responsible small lawns, you should be able to control what weeds do appear by hand pulling. For larger lawns with larger problems, herbicides can be helpful, but use them as a last resort and follow the label directions exactly.

Fungus diseases are difficult to diagnose and treat. If you do not overwater your lawn and if you allow the surface to dry out between waterings, the lawn will be less likely to suffer fungus attacks. Thatch control and careful feeding, avoiding excess nitrogen, are also useful preventatives. Chemical solutions are possible; consult a knowledgeable nursery worker

Lawn Grasses for Southern California and the Southwest

Grass	Texture	Water needs	Wear resistance	Shade tolerance
Cool-season grasses				
Colonial bent (*Agrostis tenuis*)	fine	average-light	moderate	some
Creeping bent (*Agrostis tenuis*)	fine	high	high	some
Kentucky bluegrass (*Poa pratensis*)	medium-fine	high	high	poor
Rough-stalked bluegrass (*Poa trivialis*)	fine	high	poor	good
Creeping red fescue (*Festuca rubra*)	fine	low-moderate	poor	good
Hard or sheep fescue (*Festuca ovina*)	bunchy	low	moderate	moderate
Tall fescue (*Festuca arundinacea*)	coarse-fine	moderate	good	moderate
Annual ryegrass (*Lolium multiflorum*)	coarse	moderate-high	moderate	poor
Perennial ryegrass (*Lolium perenne*)	medium-fine	high	high	some
Warm-season grasses				
Common Bermuda (*Cynodon dactylon*)	medium-fine	low	high	poor
Hybrid bermudas	fine	low	high	poor
St. Augustine grass (*Stenotaphrum secundatum*)	coarse	heavy	high	good
Seashore paspalum (*Paspalum vaginatum*)	fine	moderate	good	some
Zoysia (*Zoysia japonica, Zoysia matrella*)	fine	moderate	high	some
Zoysia tunuifolia	fine	moderate	high	some
Dichondra (*Dichondra macrantha*)	coarse	moderate-heavy	moderate	some
Native grasses				
Wheatgrass (*Agropyron cristatum*)	medium	low	moderate	low
Blue grama (*Bouteloua gracilis*)	medium	low	moderate	low
Buffalo grass (*Buchloe dactyloides*)	fine	low	good	low

Lawn Grasses for Southern California and the Southwest

Fertilizer needs	How to establish	Mowing height	Comments
low	seeds	½–1	Bent grasses appear most often in seed mixes.
moderate	seeds	½ or less	Bent grasses appear most often in seed mixes.
heavy	sod, seeds	1½–2	Do best in coastal and high-altitude areas of region.
low-moderate	seeds	1½–2	Do best in coastal and high-altitude areas of region.
low-moderate	seeds	1½–2	Widely used in Southern California as a ground cover; mow once a year.
low	seeds	1½–2	Tolerant of extreme heat, cold, drought.
low-moderate	seeds, sod	2–3	Withstands drought.
low-moderate	seeds	1½–2	Quick-sprouting, short-lived in hot weather.
moderate	seeds	1½–2	Dislikes extreme heat or cold.
heavy	seeds	½–1	Toughest of the tough in hot climates.
heavy	sod, plugs	½–1	Tifway, Santa Ana are good strains. Tifdwarf is low, slow-growing.
heavy	sod, plugs,	1½–2	Great heat resistance, tolerates saline conditions near beach.
moderate	sod, plugs	¾–1	Salt and heat resistant.
low	sod, plugs	1–2	Long dormancy, slow growth; experts restrict their use.
low	sod, plugs	n.a.	Low-growing bank or ground cover; never needs mowing.
heavy	seeds, sod, plugs	1–2 (in shade)	Tolerates heat but not hard freezing; rarely needs mowing in full sun and moderate foot traffic.
low	seeds	2	Fairway is improved strain; *A. Smithii* sometimes used.
low	seeds	1½	Bunchgrass.
low	seeds, plugs	n.a.	Maximum height of 4 inches without irrigation.

for advice. Likewise, for help in diagnosing and controlling the insects and other arthropods that can attack lawns, consult with your nursery, master gardeners, or extension representatives.

Plants for Lawns and Alternative Lawns

Whether you plan to grow a traditional turf grass lawn or plant ground covers or native grasses that need little water, there is an excellent range of plants available. The chart on pages 58–59 gives details about specific grasses. A little general information may help you choose.

Cool-season grasses

Turf grasses are divided into two classes, cool-season and warm-season. Cool-season grasses grow during the cooler months and are dormant during the hotter. Those listed will thrive in the cooler parts of the Southwest — near the ocean or at high elevations in the interior. Bent grasses (*Agrostis*) are narrow-bladed grasses that produce a velvety turf of attractive color and appearance. Where summer temperatures are not extreme, they can spread to the exclusion of other grasses in the mixture.

Fescues (*Festuca*) do not spread by rhizomes, like bluegrass (*Poa*), but form clumps instead; therefore they must be sown thickly. Bare spots do not fill in unless patched or reseeded. All tolerate cold, some shade, some drought. Their chief use is in areas where the summer is cool, near the coast or in the mountains. They may also be used to overseed winter-dormant Bermuda. Bright green color and quick cover are the virtues of the ryegrasses (*Lolium*). Both annual and perennial ryes are often used to provide winter green on dormant warm-season grasses.

Warm-season turf grasses

Widely used in the region, warm-season grasses are dormant during cooler months and grow during the warmer. Bermuda grasses (*Cynodon*) are deep-rooted and heat- and drought-tolerant. They spread rapidly by surface and underground runners, which can be a menace if the grass gets into flower beds, vegetable gardens, or shrubs. They can be overseeded with ryegrass or fescue for winter green. All develop heavy thatch.

Of the other warm-season entries on the chart, dichondra is not a grass at all but a creeping perennial with round leaves like miniature nasturtium leaves. The stems root along their length to make a reasonably tight sod that rarely needs mowing if grown in full sun and subjected to moderate foot traffic. (In shade it can grow taller and should be cut 1 to 2 inches high.) It is subject to invasion by weeds, which are hard to control, and to attack from the dichondra flea beetle.

Native grasses

All the grasses previously mentioned have been imported from abroad, even though many have become naturalized. Certain grasses native to the high, dry plains and plateaus of the West have shown themselves to make creditable lawns in those harsh climates. They need very little water once established and tolerate heat, cold, and wind. They are, of course, entirely brown and dormant in cold weather. Although they can survive with no artificial watering, all look better with a monthly deep soaking.

Ground covers

There are scores of ground covers. They are generally easy to find in nurseries, easy to grow, and conservative in water use. The following plants, which are listed in the Encyclopedia of Plants later in this book, are particularly well suited as lawn substitutes: Aaron's beard (*Hypericum calycinum*), trailing African daisy (*Osteospermum fruticosum*), agapanthus, carpet bugle (*Ajuga reptans*), coyote brush (*Baccharis pilularis*), daylily (*Hemerocallis*), gazania, trailing indigo bush (*Dalea greggii*), ivy (*Hedera*), Japanese spurge (*Pachysandra terminalis*), juniper (*Juniperus*), wild lilac (*Ceanothus*), lily turf (*Liriope, Ophiopogon*), manzanita (*Arctostaphylos*), periwinkle (*Vinca*), rosemary (*Rosmarinus officinalis*), star jasmine (*Trachelospermum jasminoides*), stonecrop (*Sedum*), and verbena.

Several other ground cover plants are worth mentioning. Australian saltbush (*Atriplex semibaccata*) is a gray-green spreading shrub 18 inches tall to 6 feet wide with insignificant flowers. It withstands heat, wind, drought, and is somewhat fire-retardant.

Ice plant is the name given to many species of succulent prostrate or low-growing plants with brilliant flowers. All require little water. Most grow only in Southern California, but *Delosperma nubigenum* (yellow) and *D. cooperi* (purple) are hardy as far north as Denver. Most brilliant in bloom are species of *Lampranthus,* which make sheets of pink, scarlet, orange, red, or purple in spring. (See the encyclopedia entry for more information on *Lampranthus* and *Delosperma.*) For good green foliage, plant *Aptenia cordifolia* or its hybrid known as red apple.

Thyme (*Thymus*) forms low or creeping shrublets with tiny, aromatic leaves and a profusion of tiny flowers. Mother of thyme, or creeping thyme (*T. praecox arcticus, T. serpyllum*), can be used to make small lawns, cover mounds, or fill in between stepping-stones. Growing from 2 to 6 inches tall, thyme becomes a mat of purplish-pink flowers in late spring. It can endure a moderate amount of foot traffic, poor soil, and casual watering, but needs some irrigation in the hottest weather. Red- or white-flowered kinds are sometimes available. Thyme is hardy anywhere when planted in sun or lightest shade.

The Gardening Year

The saying "timing is everything" certainly applies to gardening. If you are attuned to your plants' timetables, you'll be better able to plant, water, fertilize, prune, and protect them successfully. These growth cycles are directly affected by climate — the variations in moisture and temperature that occur on a daily and seasonal basis.

Determining the best times for garden chores is more difficult to prescribe for our region than others. Our varied geography — the Pacific Ocean, inland deserts, mountain ranges, and river valleys — creates many climates that differ in their high and low temperatures, first and last frost dates, and the amount and seasonal timing of rainfall, humidity, wind, and other conditions. These diverse environments support an amazing range of plants. Some tropical plants that thrive in coastal gardens won't survive 40 miles inland; climb a few thousand feet up from a lowland desert and the plant palette changes dramatically. (For more on climates, see the Introduction.)

Conditions vary considerably in your own neighborhood as

well, even around your home. We've all noticed that some spots are hotter, cooler, windier, and more or less humid than others. Note and make use of these microclimates. For example, you may be able to set out tender plants near a warm, protected south wall weeks earlier than you can in an unprotected spot with an eastern or northern exposure. In fact, the southern exposure may be the only place on your property where some plants will survive. (See "Designing Your Garden" for more on microclimates.)

As you refer to the following summaries of seasonal gardening activities, remember that they are only broad guidelines — seasons do not follow a rigid schedule from year to year. Get to know your own climate zone and microclimates. Observe the plants in your area, around your neighborhood, and in your garden. Note when certain plants begin to bloom, when leaves emerge or drop. With experience, these changes can tell you when to set out other plants as well as when to prune, fertilize, and control certain weeds and pests.

Spring

Gardening calendars often begin with spring. In most of North America, it is the traditional time to plant and prepare the garden for a new growing season. But in much of our region, fall is the best time to plant; in fact, many people plant successfully throughout the year.

Spring is a sweet-and-sour gardening season. Sometimes it is mild and even-tempered, with gradually warming days. But most years spring is a chameleon that changes every few days — now threatening to break into summer, now chilling back into winter. Gardeners need to stay on their toes, ready to protect plants from frost or to cool them with water on a 100-degree day. Check the nightly weather reports and have a protection plan and materials at hand (mulches, row covers, and so on) if freezing weather is forecast.

If you consider the average date of the last killing frost to mark the beginning of spring, it can arrive in our region from January through May. As a rule of thumb, each 1,000-foot increase in elevation delays the onset of spring by 30 days.

Key landscape plants can announce that spring is around the corner. In coastal California, look for the Chinese fringe tree (*Chionanthus retusus*). Its profuse pure white flowers can be among the first to appear. In Southern California's inland valleys, clusters of magenta flowers of Western redbud appear in the spring. In Arizona's middle-elevation Sonoran Desert, feathery cassia (*Cassia artemisiodes*) displays rich yellow blooms in early spring. High-elevation gardeners look for a flush of new growth on pines and the new, silvery tips of blue spruce. In other parts of the Southwest, the appearance of young leaves on ash, elm, cottonwood, and mulberry trees indicates that it's time to get serious about springtime gardening.

Clean up and get ready

If you didn't clean up during the cool days of winter, early spring is your last chance to get ready for the active gardening months ahead. Rake the leaves and debris from lawns to allow better air circulation, which helps prevent disease. Remove (and compost) mulches, leaves, and other materials from the flower, vegetable, and herb beds to allow the sun to warm the soil for planting. Later in the spring — after the soil has warmed and the plants have begun actively growing — spread a moisture-conserving mulch (compost, grass clippings, ground bark) around the plants.

Remove bulb flowers that are past their prime, but wait until their leaves turn brown before digging and storing the bulbs. The leaves create food that is stored in the bulb for use the following year.

Fertilizing

Apply fertilizers just before the anticipated flush of new growth so that nutrients will be available for plants when needed most. Dig in an all-purpose fertilizer around plant roots and water it in. Where the soil is cold, consider using a fertilizer that delivers nitrogen as ammonium nitrate, which is more water soluble. Check all plants for signs of iron chlorosis — yellow leaves with dark green veins. Apply iron chelates for fastest recovery.

Lawns

Fertilize lawns of cool-season grasses in mid to late spring. (This is especially important if you missed the fall feeding.) Fertilize warm-season grasses when new green blades appear beneath the dormant brown. Do not fertilize overseeded lawns late in the season. This encourages the cool-season grass to linger, slowing the reestablishment of the warm-season grass.

Spring is the time to prepare the seedbed if you plan to sow seeds for cool-grass lawns, such as bluegrass and fescue, for new lawns, or for renewing bare spots in existing lawns. You can prepare the soil now (while it's comfortable to work outside) for planting warm-season grasses in midsummer.

Check for thatch buildup. Thatch, a concentrated layer of dead grass stems that accumulates just above the soil line, can slow growth and restrict the flow of water and fertilizer to grass roots. A buildup of thatch is common in Bermuda grass. Remove it in early to mid spring by raking vigorously or with a rented power verticutter.

Pest and disease control

Protect deciduous fruit trees against pests such as scale, spider mites, and aphids with a dormant-oil spray before the flower buds swell and open. Spray the trunk, branches, and twigs thoroughly. Rake and remove garden debris to eliminate hiding places for snails, slugs, and other pests. In early to mid spring, check for aphids and whiteflies on the undersides of leaves. A stiff spray of water from a garden hose will often take care of infestations if you notice them early.

In mild-winter zones, remove emerging weeds while they're young and easy to pull, before they rob your landscape plants of moisture and nutrients. You can also apply pre-emergent sprays in early spring to prevent infestations of troublesome summer weeds such as crabgrass and spotted spurge.

Pruning

Early spring is the time to thin branches of woody plants selectively — while they are dormant and the sap is not running. Wait until late spring, after the new growth begins to thin tender plants, such as hibiscus, and to remove branches damaged by the cold. As you prune, check the stakes and supports on trees to see if the branches are developing as you like. The branches and trunks may have increased in size, so loosen or remove ties as needed.

Thin the fruit of peaches, apricots, plums, and the like before they reach marble size, spacing them 6 to 12 inches apart on the branch. Don't be timid or the fruit you harvest will end up small and misshapen. Pinch back clusters of grapes by about a fourth to a third to ensure bigger grapes. Remember that citrus normally drop fruit in late spring, so don't be alarmed when this happens.

Watering

Springtime winds can be downright fierce in some parts of the region, damaging and drying out plants. Windbreaks are required to slow down gusts of up to 60 miles an hour in California's Coachella Valley. Keep a watchful eye on your plants when the weather turns windy. If plant leaves begin to curl, irrigate deeply — this is one of the first signs of water stress. (By curling, the leaves reduce transpiration by reducing their surface area.)

Check drip irrigation systems at the beginning of spring to be certain they are operating properly. Use a soil probe or dig down to see if moisture is reaching deep enough — 2 feet or more is recommended for established trees and shrubs. If not, reset timers and/or add emitters to supply enough moisture through the late spring and summer heat.

Planting

If you didn't prepare your planting beds during winter, mix soil amendments and ammonium phosphate into the soil in early spring. Don't set out the plants until the soil begins to warm. This is particularly important for cold-winter gardeners, who may be enticed by the first warm days of spring to plant while the soil is still too cold.

Some plants can be set out before the last frost date if the soil has warmed enough. Others should wait until the danger of frost has passed. Some cold-tender species, such as bougainvillea and certain citrus (limes, lemons), should wait for mid spring and a little more warmth. Ask at your nursery if you're not sure about specific plants.

Early spring is the best time to transplant evergreens. To ease the process, dig around the plant a few weeks before making the move. The smaller root ball will create new feeder roots, making it easier for the plant to become established in its new home. When you're ready to transplant, prepare the new planting hole before you dig up the plant to get it back in the ground as quickly as possible.

In late spring, direct seed or transplant seedlings of warm-season summer annuals such as zinnias and periwinkle. Protect the seeds and young plants against hungry birds by covering them with netting or chicken wire. If cool-season annuals such as pansies and snapdragons are still blooming, plant around them or remove them to give the warm-season plants room to grow.

If you live in the desert or an inland valley, remember that the sun will be intense during the summer. Place plants where they can take advantage of the afternoon shade provided by overhangs, structures, trees, and shrubs.

Spring is the time for plant sales at many botanical gardens and arboretums. They can be excellent sources of adapted, uncommon, and native plants.

Summer

In most of the region, summertime means sunshine and heat. As early as April and sometimes sooner, daytime temperatures can reach over 100 degrees in desert areas. And it doesn't let up. In Palm Springs and Phoenix, 90 or more consecutive days of 100-degree temperatures are common. Only in the mountains and along the coast do plants and people escape the heat. Where daytime heat is oppressive, experienced gardeners limit their chores to the early morning and evening hours. Midday in June is not the time to tackle that planting of junipers infested with Bermuda grass.

In southern Arizona and parts of New Mexico, the heat is often tempered in mid-July by the summer rainy season. The welcome rains cool plants and temperatures, if only temporarily, and evaporation is rapid. Most storms provide more noise than nurture. Although rain may fall heavily for a short period, much of the water runs down desert washes before it can soak into the soil. And, unlike winter rains, summer storms are usually localized, affecting only a few square miles.

Watering

In most of the region, keeping plants watered is the most important garden chore. Every day, examine the plants you set out in late spring and water if the soil isn't moist. Make sure the watering basins around established plants are big enough. If possible, they should extend to the edge of the plant's drip line (the perimeter of its leafy canopy). Make them about 3 inches deep for shrubs and roses. Container plants require water almost every day in summer. Place them where there's some afternoon shade, if possible; they will appreciate the break.

If you live in a region with cold winters and early frosts are a possibility, gradually taper off the frequency of irrigation in late summer to slow growth. Tender new growth is most susceptible to cold damage.

Lawns

Lawns require water every few days to look their best, but they will survive on much less if they are deeply rooted. Watch for signs of heat stress — grass blades turning a bluish color, grass not straightening up after you've walked on it. From time to time, irrigate deeply to flush down the salts that can build up in soils, but don't overwater to the point of runoff.

In hot areas, early summer — when temperatures rise above 65 degrees in the evening — is the time to lay sod or plant sprigs or stolons of warm-season grasses, such as Bermuda grass and zoysia, which need heat to establish. In areas with cold winters, late summer is an excellent time to start cool-season grasses. The warm soil encourages growth, while cooling temperatures reduce stress and the need for water.

Fertilize established warm-season lawns each month in the summer. Wait until the temperatures cool in late summer before feeding cool-season grasses. During the hot months, mow cool-season grasses an inch higher. (This is most important for Kentucky bluegrass.)

Pest and disease control

Pests are most active during warm, humid periods in early summer. Examine plants often to catch infestations of aphids and spider mites before they multiply to epidemic proportion. Be sure to check the undersides of leaves. If you have grapes, look for the grape-leaf skeletonizer, a small, yellow and black caterpillar. Remove infested leaves by hand or, if the infestation is severe, check with your nursery for an appropriate control. In early summer, protect fruit trees from birds with nylon netting or a wood frame covered with wire; paper bags will protect grape clusters.

Gardeners in the semiarid Southwest should watch for signs of Texas root rot. After a summer rain, the fungus may appear on the soil surface as a tan patch that turns dark and powdery. Unfortunately, the first sign of the disease in a plant — a sudden wilting of the leaves — comes only after about half the root system has been damaged. You can guard against Texas root rot by adding sulfur to highly alkaline soil and digging in lots of organic material. Consult your nursery or county extension agent for advice on saving diseased plants.

Pull or spray summer weeds to keep them from reaching seed-production stage. Now, when it is actively growing, is the time to control Bermuda grass that has escaped into flower beds or other areas where it isn't wanted. Apply a glyphosate spray on a windless day, following all directions on the product label.

Planting

Summer is the time to plant palm trees. Palms require the heat to become established, whether you are transplanting existing palms or planting new ones. Where summers are mild, along the California coast, for instance, you can continue to plant trees, shrubs, ground cover, and perennials. Elsewhere, if possible, wait until early fall, when the soil is warm but temperatures and a corresponding need for water lessen.

Care and maintenance

Remove spent flowers from annuals and perennials to maintain their appearance and to encourage repeat bloom. Feed most plants in early summer to continue vigorous growth. Fertilize roses in midsummer, then repeat about a month later. Check their leaves for iron chlorosis as you did in the spring. Replenish organic mulches around plants to keep roots cool and to conserve moisture.

Provide supports for upright perennials such as delphinium,

phlox, and rudbeckia. Tie rapidly growing grape canes to sturdy supports with stretchable ties. Make portable shelters of shade cloth or cheesecloth to give heat-stressed plants temporary relief from the afternoon sun. Dig and store bearded iris rhizomes in mid to late summer. For best results, do not water plants for about 3 weeks before digging. If you're planning a winter garden, order the seeds in midsummer.

Fall

In most parts of the Southwest, fall is the busiest gardening season and the best time of year to plant. Days are cooler; nights are pleasant. Frost ambles across the region, arriving in Flagstaff at the end of September and in Los Angeles almost 3 months later. In all but the coldest areas, while air temperatures drop, the soil remains warm enough to encourage rapid root growth — ideal for planting.

Watering
As the temperatures drop, plants require less water. But the hot, dry winds in Southern California and the Southwest deserts, common during fall, can greatly increase water needs. During these windy spells, watch plants for signs of water stress — lackluster leaf color, curling leaves, browning at the tips of leaves. As fall progresses, it's wise to increase intervals between waterings (but not the amount) to slow plant growth in anticipation of the cold temperatures to come.

Fertilizing
The timing and extent of the drop in temperature in your area will determine when and how much you fertilize. Fertilizer encourages new growth that is highly susceptible to frost damage. This isn't a problem for annuals, so continue to fertilize them about every 2 weeks. Fertilize cold-hardy perennials, shrubs, and trees early in the season, but don't fertilize citrus, hibiscus, or other cold-tender plants late in the season unless you live along the coast or where frost is uncommon.

Lawns
If you plan to overseed your Bermuda grass lawn with a crop of lush, green, winter ryegrass, mid to late fall is the time. Bermuda grass begins to turn brown when night temperatures drop below 60 degrees. Cut the existing grass as low as possible before overseeding. If you're not going to overseed, fertilize now; the nutrients will encourage root growth, and the lawn will grow better next spring.

Planting

In most of the Southwest, fall is the best season to plant trees, shrubs, ground cover, and perennials. Roots grow rapidly in the warm soil, and diminished heat means less stress and water loss. Nurseries gear up for the fall planting season, so a good selection of container plants should be available. In early to mid fall you can sow seeds and set out transplants of winter-blooming annuals such as pansies, snapdragons, and petunias. Now is a good time to sow seeds of spring-blooming wildflowers, such as California poppies, desert marigold, and African daisies.

Plant hardy bulbs and rhizomes — amaryllis, cannas, daffodils, bearded iris, Dutch iris — as the soil begins to cool in the fall. Buy bulbs and rhizomes as soon as they arrive at the nursery — late summer to early fall — for best quality and selection. Chilling some bulbs (tulips, particularly) in the crisper compartment of the refrigerator for a few weeks before planting can help increase bloom in spring. Lift and divide established but overcrowded plantings of spring-blooming perennials such as iris.

Don't forget the fall plant sales at botanical gardens and arboretums. You can buy some nice plants and also be able to see what they'll look like when mature.

Cleanup

In the cold-winter mountains and high deserts, fall is the time to clean up the garden and prepare plants for the winter. Remove (and compost) leaves and debris — dying annuals, the frost-killed foliage of herbaceous perennials, spoiled fruit and vegetables — to discourage insect and animal pests. Police weeds to prevent winter rains and winds from scattering their seeds or their progeny will greet you in the spring.

Winter

Winter best illustrates the great contrasts in the region's climates. Most of coastal California does not have winter or, more accurately, a killing frost, and gardening continues apace. Where winters are mild but susceptible to frosts, gardeners make creative use of the warmer areas on their property. In the high deserts and mountains, winter is harsh and outdoor gardening practically comes to a standstill. But even in these regions, there are a few outdoor gardening chores, house plants to tend, and seed catalogs and gardening books to fuel dreams for warmer days.

Plant protection

In cold, high-elevation climates, plants need protection. Knock the snow from branches as it accumulates or the branches may break under the load. Mulch perennial beds and small shrubs after the ground has frozen a couple of inches deep. The mulch will keep the ground frozen so that plants won't be heaved out of the soil by repeated freezing and thawing, which exposes their roots and, sometimes, kills the plant.

In regions with mild winters, be ready to protect citrus, bougainvillea and other tender plants from freezing temperatures. Have row covers, burlap, carpet scraps, or old blankets on hand for covering plants and wrapping the trunks of young citrus and other tender trees and shrubs. A cold snap can come quickly — pay attention to nightly weather forecasts.

Watering

In winter, cloudiness can be widespread and gentle rains can occur over large areas, sometimes lasting for several days. Nevertheless, if rain is scarce, you will need to water. In warm and mild regions, water spring-blooming annuals regularly. Irrigate permanent landscape plants deeply about every 2 to 3 weeks. In cold regions, if water isn't supplied by melting snow, irrigate when the temperature is above freezing. Well-watered plants are better able to survive cold snaps and desiccating winds. Wherever the soil freezes, flush and drain irrigation systems to rid the lines of mineral deposits and keep freezing water from cracking them.

Pruning

Prune roses and deciduous trees and shrubs in late winter, while they are dormant. (Don't prune spring-flowering shrubs.) When the buds on rose canes begin to swell, it's all right to prune. This can be as early as mid-December in the low deserts and mild-winter regions of Southern California, January in intermediate deserts, and as late as March or April in higher elevations. Prune evergreen trees that require control or shaping in late winter. In windy areas, trees may require some thinning to allow strong winds to blow through the branches.

Lawns

Fertilize fall-seeded ryegrass with a high-nitrogen fertilizer at 6-week intervals through the winter to keep it green and vigorous. Water dormant Bermuda grass lawns about every 3 weeks.

Planting

In regions with mild winters, continue to plant spring-blooming annuals. Pansies, alyssum, snapdragons, and stock will be available as bedding plants at nurseries. Late winter tending toward early spring is also an acceptable time to plant selected flowering perennials, such as coreopsis, geranium, Shasta daisy, and gaillardia, and spring-blooming bulbs, such as gladiolus. And, if yours is an edible landscape and you didn't plant cool-season vegetables (peas, broccoli, lettuce) in the fall, you may be able to squeeze them in now and harvest before the heat of late spring.

Start seeds of selected annuals and warm-season vegetables indoors. You still have time to order from catalogs with their huge selection of varieties, many of which aren't available at nurseries.

In all but the coldest regions, you'll usually find a good selection of bare-root plants (roses, fruit trees, berries, asparagus, strawberries) at the nursery in late winter. These can be planted from mid-December through January in the low deserts and inland valleys and from March through April in high elevations.

The Color Plates

The plants shown in the plates on the following pages were selected for their proven performance in gardens and landscapes of the Southwest. They are grouped according to plant types: trees and palms, shrubs, perennials and succulents, ground covers, and vines. Each plate is accompanied by a short description, including the plant's botanical and common names, its height or spread, the time of bloom (if appropriate), a comment on its uses or culture, its hardiness zone rating, and the page on which you will find its encyclopedia entry.

A Word about Color

Color, more than many other visual attributes, is in the eye of the beholder. What one person describes as blue, another may call lavender or even purple. And it is not just the names of colors that vary. Light and shade, time of day, and other colors nearby can all affect what we see. A leaf that appears rich red in the midday sun may be a deep lavender in late-afternoon shade.

As you look at the photos on the following pages, remember that the camera, no less than the eye, captures color as it appears at a certain moment. Add to that the natural variation among plants and the difficulty of reproducing colors precisely, and you will understand that you should not count on your plant having exactly the color you see in the photograph.

Trees and Palms

Acacia baileyana   Cootamundra   Prefers sun
                       Wattle   Zones 9, 10
                       Height: 30–40 ft.   p. 218
                       Blooms in winter

Albizia julibrissin Hardy Silk Tree   Tolerates drought,
'Rosea'   Height: 20–40 ft.   wind, salt
                       Blooms in summer   Zones 6–9
                                            p. 223

Arbutus unedo

Strawberry Tree
Height: to 35 ft.
Flowers and fruit
in fall

Fairly drought
tolerant
Zones 6–10
p. 227

Arecastrum
romanzoffianum

Queen Palm
Height: to 50 ft.
Flowers and fruit
year-round
Full sun

Moist air
Zone 10;
semihardy in 9
p. 228

Brachychiton populneus

Bottle Tree
Height: 30–50 ft.
Evergreen
Blooms in spring
Fruit in fall

Very drought tolerant
Zones 8–10
p. 233

Brahea armata

Blue Palm
Height: to 40 ft.
Blooms summer to fall

Fruit fall to winter
Zones 9, 10
p. 233

***Calocedrus
decurrens***

*California Incense
Cedar
Height: to 100 ft.
Tolerates poor soil*

*Useful screen or
windbreak
Zones 5–10
p. 237*

Casuarina stricta

*Mountain She-Oak
Height: to 35 ft.
Tough and hardy
Good desert tree*

*Zone 9
p. 241*

Cedrus atlantica
'**Glauca**'

Blue Atlas Cedar
Height: to 60 ft.
Evergreen

Drought tolerant
Zones 6–10
p. 242

Ceratonia siliqua

Carob
Height: 20–50 ft.
Evergreen
Blooms in spring

Drought tolerant
Zones 9, 10
p. 244

Cercidium
floridum

Palo Verde
Height: to 30 ft.
Blooms in spring
Good desert tree

Native to
Southwest
Zones 8–10
p. 244

Chamaerops
humilis

European Fan
Palm
Height: to 20 ft.
Slow-growing

One of the
hardiest palms
Zones 8–10
p. 247

Chorisia speciosa *Floss Silk Tree* *Needs excellent*
Height: to 60 ft. *drainage*
Showy flowers in *Zones 9, 10*
fall *p. 248*

Cinnamomum *Camphor Tree* *Thrives in heat*
camphora *Height: to 50 ft.* *Zones 8–10*
Evergreen *p. 249*
Fragrant flowers in
spring

**Citrus
× paradisi**

*Marsh Grapefruit
Height: to 30 ft.
Dwarf trees to 15
ft.*

*Evergreen
Fragrant
Zones 9, 10
p. 251*

**Cordyline
australis**

*Giant Dracaena
Height: to 30 ft.
Evergreen
White flowers in
spring*

*Drought tolerant
Zones 8–10
p. 253*

**Cupaniopsis
anacardioides**

Carrot Wood
Height: to 40 ft.
Evergreen
Good lawn tree

Tolerates wet soil,
salt
Zone 10;
semihardy in 9
p. 256

× **Cupressocyparis
leylandii**

Leyland Cypress
Height: to 100 ft.
Evergreen
Needs full sun

Fast-growing
Tolerates salt
Zones 6–10
p. 257

Cupressus glabra   *Smooth-barked*   p. 258
                         Arizona Cypress
                         Height: to 40 ft.
                         Fast-growing
                         Good desert tree
                         Zones 8–10

Cupressus   *Columnar Italian*   Zones 8–10
sempervirens   *Cypress*   p. 258
                        Height: to 75 ft.
                        Best used in
                        groups

Dalea spinosa   Smoke Tree   Zones 9, 10
                    Height: to 12 ft.   p. 259
                    Blooms in spring
                    Native to
                    Southwest

Diospyros kaki   Kaki   Fall color
                     Height: to 30 ft.   Zone 5
                     Edible fruit in   p. 262
                     November

Elaeagnus angustifolia

*Russian Olive
Height: to 20 ft.
Fragrant flowers in spring
Fruit in fall*

*Extremely drought tolerant
Zones 3–9
p. 265*

Eriobotrya japonica

*Loquat
Height: to 30 ft.
Fragrant flowers in winter*

*Fruit in spring
Zones 8–10
p. 267*

**Eucalyptus
citriodora**

*Lemon-scented
Gum
Height: 50–75 ft.
Strongly scented*

*Easy to grow
Zones 9, 10
p. 269*

**Eucalyptus
nicholii**

*Narrow-leaved
Black Peppermint
Height: to 40 ft.
Peppermint
scented*

*Good for street or
garden
Zones 9, 10
p. 270*

**Eucalyptus
sideroxylon**

*Red Ironbark
Height: to 80 ft.
Blooms from fall
to spring*

*Drought tolerant
Zones 9, 10
p. 270*

**Eucalyptus
spathulata**

*Narrow-leafed
Gimlet
Height: to 20 ft.*

*Good desert tree
Zones 9, 10
p. 270*

Ficus carica   Common Fig   Popular desert tree
                        Height: to 30 ft.   Zones 8–10
                        Edible fruit   p. 274

Ficus microcarpa   Indian Laurel   Zone 10;
                        Height: to 40 ft.   semihardy in 9
                        Good street tree   p. 274

Fraxinus oxycarpa

Ash
Height: to 35 ft.
Fall color
Useful street or
garden tree

Not suitable for
very dry sites
Zone 6
p. 277

Fraxinus velutina

Arizona Ash
Height: to 50 ft.
Fall color

Fast-growing
Zone 6
p. 277

Geijera parviflora   *Australian Willow   Zone 9
Height: to 30 ft.   p. 282
Evergreen
Excellent street or
garden tree*

Ginkgo biloba   *Ginkgo   Tolerates drought,
Height: to 80 ft.   wet soil, salt
Fall color   Zones 5–9
Full sun   p. 284*

Ilex
× *altaclarensis*
'Wilsonii'

Wilson Holly
Height: to 30 ft.
Evergreen
Vigorous grower

Lots of berries
Zone 8
p. 290

Jacaranda
mimosifolia

Jacaranda
Height: to 40 ft.
Blooms in spring
Fruit in fall

Drought tolerant
Zone 10;
semihardy in 9
p. 292

**Koelreuteria
paniculata**

Golden-rain Tree
Height: to 40 ft.
Blooms in summer
Flowers in long
clusters

Tolerates drought
and heat
Zone 5
p. 295

Laurus nobilis

Laurel
Height: to 40 ft.
Evergreen
Slow-growing

Drought tolerant
when established
Zones 8–10
p. 298

Liquidambar styraciflua

*Sweet Gum
Height: to 75 ft.
Fall color*

*Moist, acid soil
Zones 7–10
p. 304*

Magnolia grandiflora

*Southern Magnolia
Height: to 80 ft.
Evergreen
Large, fragrant
flowers*

*Fine specimen tree
Zones 7–9
p. 307*

Maytenus boaria

*Mayten Tree
Height: to 30 ft.
Evergreen*

*Average soil with
good drainage
Zones 9, 10
p. 308*

***Melaleuca
linariifolia***

*Flaxleaf Paperbark
Height: to 30 ft.
Blooms in late
summer
Tolerates drought,
heat*

*Zone 10;
semihardy in 9
p. 309*

Olea europaea   *Olive*   *Drought tolerant*
                    Height: to 30 ft.   *Zone 9; semihardy*
                    Evergreen   *in 8*
                    Edible fruit   *p. 315*
                    Fruitless cultivars
                    available

Olneya tesota   *Desert Ironwood*   *Native to*
                    Height: 25–30 ft.   *Southwest*
                    Evergreen   *Zone 9*
                    Thrives in desert   *p. 316*
                    heat

**Parkinsonia
aculeata**

*Jerusalem Thorn
Height: 20–30 ft.
Drought tolerant
when established*

*Zones 8–10
p. 320*

**Phoenix
canariensis**

*Canary Islands
Date Palm
Height: to 60 ft.
Fruit fall to winter
Rich, well-drained
soil*

*Not drought
tolerant
Zones 9, 10
p. 326*

Pinus edulis

Piñon
Height: to 30 ft.
Evergreen
Drought tolerant

Edible seeds
Zones 4–10
p. 328

Pinus eldarica

Afghanistan Pine
Height: to 60 ft.
Evergreen
Tolerates desert
heat and wind

Zones 7–10
p. 328

Pinus halepensis   *Aleppo Pine*   *Zones 8–10*
                       Height: to 60 ft.   *p. 329*
                       Evergreen
                       Tolerates drought,
                       heat, wind, salt

Pinus pinea   *Italian Stone Pine*   *Zone 9*
                       Height: to 80 ft.   *p. 329*
                       Evergreen
                       For large
                       properties

**Pinus
thunbergiana**

*Japanese Black
Pine
Height: 20–80 ft.
Evergreen
Tolerates wind,
salt spray*

*Useful for coastal
areas
Zones 5–9
p. 329*

Pistacia chinensis

*Chinese Pistache
Height: to 60 ft.
Fall color*

*Drought tolerant
Zones 7–9
p. 329*

Pittosporum
eugenioides

Pittosporum
Height: to 40 ft.
Evergreen
Often used as a
hedge, clipped to
4–10 ft.

Zones 9, 10
p. 330

Pittosporum
undulatum

Victorian Box
Height: to 40 ft.
Evergreen
Blooms in spring
Fragrant

May be sheared as
screen
Zones 9, 10
p. 331

Platanus
racemosa

California
Sycamore
Height: to 100 ft.
Fast-growing

Smaller Arizona
species available
Zone 7
p. 331

Podocarpus
gracilior

Fern Pine
Height: to 60 ft.
Evergreen
Needs regular
watering

Zones 9, 10
p. 332

Populus alba   White Poplar   Zone 5
                  Height: to 50 ft.   p. 333
                  Fast-growing
                  Good screen or
                  windbreak

Populus fremontii   Western   Needs watering in
                      Cottonwood   desert areas
                      Height: to 60 ft.   Zone 8
                      Good fall color   p. 333
                      Grow male plants
                      only

Prosopis glandulosa

*Mesquite
Height: to 30 ft.
Blooms spring to summer
Drought tolerant*

*Native to Southwest
Zones 7–9
p. 333*

Prunus cerasifera 'Thundercloud'

*Cherry Plum
Height: 15–30 ft.
Flowers in early spring
Moist, well-drained soil*

*Sun
Zone 5
p. 334*

Prunus lyonii   *Catalina Cherry*   *Drought tolerant*
                       Height: to 40 ft.   *Zone 7*
                       Evergreen   *p. 335*
                       Edible fruit

Prunus mume   *Flowering Apricot*   *Full sun*
                      Height: to 20 ft.   *Zone 5*
                      Blooms January to   *p. 335*
                      March

Pyrus calleryana *Bradford Pear*   p. 337
'Bradford'   *Height: to 30 ft.*
Blooms in spring
Fall color
Zones 5–9

Quercus agrifolia *Coast Live Oak*   Zones 8–10
   Height: to 70 ft.   p. 338
Evergreen
Native to
California

Quercus coccinea   *Scarlet Oak*   *Zones 5–9*
                        Height: to 80 ft.   *p. 339*
                        Fall color
                        Tolerates alkaline
                        soil

Quercus suber   *Cork Oak*   *Picturesque bark*
                        Height: to 60 ft.   *Zones 7–9*
                        Evergreen   *p. 339*

Rhus lancea

*African sumac
Height: to 25 ft.
Evergreen
Tolerates intense
heat and drought*

*Zones 9, 10
p. 340*

**Robinia
× ambigua
'Idahoensis'**

*Hybrid Locust
Height: to 40 ft.
Full sun
Tolerates heat and
drought*

*Zone 4
p. 341*

Sapium sebiferum   *Chinese Tallow*   *Tolerates dry or*
                       Tree   *wet, acid or*
                       Height: to 50 ft.   *alkaline soil*
                       Fall color   *Zones 8, 9*
                                             p. 345

Schinus molle   *California Pepper*   *Tolerates drought*
                    Tree   *and heat*
                    Height: to 40 ft.   *Zones 9, 10*
                    Evergreen   *p. 346*
                    Blooms in summer

Schinus terebinthifolius

Brazilian Pepper Tree
Height: to 30 ft.
Evergreen

Extremely drought tolerant
Zone 10
p. 346

Sophora japonica

Pagoda Tree
Height: to 70 ft.
Blooms in summer
Flowers in long clusters

Fruit fall to winter
Zones 5–8
p. 349

**Tabebuia
chrysotricha**

*Golden Trumpet
Tree
Height: to 25 ft.
Blooms most
heavily in spring*

*Fast-growing
Zone 10
p. 352*

Tristania conferta

*Brisbane Box
Height: to 50 ft.
Endures drought
when established*

*Zones 9, 10
p. 353*

Ulmus parvifolia

Chinese Elm
Height: to 60 ft.
Fast-growing
Excellent shade
tree

Resistant to Dutch
elm disease
Zones 5–10
p. 354

*Vitex agnus-
castus*

Lilac Chaste Tree
Height: to 20 ft.
Flowers in long
clusters

Zone 7
p. 358

Shrubs

Acacia greggii Catclaw Acacia Zones 7–10
Height: to 20 ft. p. 219
Blooms in summer
Native to
Southwest

Atriplex Four-wing Alkaline soil
canescens Saltbush Fire resistant
Height: 3–6 ft. Zones 4–10
Width: 4–8 ft. p. 229
Evergreen

Aucuba japonica   Japanese Aucuba   Zone 7
                          Height: 4–10 ft.   p. 230
                          Evergreen
                          Requires male and
                          female for berries

Bauhinia   Purple Orchid   Messy seed pods
variegata   Tree   Zone 10
                          Height: to 30 ft.   p. 231
                          Blooms January
                          through spring

Buddleia davidii   Orange-eye   Flowers in clusters
                        Butterfly Bush   Zones 5–9
                        Height: 6–10 ft.   p. 234
                        Blooms summer to
                        fall

Caesalpinia   Red Bird of   Good desert plant
pulcherrima   Paradise   Zones 9, 10
                        Height: to 10 ft.   p. 235
                        Full sun

Calliandra eriophylla

*Fairy Duster
Height: to 3 ft.
Evergreen
Blooms in late winter*

*Drought tolerant
Native to
Southwest
Zone 10
p. 236*

Callistemon citrinus

*Crimson Bottle-
Brush
Height: 10–20 ft.
Blooms spring to summer
Fast-growing*

*Acid soil
Easily trained as espalier
Zone 9
p. 236*

Camellia
sasanqua
'Showa no Sakae'

Sasanqua Camellia
Height: 6–10 ft.
Evergreen
Acid soil

Blooms fall to
winter
Zones 8–10
p. 238

Carissa
macrocarpa

Natal Plum
Height: to 15 ft.
Evergreen
Blooms year-round

Fragrant
Zone 10
p. 239

**Cassia
artemisioides**

*Wormwood Senna
Height: to 4 ft.
Evergreen
Blooms early
spring to summer*

*Very drought
tolerant
Zones 9, 10
p. 240*

Cassia nemophila

*Feathery Cassia
Height: to 4 ft.
Evergreen
Hardier than* C.
artemisioides

*Zones 9, 10
p. 240*

Ceanothus
× 'Julia Phelps'

Wild Lilac
Height: to 7 ft.
Blooms in spring
Fussy about
temperature and
drainage

Zones 9, 10
p. 241

Ceanothus
× 'Ray Hartman'

Wild Lilac
Height: to 20 ft.
Tall shrub or small
tree

Zones 9, 10
p. 242

**Ceanothus
thyrsiflorus**

*Blue Blossom
Height: to 30 ft.
Tall shrub or small
tree*

*Dwarf form
available
Zones 8–10
p. 242*

**Cercis
occidentalis**

*Western Redbud
Height: 10–15 ft.
Blooms in early
spring*

*Zones 5–9
p. 245*

Cercocarpus ledifolius

*Curl-leaf Mountain Mahogany
Height: to 12 ft., usually lower
Evergreen*

*Extremely drought tolerant
Zones 5–9
p. 246*

Chaenomeles speciosa 'Toyo Nishiki'

*Common Flowering Quince
Height: 6–10 ft.
Dwarf forms available*

*Blooms in spring
All zones
p. 246*

Chilopsis linearis *Desert Willow* *Zones 9, 10*
Height: to 25 ft. *p. 247*
Fast-growing
Native to
Southwest

× **Chitalpa** *Chitalpa* *Drought tolerant*
Height: to 30 ft. *Zones 7–10*
Shrub or small tree *p. 247*
Blooms summer
through fall

Cistus ladanifer

Crimson-spot
Rockrose
Height: to 5 ft.
Evergreen
Fragrant leaves

Fire resistant,
drought tolerant
Zones 9, 10
p. 250

**Cotoneaster
lacteus**

Parney
Cotoneaster
Height: to 12 ft.
Evergreen

Useful as hedge
Zone 7
p. 256

Dodonaea viscosa 'Purpurea'

Purple Hop Bush
Height: to 15 ft.
Evergreen
Tolerates most
soils, drought,
heat, wind

Useful as screen
Zone 8
p. 264

Elaeagnus pungens

Thorny Elaeagnus
Height: to 15 ft.
Evergreen
Blooms in fall

Fragrant
Zones 7–9
p. 265

Encelia farinosa   Brittlebush   Zones 8, 9
Height: to 5 ft.   p. 266
Aromatic
Native to
Southwest

Eriogonum   California   Full sun
fasciculatum   Buckwheat   Zones 8–10
Height: 3 ft.   p. 267
Blooms in summer
Flowers good for
drying

Erythrina crista-galli

Cockspur Coral Tree
Height: to 20 ft.
Treelike in frost-free areas

Blooms spring through fall
Zones 8–10
p. 269

Euryops pectinatus

Gray-leaved Euryops
Height: to 3 ft.
Evergreen

Blooms most of year
Zones 9, 10
p. 271

Fatsia japonica   Japanese Aralia   Needs water
                          Height: 10–12 ft.   Zone 8
                          Evergreen   p. 272
                          Best in full shade

Feijoa sellowiana   Pineapple Guava   Edible petals
                          Height: to 20 ft.   Zone 8
                          Evergreen   p. 272
                          Blooms in spring

Forestiera neomexicana

*Desert Olive
Height: to 10 ft.
Fast-growing,
weedy*

*For hedges in
harsh, dry climates
Zones 5–10
p. 275*

Fouquieria splendens

*Ocotillo
Height: 10–20 ft.
Leafless except
after rains*

*Dry soil
Full sun
Zone 8
p. 275*

Fremontodendron × 'California Glory'

Flannel Bush
Height: to 20 ft.
Evergreen
Cavagnaro
Blooms in spring

Very drought tolerant
Fast-growing
Zone 9
p. 279

Gardenia jasminoides

Gardenia
Height: 2–5 ft.
Blooms spring to fall

Heavily scented
Zone 8
p. 280

Garrya elliptica *Silktassel* Zone 8
Height: to 10 ft. p. 280
Evergreen
Good as specimen
or screen

Heteromeles *Toyon* *Attracts birds and*
arbutifolia *Height: 10–25 ft.* *bees*
Evergreen *Zone 8*
Blooms in spring p. 287
Red fruit in fall

| **Hypericum** **calycinum** | Aaron's-beard Height: to 12 in. Evergreen Blooms in summer | Good for sandy soil Zone 5 p. 289 |

| **Ilex cornuta** | Chinese Holly Height: 8–15 ft. Evergreen | Zone 7 p. 290 |

Ilex vomitoria

Yaupon
Height: 15–25 ft.
Evergreen
Acid or alkaline
soil

Tolerates salt spray
Zone 7
p. 290

Juniperus
chinensis
'Torulosa'

Chinese Juniper
Height: to 15 ft.
Evergreen
Easy to grow

Other cultivars for
many uses
All zones
p. 293

Justicia
californica

Chuparosa
Height: to 5 ft.
Blooms in spring
Full sun

Drought tolerant
Zone 5
p. 294

Lantana camara

Lantana
Height: to 4 ft.
Blooms year-round
Drought tolerant
when established

Zone 9
p. 297

Larrea tridentata *Creosote Bush* *Full sun*
Height: to 10 ft. *Zone 7*
Evergreen *p. 298*
Aromatic

Lavandula *English Lavender* *Sun*
angustifolia *Height: 1–3 ft.* *Zones 5–6*
Blooms in summer *p. 299*
Dry, well-drained
soil

**Lavandula
stoechas**

Spanish Lavender
Height: 1–3 ft.
Blooms in early
summer
Dry, well-drained
soil

Sun
Zone 9
p. 299

**Leptospermum
laevigatum**

Australian Tea
Tree
Height: to 30 ft.
Full sun
Can be staked as
tree or clipped for
hedge

Zone 9
p. 300

Leucophyllum frutescens

Texas Ranger
Height: 6–8 ft.
Blooms in summer
Good for hot, dry,
windy areas

Zone 9
p. 301

Mahonia nevinii

Nevin Mahonia
Height: 3–10 ft.
Evergreen
Tolerates heat,
sun, shade

Zone 9
p. 308

Myrtus communis
'Compacta'

Compact Myrtle
Height: 2–3 ft.
Evergreen
Blooms in summer

Tolerates dry soil
Zone 9
p. 312

**Nandina
domestica**

Heavenly Bamboo
Height: 6–8 ft.
Handsome red
berries

Tolerates shade
Zone 7
p. 313

Nerium oleander
Common Oleander
Height: 8–20 ft.
Evergreen

Blooms in summer
Zones 8–10
p. 314

Osmanthus fragrans
Fragrant Tea Olive
Height: to 25 ft.
Evergreen
Blooms most heavily in spring and summer

Zone 8
p. 318

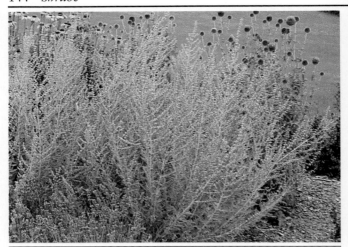

**Perovskia
atriplicifolia**

*Azure Sage
Height: 3–5 ft.
Blooms
midsummer to fall*

*Full sun
Zones 5–6
p. 324*

**Philodendron
selloum**

*Split-leaf
Philodendron
Height: leaves to 3
ft.
Rich soil*

*Ample water
Shade
Zones 9–10
p. 325*

Phormium tenax
'Variegatum'

New Zealand Flax
Height: 8–15 ft.
Smaller varieties
available
Grown for foliage

Sun or partial
shade
Needs water
Zone 9
p. 326

Photinia
× *fraseri*

Fraser Photinia
Height: to 15 ft.
Evergreen
Useful as hedge or
screen

Zone 8
p. 327

Pittosporum crassifolium

*Pittosporum
Height: to 25 ft.
Can be kept low
with pruning
Withstands sea
winds*

*Excellent screen or
hedge
Zones 9–10
p. 330*

**Pittosporum
tobira
'Variegata'**

*Japanese
Pittosporum
Height: to 6 ft.
Evergreen
Blooms in spring*

*Dry soil
Zone 9
p. 330*

Prunus
caroliniana

Carolina Cherry
Laurel
Height: 20–30 ft.
Blooms in early
spring

Fragrant
Zone 7
p. 334

Punica granatum

Pomegranate
Height: 10–20 ft.
Blooms in spring
Fall color

Useful as hedge
Zone 7
p. 336

Pyracantha × 'Mohave'

Pyracantha
Height: 12–15 ft.
Evergreen
For screen, hedge,
or espalier

Zone 7
p. 337

Rhaphiolepis umbellata

Yeddo
Rhaphiolepis
Height: 4–6 ft.
Evergreen
Blooms in spring

Tolerates dry soil
Zone 8
p. 340

Rhus ovata   *Sugar Bush*   *Blooms in spring*
                  Height: 5–10 ft. *Zone 9*
                  Evergreen   *p. 341*

Rhus typhina *Staghorn Sumac*   *Tolerates dry soil*
                  Height: to 30 ft. *Zone 4*
                  Fall color   *p. 341*

Rosa   *Climbing Peace*   Zone 4
'Climbing Peace'   *Rose*   *p. 342*
                     Height: 8–10 ft.
                     Long-blooming
                     Can be trained
                     against fence, wall,
                     or pillar

Salvia greggii   *Autumn Sage*   *Full sun or partial*
                        Height: to 4 ft.   *shade*
                        Evergreen   *Zone 8*
                                                p. 344

Salvia leucantha   Mexican Bush   Blooms in summer
                        Sage   and fall
                        Height: 3–4 ft.   Zone 8
                        Width: 3–4 ft.   p. 344

Simmondsia   Goat Nut   Zone 10
chinensis   Height: 6–7 ft.   p. 348
                   Evergreen
                   Edible fruit yields
                   jojoba oil

Sophora
secundiflora

Mescal Bean
Height: to 25 ft.
Evergreen

Slow-growing
Zones 9, 10
p. 349

Syringa vulgaris

Common Lilac
Height: to 15 ft.
Blooms in spring

Very fragrant
Zone 4
p. 351

Tecoma stans

Yellowbells
Height: to 20 ft.
Blooms from
summer to
midwinter

Good desert plant
Zones 9, 10
p. 352

Ungnadia
speciosa

Mexican Buckeye
Height: to 30 ft.
Blooms in spring

Drought tolerant
Zone 7
p. 355

Viburnum
× carlcephalum

Fragrant Snowball
Height: 8–10 ft.
Blooms in spring

Fragrant
Zone 4
p. 356

Viburnum
suspensum

Sandankwa
Viburnum
Height: 6–12 ft.
Evergreen

Drought tolerant
Zone 9
p. 356

Viburnum tinus   *Laurustinus*   *Zone 7*
                        Height: 7–10 ft.   *p. 357*
                        Evergreen
                        Blooms winter to
                        spring

Xylosma   *Xylosma*   *Zones 9, 10*
congestum   *Height: 8–10 ft.*   *p. 360*
                        Evergreen
                        Useful screen or
                        hedge

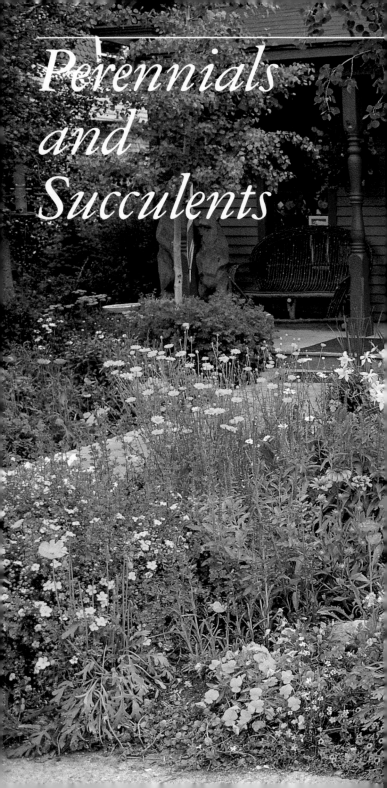

Perennials and Succulents

Acanthus mollis
'Latifolius'

Bear's-breech
Height: 3–4 ft.
White, lilac, or
rose flowers

Dry soil
Zone 8
p. 219

Achillea
× 'Coronation
Gold'

Fernleaf Yarrow
Height: to 3 ft.
Blooms in summer

Sun
Zone 4
p. 220

Agapanthus orientalis

African Lily
Height: 2–3 ft.,
flower stalks to 5 ft.
Blooms in summer

Sun or light shade
Zones 8, 9
p. 220

Agave attenuata

Agave
Height: leaves to 2½ ft.
Good soil

Tender to desert sun
Zone 10
p. 222

Agave victoriae-reginae

Victoria Regina
Agave
Rosettes 1 ft.
across
Good for
containers, rock
gardens

Drought tolerant
Zones 9, 10
p. 222

Agave vilmoriniana

Octopus Agave
Rosettes to 3 ft.
wide
Drought tolerant
Excellent container
plant

Zones 9, 10
p. 222

Aloe arborescens
Tree Aloe
Height: 15–18 ft.
Blooms in winter

Well-drained soil
Zones 9, 10
p. 224

Aloe saponaria
Aloe
Ground-hugging
clumps
Blooms in spring
and summer

Well-drained soil
Zones 9, 10
p. 224

**Alstroemeria
Evergreen
Hybrids**

Alstroemeria
Height: 18–36 in.
Excellent cut
flower

Needs water
Zones 7–10
p. 224

**Aquilegia
chrysantha**

Golden Columbine
Height: 3–4 ft.
Blooms in spring
and summer

Native to
Southwest
Zone 5
p. 226

Aquilegia
'McKana' hybrids

Columbine
Height: 1–3 ft.
Blooms in late
spring

Zone 5
p. 226

Asparagus
densiflorus
'Sprengeri'

Sprenger
Asparagus
Height: stems to 6
ft., usually shorter
Sun or light shade

Drought tolerant
Zones 9, 10
p. 229

Canna hybrids   *Common Garden*   *Blooms in summer*
                     Canna   *Zone 8*
                     Height: 3–6 ft. *p. 239*

Centranthus   *Red Valerian*   *Sun*
ruber   *Height: 1–3 ft.*   *Zone 5*
                   Blooms in summer   *p. 243*

Chrysanthemum coccineum 'Brenda'

Pyrethrum
Height: 1–3 ft.
Blooms in early summer

Moist soil
Sun
Zone 4
p. 249

Chrysanthemum × morifolium

Florist's Chrysanthemum
Height: to 4 ft.
Blooms in fall

Moist soil
Sun
Zone 5
p. 249

Coreopsis
auriculata
'Nana'

Dwarf Eared
Coreopsis
Height: 12–18 in.
Blooms in early
summer

Sun to partial
shade
Zone 4
p. 254

Coreopsis
verticillata
'Moonbeam'

Threadleaf
Coreopsis
Height: 1½–2 ft.
Blooms in summer
and fall

Drought tolerant
Zone 4
p. 254

Cortaderia selloana	*Pampas Grass* Height: 8–12 ft. Year-round interest	Zone 8 p. 255

Dasylirion wheeleri	*Desert Spoon* Height: leaves 3 ft., flower stalk to 15 ft.	Full sun, heat Zones 7–9 p. 259

Dianthus | Sweet William | Self-seeding
barbatus | Height: 1–2 ft. | biennial
  | Blooms in early | Zone 6
  | summer | p. 261
  | Well-drained soil

Dianthus | Grass Pink | Well-drained soil
plumarius | Height: 9–18 in. | Sun
'Agatha' | Blooms June to | Zone 4
  | October | p. 261

Dietes vegeta

African Iris
Height: 2–4 ft.
Blooms in late
spring

Well-drained soil
Sun
Zone 8
p. 262

**Echium
fastuosum**

Pride of Madeira
Height: 3–6 ft.
Tolerates wind,
poor soil

Zones 9, 10
p. 264

Eriogonum
umbellatum

Sulphur-Flower
Height: 12 in.
Width: 3 ft.
Very drought
tolerant

Flowers attractive
when dried
Zones 4–10
p. 268

Festuca ovina
glauca

Blue Fescue
Height: 8–12 in.
Evergreen

Zone 4
p. 273

**Freesia
× hybrida**

*Freesia
Height: 1½–2 ft.
Blooms in winter
Pale colors most
fragrant*

*Zone 9
p. 278*

**Gaillardia
grandiflora**

*Blanket Flower
Height: 8–36 in.
Blooms in summer
Needs well-drained
soil*

*Zone 4
p. 279*

Gerbera
jamesonii

Transvaal Daisy
Height: stems to
18 in.
Well-drained soil

Sun or light shade
Zone 9
p. 283

Hemerocallis
'Stella d'Oro'

Daylily
Height: 12–18 in.
Other cultivars to
36 in. or higher

Long-lived,
carefree
Zone 5
p. 286

Hesperaloe
parviflora

Red Yucca
Height: flower
stalks 3–4 ft.
Evergreen rosettes
Desert plant

Good container
plant
Zone 5
p. 287

Heuchera
sanguinea

Coral Bells
Height: flower
stalks 1–2 ft.
Attractive leaves
Fertile, well-
drained soil

Native to
Southwest
Zone 4
p. 288

Iberis
sempervirens

Candytuft
Height: to 12 in.
Evergreen

Blooms in spring
Zone 4
p. 289

Iris kaempferi
'Azure'

Japanese iris
Height: 2–3 ft.
Blooms in summer
Sun to partial
shade

Moist, acid soil
Zone 5
p. 291

Kniphofia uvaria   *Red-hot Poker*   *Zone 5*
Height: 2–6 ft.   *p. 295*
Blooms from early
summer until frost

Liatris spicata   *Gay-feather*   *Sun*
Height: 4–6 ft.   *Somewhat drought*
Shorter cultivars   *tolerant*
available   *Zone 4*
Blooms in summer   *p. 301*

Lilium candidum   Madonna Lily   Oldest garden
Height: 3–4 ft.   flower
Leaves evergreen   Zone 5
Fragrant flowers in   p. 302
summer

Limonium perezii   Sea Lavender   Full sun
Height: 1 ft.   Good dried flower
Best in sandy,   Zones 9, 10
moist soil   p. 303

Linum perenne

*Perennial Blue
Flax
Height: 1–2 ft.
Blooms in summer*

*Sun
Zone 5
p. 303*

**Melampodium
leucanthum**

*Blackfoot Daisy
Height: to 12 in.
Blooms most of
year
Sun*

*Tolerates heat and
drought
Zones 6–10
p. 310*

Miscanthus
sinensis
'Gracillimus'

Maiden Grass
Height: to 5 ft.
Tolerates wet soil

Many cultivars
Zone 5
p. 311

Muhlenbergia
dumosa

Giant Mullee
Height: leaves 2–3
ft.
Blooms in summer
and fall

Full sun
Good for erosion
control
Zone 7
p. 311

Oenothera missouriensis

Missouri Primrose
Height: 3–6 in.
Trailing branches
Blooms in summer

Dry soil
Sun
Zone 5
p. 314

Opuntia ficus-indica

Prickly Pear
Height: stem to 15 ft.
Full sun
Very drought tolerant

Edible fruit
Zones 9, 10
p. 317

Opuntia
microdasys

Bunny Ears
Height: 2 ft.
Width: 4–5 ft.
Full sun

Very drought
tolerant
Zones 9, 10
p. 318

Opuntia violacea
'Santa-Rita'

Dollar cactus
Height: 8 ft.
Few or no spines
Very drought
tolerant

Zones 9, 10
p. 318

Pelargonium × hortorum

Zonal Geranium
Height: 1–3 ft. or
more
Needs regular
watering

Good container
plant
Zones 9, 10
p. 322

Pennisetum setaceum

Fountain Grass
Height: flower
spike to 3 ft.
Fertile soil

Sun
Zone 8
p. 322

Penstemon barbatus

Beardlip Penstemon
Height: 2–3 ft.
Blooms in summer
Well-drained soil

Sun or partial shade
Zones 9, 10
p. 323

Penstemon eatonii

Eaton's Penstemon
Height: 2–3 ft.
Blooms in summer
Well-drained soil
Heat and drought tolerant

Native to Southwest
Zone 7
p. 323

Penstemon
heterophyllus
purdyi
'Blue Bedder'

Blue Bedder
Penstemon
Height: to 2 ft.
Blooms from April
to July

Zones 9, 10
p. 323

Phlomis fruticosa

Jerusalem Sage
Height: to 4 ft.
Reblooms if
watered in summer

Full sun
Zone 5
p. 325

Salvia farinaceae
'Catima'

Mealy-Cup Sage
Height: to 3 ft.
Blooms in summer
Sun to partial
shade

Zone 8
p. 344

Sedum
× 'Autumn Joy'

Autumn Joy
Sedum
Height: to 2 ft.
Blooms from mid-
to late summer

Sun to partial
shade
Zone 4
p. 347

Senecio cineraria

Dusty Miller
Height: to 2½ ft.
Grown for foliage
Good for hot, dry
climates

Zone 5
p. 347

Stachys
byzantina

Lamb's-ears
Height: to 18 in.
Grown for silvery
foliage

Sun
Tolerates dry soil
Zone 5
p. 350

Yucca elata

Soaptree Yucca
Height: trunk to
20 ft.
Blooms in summer

Well-drained soil
Full sun
Zones 8–10
p. 360

Yucca whipplei

Our Lord's Candle
Height: flower
clusters to 10 ft.,
leaves 18 in. long

Full sun
Zones 6–10
p. 360

Zauschneria californica

California Fuchsia
Height: 1–2 ft.
Blooms in late summer

Tolerates poor, dry soil
Zone 5
p. 361

Zinnia grandiflora

Zinnia Grandiflora
Height: to 10 in.
Blooms from spring to fall

Needs sun, good drainage
Zone 4
p. 361

Ground
Covers

Acacia redolens
'Prostrata'

Acacia
Height: 1–2 ft.
Evergreen
Blooms in spring

Quick cover for
dry, sunny banks
Zones 9, 10
p. 219

Ajuga reptans
'Burgundy Glow'

Common Blue
Bugleweed
Height: to 6 in.
Tolerates shade

Easy to grow
All zones
p. 222

Arctostaphylos *Emerald Carpet*   *Tolerates heat and*
× 'Emerald Carpet' *Manzanita*   *drought*
                 Height: to 15 in.   *Zone 8*
                 Evergreen   *p. 227*
                 Blooms in winter

Arctostaphylos *Bearberry*   *Berries in fall*
uva-ursi *Height: to 12 in.*   *All zones*
'Point Reyes' *Evergreen*   *p. 228*
                 Blooms in spring

Baccharis
pilularis
'Twin Peaks'

Dwarf Coyote
Brush
Height: to 2 ft.
Evergreen

Full sun
Zone 7
p. 231

Ceanothus
griseus
horizontalis
'Yankee Point'

Carmel Creeper
Height: 18–30 in.
Width: 5–15 ft.
Evergreen

Blooms in spring
Zone 8
p. 241

Cistus salviifolius *Sageleaf Rockrose* *Sun*
Height: to 2 ft. *Fire resistant*
Width: 6 ft. *Zones 9, 10*
Dry, alkaline soil *p. 251*

Cotoneaster *Creeping* *Well-drained soil*
adpressus *Cotoneaster* *Sun*
Height: to 12 in. *Zone 5*
Pink flowers *p. 256*
Red berries

Cotoneaster
dammeri
'Skogsholm'

Bearberry
Cotoneaster
Height: to 12 in.
Evergreen

White flowers
Red berries in fall
Zone 5
p. 256

Dalea greggii

Trailing Indigo
Bush
Width: to 3 ft.
Blooms in spring
Useful desert plant

Native to
Southwest
Zones 9, 10
p. 259

Delosperma cooperi

*Hardy Ice Plant
Height: to 6 in.
Evergreen
Good for erosion
control*

*Zones 9, 10
p. 260*

Fragaria chiloensis

*Beach Strawberry
Height: 6–8 in.
Fruit edible but
rarely seen*

*Zone 5
p. 276*

Gazania rigens leucolaena

Trailing Gazania
Height: 6–10 in.
Blooms spring to
fall

Best in dry desert
gardens
Zone 9
p. 281

Juniperus chinensis 'Sargentii'

Sargent Juniper
Height: to 18 in.
Width: 8–10 ft.

Evergreen
Zone 5
p. 293

***Juniperus
conferta*
'Blue Pacific'**

*Shore Juniper
Height: 18 in.
Evergreen
Good seashore
plant*

*Zone 6
p. 293*

***Juniperus
horizontalis*
'Wiltonii'**

*Blue Rug Juniper
Height: to 6 in.
Evergreen
Sandy, rocky soil*

*Sun
Zone 3
p. 294*

Lampranthus spectabilis

Trailing Ice Plant
Height: to 12 in.
Blooms in spring
Tolerates dry soil

Full sun
Zone 9
p. 296

Lantana montevidensis

Weeping Lantana
Vinelike shrub
Height: 18 in.
Good for walls,
banks, baskets

Zone 9
p. 297

Liriope muscari
'Variegata'

Blue Lily Turf
Height: to 18 in.
Evergreen

Zone 6
p. 305

Liriope spicata

Creeping Lily Turf
Height: to 18 in.
Evergreen

Zone 5
p. 305

Mahonia repens   Creeping Mahonia   Tolerates shade
                          Height: to 12 in.   Zone 5
                          Evergreen   p. 308
                          Blooms in spring

Myoporum   Myoporum   Drought tolerant
parvifolium   Height: 3 in.   Zone 10
                          Width: 9 ft.   p. 312
                          Evergreen
                          Quick ground
                          cover

**Oenothera
berlandieri**

*Showy Primrose
Height: 6–18 in.
Sun
Native to
Southwest*

Zone 5
p. 315

**Ophiopogon
japonicus**

*Mondo Grass
Height: to 12 in.
Evergreen*

Sun or shade
Zone 7
p. 317

Osteospermum fruticosum   *Trailing African Daisy*   *Drought tolerant*
                               Height: to 12 in.   *Zone 9*
                               Evergreen   *p. 319*
                               Blooms in late winter, early spring

Rosmarinus officinalis 'Prostratus'   *Trailing Rosemary*   *Tolerates dry soil*
                                           Height: to 2 ft.   *Zone 7*
                                           Evergreen   *p. 343*

Santolina
chamaecyparissus

Lavender Cotton
Height: 1–2 ft.
Evergreen
Blooms in summer

Drought tolerant
Zone 4
p. 345

Sedum spurium
'Dragon's Blood'

Two-row
Stonecrop
Height: to 6 in.

Blooms in summer
Zone 4
p. 347

Trachelospermum
jasminoides

Star Jasmine
Vine used as
ground cover
Evergreen

Fragrant
Slow-growing
Zones 9, 10
p. 353

Verbena
bipinnatifida

Verbena
Sprawling plant
Thrives in heat
and sun

Zone 4
p. 355

Vinca major   Big Periwinkle   Prefers light shade
                         Height: to 18 in.   Zone 7
                         Evergreen   p. 357
                         Blooms in spring

Vines

Antigonon
leptopus

Coral Vine
Height: to 30 ft.
Blooms
midsummer to fall

Full sun
Zone 8
p. 225

Bougainvillea
'Barbara Karst'

Bougainvillea
Handsome, most
popular tropical
vine
Good for covering
arbors

Easy to grow
Zone 9
p. 232

**Clematis
× jackmanii**

*Hybrid Clematis
One of many
cultivars
Blooms in early
summer*

*Most popular
hardy vine in U.S.
Zone 5
p. 253*

**Clematis
montana rubens**

*Anemone Clematis
Height: to 25 ft.
Blooms in early
spring*

*Prune after
flowering
Zones 7–10
p. 253*

Clematis paniculata

Sweet Autumn Clematis
Fragrant flowers in fall

Scrambles up and over any support
Zones 5–10
p. 253

Distictis buccinatoria

Blood-red Trumpet Vine
Height: to 18 ft.
Evergreen

Long-flowering
Zone 9
p. 263

Euonymus
fortunei
'Colorata'

Winter Creeper
Can trail or climb
Evergreen
Purple leaves in
winter
Tolerates shade
Zone 4

p. 271

Ficus pumila

Creeping Fig
Height: to 40 ft.
Evergreen

Clings by suckers
Zone 9
p. 274

Gelsemium sempervirens

Carolina Jessamine
Height: 10–20 ft.
Evergreen
Blooms in spring

Very fragrant
Zone 7
p. 283

Hedera canariensis

Algerian Ivy
Good wall or ground cover
Evergreen

Fast-growing
Zone 9
p. 285

Hedera helix　　*English Ivy*　　　　　*Tolerates shade*
　　　　　　　　　Can creep or climb　*Zone 6*
　　　　　　　　　Evergreen　　　　　*p. 285*

Lonicera　　*Goldflame*　　　　*Zone 4*
heckrottii　　*Honeysuckle*　　　*p. 305*
　　　　　　Height: to 12 ft.
　　　　　　Long-blooming,
　　　　　　spring and summer

**Macfadyena
unguis-cati**

Cat's-claw
Height: 30–40 ft.
Quick-climbing
Clings to any
surface

Endures heat, sun
Zones 9, 10
p. 306

**Parthenocissus
tricuspidata**

Boston Ivy
Height: to 60 ft.
Semi-evergreen
Brilliant fall color

Outstanding wall
cover
Zone 5
p. 320

Passiflora
× alatocaerulea

Passion-flower
Height: to 20 ft.
Fast-growing
Good for fences,
trellises

Zones 8–10
p. 321

Rosa banksiae

Lady Banks' Rose
Height: 15–30 ft.
Evergreen
Blooms in spring

Good for fences,
walls
Zone 7
p. 342

Solanum jasminoides

Potato Vine
Height: 25–30 ft.
Evergreen
Blooms most of
year

Fast-growing
Zones 9, 10
p. 349

Wisteria sinensis

Chinese Wisteria
Height: to 40 ft.
Blooms in spring
Sun

Slow to become
established
Zone 4
p. 359

Encyclopedia
of Plants

Acacia
A-kay′si-a; a-kay′sha
Leguminosae. Pea family

Description
About 800 species of fast-growing, usually evergreen tropical and subtropical shrubs and trees. Attractive, free-flowering, and easy to grow outdoors in warm climates. Most species, once established, are drought resistant. They are short-lived, only about 30 years.

Some species thorny. Compound leaves with numerous small leaflets. In many species leaves are reduced to a single leaflike organ called a phyllode. Flowers, usually yellow, very small but crowded into dense, finger-shaped or globular spikes or racemes. Fruit like a pea pod, sometimes woody or twisted at maturity.

How to Grow
Acacias prefer sun, tolerate a wide range of soils. Pinch shrubby forms to encourage bushiness. Thin crown of tree to admit sunlight and remove lower branches to shape it. Easy to grow from seed.

baileyana p. 78
Cootamundra wattle; Bailey acacia. Showy shrub or small tree, 30–40 ft. high, without spines and with beautiful, feathery, bluish gray foliage. Bears abundant clusters of brilliant yellow flowers in winter. Messy brown fruit in late spring. Very popular in California as a specimen tree. Australia. Zones 9–10.

decora
Graceful wattle. Shrub to 6–8 ft. Phyllodes 2 in. long, bluish green. Flowers bright yellow in 2-in. clusters, most abundant in spring. Good hedge or screen. Australia. Zone 8.

greggii p. 118
Catclaw acacia. Thorny shrub or tree to 20 ft. Pale yellow flowers in summer. Texas to Arizona. Zones 7–10.

redolens 'Prostrata' p. 190
(Often sold as *A. ongerup.*) A dense evergreen, 1–2 ft. high, with bright green, vanilla-scented foliage (phyllodes), 2-in. clusters of yellow flowers in spring. Good for quickly covering dry, sunny banks. Australia. Zones 9–10.

smallii
Tree to 30 or 35 ft. with thorny branches. Feathery leaves fall in winter. Yellow, fragrant flowers in spring. (Often sold as *A. farnesiana,* a similar but cold-tender plant.) Southern California to Texas. Zones 7–10.

Acanthus
A-kan'thus. Bear's-breech
Acanthaceae. Acanthus family

Description
About 30 perennial herbs or shrubs, native to the Mediterranean region, Africa, and Asia. Large leaves are frequently prickly, somewhat thistlelike. Flowers in long, erect spikes.

How to Grow
Plants flower more profusely when grown in the sun, but foliage is most lush and attractive in shade. Soil must be well drained; too much water can be fatal. Good in dry areas, but summer-deciduous if bone-dry.

mollis p. 158
Bear's-breech. Perennial to 3 or 4 ft. Leaves toothed, not spiny. White, lilac, or rose flowers in 18-in. spike. Propagate by division; pieces of root can develop into new plants. Mediterranean region. Zone 8.

Achillea
A-kil'lee'a. Yarrow
Compositae. Daisy family

Description
Many perennial herbs, mostly from the north temperate zone.

Clumps of foliage, often fernlike. Clusters of small flowers on upright stems.

How to Grow
Achilleas take full sun, ordinary garden soil. Propagate by division in spring or fall. Species and some garden strains can be grown from seed. Many species will crowd out other plants.

× 'Coronation Gold' *p. 158*
Vigorous, heat-tolerant. 3 ft. high. Leaves, to 10 in. long, have a strong, spicy odor. Flower heads mustard yellow, in clusters to 4 in. wide. Zone 4.

× 'Moonshine'
2 ft. high, with silvery-gray leaves. Sulfur-yellow flowers in clusters 3–4 in. wide. Grows well in dry, sunny areas. Excellent for cutting and drying. Zone 4.

Summer Pastels
2 ft. high. Finely divided foliage, deep green to gray-green. Flowers white or cream to fawn, pink, salmon, pale yellow, even red. Grow from seed or division. Named varieties sometimes available as plants. Zone 4.

Agapanthus
Ag-a-pan'thus
Amaryllidaceae. Amaryllis family

Description
Rhizomatous herbs with showy flowers. Often grown in tubs or pots in cold-winter areas, in gardens in mild-winter areas. Long, narrow leaves at the base. A ball-shaped cluster of flowers sits atop a slender stalk.

How to Grow

The species below grows well in full sun or light shade, tolerates many kinds of soils. Best with ample water, but can take some drought when established. Divide every 5–6 years. Appreciates heavy feeding, endures without it.

orientalis p. 159

African lily; lily-of-the-Nile. Very showy. Leaves numerous, rather thick, 1–2 ft. long and nearly 3 in. wide. In summer, dense clusters of blue flowers (often 40–100) bloom on stalks to 5 ft. tall. Many hybrid cultivars, in a range of sizes and flower colors. 'Peter Pan', to 18 in., with deep blue flowers, is a favorite. South Africa. Outdoors in zones 8, 9.

Agave
Ah-gah'vee
Agavaceae. Agave family

Description

Large to gigantic perennials with succulent leaves in rosettes. Individual rosettes flower after many years, then die, usually leaving offsets that can be removed for propagation. Flowers in clusters, usually greenish or whitish. Smaller kinds are useful container plants.

How to Grow

Most grow in any soil and need no water once established. They may shrivel in extreme drought, but fill out when watered.

americana

Century plant. Thick, fleshy blue-green leaves to 6 ft. long, with spiny edges and stout spine at the tip. Flower stalk 10–40 ft. high after 10–20 years. Mexico. Zones 9–10.

attenuata p. 159
Soft, spineless, gray-green leaves to 2½ ft. Eventually develops short trunks, numerous offsets. Narrow flower stalk rises several feet, then bends to the ground. Likes water, good soil; tender to frost and desert sun. Mexico. Zone 10.

victoriae-reginae p. 160   *Pictured above*
Tight, dark-green rosettes 1 ft. across, marked with narrow white lines. Rarely blooms. Excellent pot or rock garden plant. Mexico. Zones 9–10.

vilmoriniana p. 160
Octopus agave. Twisted, pale to yellowish green leaves, 3–4 in. wide in rosettes to 3 ft. wide. Container favorite. (Often sold as *A. mayoensis.*) Mexico. Zones 9–10.

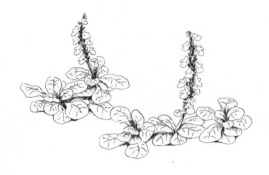

Ajuga
Aj-oo′ga. Bugleweed
Labiatae. Mint family

Description
European annual or perennial herbs, sometimes weedy, but a few cultivated in borders and rock gardens for their profusion of blooms. Oval leaves to 2½ in. long; flowers in close clusters or spikes in spring or early summer.

How to Grow
Easy to grow in full sun or light shade, in ordinary, well-drained garden soil. Plant seedlings in spring or early fall, 6–18 in. apart depending on mature size. Water in summer.

reptans p. 190   *Pictured above*
Common blue bugleweed. Excellent perennial ground cover. Dark green clustered leaves, 3–6 in. high. Spreads by runners to form thick carpet. Small blue or purplish flowers. 'Bronze

Beauty' has bronze foliage and blue flowers. 'Burgundy Glow' has green, white, and dark pink to purple leaves. These varieties hold color best in some shade. All zones.

Albizia
Al-bizz'i-a
Leguminosae. Pea family

Description
More than 100 species of deciduous trees and shrubs from central Asia. Compound leaves with numerous small leaflets. Small flowers in rounded heads have showy stamens. Long seedpods.

How to Grow
The species below prefers full sun, will tolerate either acid or alkaline soil if well drained. Also tolerates wind, drought, salt spray, and air pollution. Choose container-grown plants.

julibrissin p. 78
Hardy silk tree (sometimes incorrectly called mimosa). Grows 20–40 ft. high with broad, spreading, low-branched crown. Tiny leaflets fold up at night. Blooms in summer, bright pink flowers with prominent tufted stamens that give the tree a soft, fluffy appearance. 'Rosea' is most widely grown cultivar; its flowers are richer pink, somewhat hardier than the species. Zones 6–9.

Aloe
A'low; a-low'ee
Liliaceae. Lily family

Description
Succulent plants from Africa and southwest Asia. Rosettes of

thick, fleshy leaves. Some hug the ground, others are treelike. All have showy spikes of tubular flowers in red, orange, or yellow.

How to Grow
Easy to grow. Plant in containers in cool-winter areas; otherwise plant in well-drained soil. Propagate by offsets or cuttings.

arborescens p. 161 *Pictured above*
Tree aloe. Branching plants to 15–18 ft. Rosettes of gray-green leaves with toothed edges. In winter, long spikes of bright red to orange or yellow flowers. South Africa. Zones 9–10.

saponaria p. 161
Ground-hugging clumps of broad, dark green leaves heavily marked with white spots. Forms offsets freely. Branched clusters of orange-red to coral flowers in spring and summer. South Africa. Zones 9–10.

Alstroemeria
Al-stro-meer′i-a
Amaryllidaceae. Amaryllis family

Description
About 50 species of South American herbs, a few of which are grown in greenhouses or outdoors for their showy, lilylike flowers. Flowers clustered atop slender stems. Some are evergreen, some summer-dormant. All are splendid cut flowers.

How to Grow
Plant in sun or light shade in average to rich soil; water amply when in leaf or bloom. Buy in containers or grow from seed.

aurantiaca
Evergreen in mild-winter climates, plant is 3–4 ft. tall, with
sheaves of dark-spotted yellow, orange, or red flowers in late
spring and summer. Often invasive. Zones 7–10.

Evergreen Hybrids *p. 162*
Shorter than Ligtu hybrids, with fewer but larger flowers to
the cluster. Flowers white to pink, red, purple, orange, or
yellow, often with white markings, green petal tips, and dark
throat spots. Dormant in cold winters. Nearly everblooming
if flower stalks are pulled from ground, not cut. Zones 7–10.

Ligtu Hybrids
Widely grown plants, summer-dormant, bloom in late spring.
Big clusters of pink, salmon, orange, yellow, or cream flowers
with yellow markings and dark spots on stems 1½–5 ft. tall.
Self-seed freely once established. Zones 7–10.

Antigonon
An-tig'o-non
Polygonaceae. Knotweed family

Description
One of this small group of showy, tropical American, tendril-
climbing vines is widely grown for its profuse bloom.

How to Grow
Coral vine thrives in full sun, tolerates a wide range of soils.
May go dormant in summer without adequate moisture. Prop-
agate from seeds or cuttings.

leptopus *p. 208*
Coral vine; mountain rose; confederate vine. To 30 ft. high
or more. Leaves arrow- or heart-shaped, 1–3 in. long; lower
leaves are larger. Numerous tiny flowers in drooping racemes
ending in a tendril; pink to red, rarely white. Blooms midsummer to autumn. Mexico. Zone 8.

Aquilegia
A-kwee-lee'je-a. Columbine
Ranunculaceae. Buttercup family

Description
About 75 species of herbaceous perennials. Airy foliage and showy flowers with long spurs.

How to Grow
Some types are best for rock gardens, others for open borders. In borders they do best in well-drained, sandy loam. Grow from seed or divide in spring.

chrysantha p. 162
Golden columbine. Well-branched plants, 3–4 ft. high, carry 3-in. golden yellow flowers with long spurs in spring, summer. Native to the Southwest. Zone 5.

Hybrids p. 163 *Pictured above*
Plants are 1–3 ft. high. In late spring, 2-in. flowers, in red, yellow, blue, white, or purple. Prey to leaf miners. Cultivars include 'Dragon Fly', with large flowers in mixed colors; white 'Snow Queen'; and 'Nora Barlow', double-flowered with pink and red petals tinged with green. Zone 5.

Arbutus
Ar-bew'tus
Ericaceae. Heath family

Description
Some 14 species of broadleaf evergreen trees grown in tem-

perate and warm climates for their ornamental flowers and striking bark. Urn-shaped flowers are white or pink and bloom in loose terminal clusters. Bark is usually reddish and is rough and shedding. Fleshy fruit is red or orange.

How to Grow

The species listed below needs watering only during periods of drought but should be protected from drying winds. Plant in full sun and dry, sandy, acid soil that is well drained. Grows as a shrub unless trained into a tree with a central leader. Shredding bark and dropped fruit can be messy. Good as a hedge or screen; can be used as a specimen plant.

unedo p. 79

Strawberry tree. Slow-growing to 10–35 ft. Branches become gnarled when mature. Toothed, 3½-in. leaves are dark green with red stems. Drooping, 2-in.-long flower clusters appear in fall at the same time as the small round fruits, edible but flavorless. Southern Europe, Ireland. Zones 6–10.

Arctostaphylos

Ark-to-staff′i-los
Ericaceae. Heath family

Description

About 50 species of evergreen woody plants, mostly North American, ranging in size from small trees to prostrate ground covers. Crooked branches, handsome bark and leaves. Small urn- or bell-shaped flowers, often nodding. Fruit fleshy, red or brown, often showy.

How to Grow

All species perform best in sandy or rocky, acid soil in full sun or partial shade. Can be propagated from top cuttings or, in creeping species, by transplanting sods.

× 'Emerald Carpet' p. 191

Emerald Carpet manzanita. Dense, uniform, wide-spreading carpet to 15 in. high. Small oval leaves are shiny emerald green. Pale pink flowers in midwinter. Tolerates heat and drought. Resists fungus if watered deeply and infrequently. Prefers neutral or slightly acid soil. 'Sea Spray', dense and compact, hugs the ground; new leaves, shiny bronze, turn dark green. 'Winter Glow' has round leaves with reddish margins; entire leaf turns copper in winter. All zone 8.

uva-ursi 'Point Reyes' *p. 191*
Bearberry; kinnikinnick. To 12 in. high; the stems, often 5–6 ft. long, root at the joints. Small, dark green leathery leaves turn bronze in winter. Bell-shaped, waxy pink flowers bloom in spring, followed by long-lasting red fruit. All zones.

Arecastrum
A-re-kas'trum
Palmae. Palm family

Description
One species of this genus of South American feather palms is widely grown for ornament in southern California in greenhouses and outdoors, frequently as a street tree. It is effective in small, clustered groves with individual trees of varied ages and heights.

How to Grow
Widely cultivated by florists for its feathery foliage, queen palm needs a warm, moist atmosphere and plenty of water. Outdoors it prefers full sun and is easily grown in ordinary soil. Spray with water to control spider mites. Fast-growing but susceptible to cold.

romanzoffianum *p. 79*
Queen palm; plumy coconut. Trunk straight, reaching 50 ft. Old specimens often clothed with a few dead leaves. In mature plants, bright green, gracefully arching compound leaves are 7–12 ft. long; much smaller in pot or tub specimens. Numerous leaflets never more than 1 in. wide. Flower clusters 3–4 ft. long, creamy white to yellow, emerge from crown of leaves. Large, hanging clusters of numerous yellow fruits, not over 1½ in. long. Flowers and fruit occur intermittently throughout the year. Often sold as *Cocos plumosa, C. romanzoffiana,* and *Syagrus romanzoffianum.* Brazil to Argentina. Zone 10; semihardy in 9.

Asparagus
As-pa'ra-gus
Liliaceae. Lily family

Description
Ornamental species are perennials, shrubs, or vines with fine, leaflike branches. Tiny white flowers are followed by small red, brown, or black berries.

How to Grow
All are tough plants that thrive in sun or light shade. Look best with average water, but tolerate drought once established.

densiflorus 'Sprengeri' *p. 163*
Sprenger asparagus. Sprawling or trailing stems can reach 6 ft., are usually much less. Branches are bright green, 1 in. long. Hanging-basket plant that serves as a tough ground cover where frosts are rare. South Africa. Zone 9–10.

Atriplex
At'ri-plex. Saltbush; orach
Chenopodiaceae. Goosefoot family

Description
About 100 species of annual and perennial herbs and evergreen and deciduous shrubs grown primarily for their dense, attractive gray or silvery foliage. Clustered spikes of small flowers are not showy. These plants often grow naturally in saline soil, thus the common name saltbush.

How to Grow
Saltbush needs dry, well-drained soil. Extremely drought tolerant. Grows well in full sun. Start from seeds. Use in hedges or massed plantings.

canescens *p. 118*
Four-wing saltbush. Grows 3–6 ft. high, 4–8 ft. wide. Covered with minute gray scales. Narrow, evergreen leaves 2 in. long. Grows well in alkaline soil. Fire resistant. Western U.S. Zones 4–10.

Aucuba
Aw-kew′ba
Cornaceae. Dogwood family

Description
A small genus of Asiatic evergreen shrubs, very popular as foliage plants, especially for dark places: under overhangs, in entries, even as a house plant.

How to Grow
A. japonica grows vigorously. In the open, it spreads; in a tub, its brightly colored berries are better seen. Grow from semi-hardwood cuttings or seeds.

japonica p. 119   *Pictured above*
Japanese aucuba. 4–10 ft. high and wide. Glossy dark green leaves are more or less oval, 4–8 in. long. Berries are ½ in. long, mostly scarlet; not produced without male plants. 'Variegata', often called gold-dust tree, has yellow-spotted leaves. Blooms in spring. Himalayas to Japan. Zone 7.

Baccharis
Bak′kar-is
Compositae. Daisy family

Description
About 350 species of erect or trailing shrubs, sometimes evergreen. Their habitats are diverse, from marsh to desert. Leaves are thick and fleshy. Small, off-white flowers are tubular, crowded in small heads. Fruit a conspicuous cottony seed.

How to Grow
The species below will tolerate drought but grows best in moderately rich, moisture-retentive soil in full sun. Prune annually in early spring to remove old arching branches and maintain density. To avoid mess and seeding problems of female plants, choose male plants grown from cuttings.

pilularis p. 192
Dwarf coyote brush. Forms dense evergreen mat 1–2 ft. high, spreading to 6 ft. Small leaves; inconspicuous flowers in fall. Very reliable ground cover in the West and Southwest, but susceptible to spider mites. 'Twin Peaks' is a lower, denser, all-male cultivar with small, dark green leaves. 'Pigeon Point' is faster-growing and forms a mound. Coastal bluffs of California. Zone 7.

Bauhinia
Baw-hin'i-a
Leguminosae. Pea family

Description
Some 300 species of tropical shrubs, trees, and woody vines. A few species are among the most spectacular tropical flowering trees. Leaves compound or simple, much resembling those of redbud, to which it is related. Showy flowers. Fruit a long, flat pod.

How to Grow
These trees are slow-growing. They bloom in winter and very early spring; some species then drop their leaves. Need well-drained soil and moderate moisture. No serious pests. They are winter-hardy only in southern California, the low desert, and Arizona.

variegata p. 119
Purple orchid tree. Big shrub easily trained into a 30-ft. tree. Flowers, pink to purple, 2–3 in., appear from January through spring while plants are leafless. Messy seed pods follow. Often sold as *B. purpurea*. India. Zone 10.

Bougainvillea
Boo-gen-vill'ee-a
Nyctaginaceae. Four o'clock family

Description
The 10 known species, all South American, are perhaps the most handsome, and certainly the most widely planted, ornamental vines of the tropics. They are great favorites in the Southwest. Tall-growing woody vines (some cultivars shrubby) with small flowers — the color comes from 3 large, showy bracts surrounding each flower.

How to Grow
Bougainvilleas grow easily in any well-drained soil in sun but benefit from some afternoon shade in hottest areas. Transplant with care to keep from damaging fragile root ball. Limit watering in midsummer to encourage flowering. Plants withstand drought. Prune heavily to control size, encourage blooming side shoots. Among the finest creeping vines for covering an arbor, porch, or corner of a house.

Hybrids *p. 208*
'Barbara Karst' and 'San Diego Red', both red, are among the hardiest and most reliable. Other varieties have white, pink, purple, orange, or multicolored flowers. Double varieties exist, but aging bracts hang on, and the effect is messy. Brazil. Zone 10; borderline zone 9.

Brachychiton
Brack-i-ky'ton. Bottle tree
Sterculiaceae. Chocolate family

Description
A small genus of mostly deciduous Australian trees, named for the bottlelike swelling at the base of the trunk. Useful as shade trees and windbreaks. Clusters of bell-shaped flowers are followed by boat-shaped seedpods that can be used in dried flower arrangements. Many species lose their leaves after flowering.

How to Grow
Bottle trees are not particular about soil. They are very drought tolerant and need little pruning. Propagate from seeds or cuttings.

populneus *p. 80*
Bottle tree; kurrajong. Broadleaf evergreen tree to 30–50 ft. high, 30 ft. wide. Its 3-in.-long leaves shimmer in the breeze. The ½-in.-wide yellowish white flowers are reddish inside and sometimes have dark spots on the outside. They bloom in 3-inch clusters in late spring. Woody, canoe-shaped seedpods, 2–3 in. long, form in fall and can be messy. Zones 8–10.

Brahea
Bra'hee-a
Palmae. Palm family

Description
A small genus of medium-sized ornamental fan palms. Most are native to Mexico. Stout trunks are usually covered toward the top with dead and drooping leaves. Leaves divided to the middle or deeper with many slender segments. Flowers in clusters or single.

How to Grow
These plants are tolerant of various soil conditions but fare poorly in wet areas or shade. They withstand wind, heat, and drought.

armata *p. 80*
Blue palm; Mexican blue palm. Not more than 40 ft. high. As usually seen, trunks are cleaned. Silvery blue, waxy leaves are cut deeply into nearly 50 segments on a spiny leafstalk up

to 15 ft. long. Spectacular flowering cluster, 6–20 ft. long, creamy white, protrudes beyond the crown of leaves and often to the ground. Blooms from summer to fall. Fleshy orange fruit, nearly round, ¾ in. long, from fall to winter. Lower California. Zones 9–10.

edulis
Guadalupe palm. Fan palm to 30 ft., with heavy, smooth trunk and green leaves to 6 ft. wide. Slow-growing, choice. Guadalupe Island, Baja California. Zones 9–10.

Buddleia
Bud′li-a. Butterfly bush
Loganiaceae. Buddleia family

Description
About 100 species of mostly tropical shrubs that attract butterflies in profusion when in flower.

How to Grow
Plants need a sunny location and rich but not heavy, well-drained soil. Cut winter-killed tops back to the ground, as the roots usually survive.

davidii p. 120 *Pictured above*
Orange-eye butterfly bush. The best known of the cultivated species and the hardiest. Vigorous deciduous or semi-evergreen shrub 6–10 ft. high, often much lower if cut back for winter. Leaves oval to lance-shaped, 6–9 in. long, green above, white and felty beneath. Fragrant flowers are lilac, orange at the throat, usually in nodding spike 5–12 in. long. Blooms summer to fall. Of the many cultivars, 'Charming' has deep pink flowers, 'Black Knight' dark purple flowers, 'Dubonnet' reddish purple flowers. China. Zones 5–9.

Caesalpinia
See-zal-pin′i-a
Leguminosae. Pea family

Description
A genus of about 70 showy tropical trees or shrubs. Commonly cultivated species are shrubs with compound, featherlike leaves. Flowers have 5 broad, separate, showy petals and protruding stamens. Fruit a narrow, flattened pod. Good plants for desert climates.

How to Grow
These plants thrive in full sun and almost any well-drained soil. Soak seeds in warm water for several hours to encourage germination; sow in pots. Transfer outdoors when plants are 1–2 ft. high.

gilliesii
Bird of paradise bush. Evergreen shrub (deciduous in cold winters) with ferny foliage; yellow flowers, in clusters, have tufts of long red stamens. Blooms all summer. Argentina, Uruguay. Zones 9–10.

pulcherrima *p. 120* *Pictured above*
Red bird of paradise. Deciduous shrub to 10 ft. Orange or red flowers with red stamens. May freeze to ground in cold winters, but will come back fast. Argentina, Uruguay. Zones 9–10.

Calliandra
Kal-li-an'dra
Leguminosae. Pea family

Description
A large genus of tropical evergreen shrubs and trees that differ only slightly from those in the genus Acacia. However, these plants are not usually thorny.

How to Grow
Calliandras require a sunny location and well-drained soil. They grow well only in the warmest region of zone 10. Propagate by seeds or by cuttings over bottom heat.

eriophylla p. 123
Fairy duster, false mesquite. Airy, open shrub to 3 ft. with ferny foliage, tiny leaflets. Flowers in late winter. Drought tolerant. Native to the Southwest. Zone 10.

haematocephala
Pink powder puff. Shrub to 10 ft. or more with larger leaflets and bigger (2–3-in.) flowers than *C. eriophylla*. Blooms in winter. Needs ample water. Tender to frost. Bolivia. Zone 10.

Callistemon
Kal-lis-tee'mon; kal-lis'tee-mon. Bottle-brush
Myrtaceae. Myrtle family

Description
Showy Australian evergreen shrubs and trees. Small leaves, usually narrow and pointed. Minute flowers in very showy, dense spikes, with numerous handsome protruding stamens. Fruit a somewhat woody capsule that persists on the branches for many years.

How to Grow
Bottle-brushes are easy to grow in any soil. Drought tolerant, but prefer moist, well-drained soil. Thrive in full sun. Prune heavily every 3 years for best flowers and fruit.

citrinus p. 121
Crimson bottle-brush. Popular, dramatic shrub, 10–20 ft. high. Leaves lance-shaped, 2½ in. long. Flower spikes 2–4 in. long, not dense, with bright red stamens. Blooms spring to

summer. Does best in acid soil, especially on beach fronts. Grows fast and is easily trained as espalier. Zone 9.

viminalis
Weeping bottle-brush. Big shrub or tree to 30 ft. Narrow profile with strongly weeping branches, bright red brushes in spring and summer, with some bloom at other times. Needs ample water. Zone 9.

Calocedrus
Kal-oh-see'drus
Cupressaceae. Cypress family

Description
Narrowly upright conifers with dark green scalelike foliage in flat sprays.

How to Grow
These trees are adapted to a variety of climates; they prefer well-drained soil and need little water once established.

decurrens p. 81
California incense cedar. Grows slowly at first, then moderately fast to nearly 100 ft. Tolerates poor soil. Useful as background plant, screen, windbreak. Resembles smaller giant sequoia. Oregon to Baja California. Zones 5–10.

Camellia
Ka-mee'li-a
Theaceae. Tea family

Description
Asiatic evergreen shrubs or small trees, widely grown for their typically red, waxlike flowers, very showy and lasting, stalkless. Other colors and some double flowers in the many horticultural forms (over 3,000 named kinds).

How to Grow
Easy to grow by transplanting from containers into moist, well-drained, acid soil. The root systems are shallow, so mulch the area around the plant. Vigorous, mature plants can survive

on rainfall. Camellias flower best in partial shade. Propagate from cuttings of current season's growth. Seedlings give unpredictable results.

japonica
Common camellia; Japanese camellia. A shrub or, rarely, a tree to 20–25 ft. Shiny, dark green oval leaves 3–4 in. long. Flowers 3–6 in. wide, waxy, with roundish petals. Several hundred cultivars are grown in the U.S., with single or double flowers ranging from white to dark red. Blooms fall to spring. China and Japan. Zone 8.

reticulata
Open, lanky shrubs to 10 ft., eventually small trees. Leaves not shiny. Flowers large to very large, pink to red, single to double, in late winter, early spring. Not as hardy as C. *japonica*. China. Zones 9–10.

sasanqua p. 122
Sasanqua. Shrubs with smaller flowers than C. *japonica* and smaller leaves on willowy branches. Good for espalier; low-growing forms for ground cover, upright for hedges and screens. Tolerates drought. Profuse flowering in fall to early winter in shades of white, pink, and red. Long-blooming varieties of C. *hiemalis* 'Shishi Gashira' and 'Showa no Sakae' are often sold as sasanquas. Japan. Zones 8–10.

Canna
Kan'na
Cannaceae. Canna family

Description
Very useful, handsome, much-hybridized tropical herbs. Mostly tuberous roots and stately, broad, often reddish purple

leaves. Very showy clusters of flowers on tall stalks. Nearly all of the flower color comes from the enlarged, petallike stamens.

How to Grow
In frost-free areas cannas can be grown as perennials; elsewhere as summer bedding plants. Plant in rich soil, water thoroughly during droughts. Dig before frost and store rootstocks like dahlias. In spring, divide rootstock into pieces, each with 1–2 buds. Plant 6 in. deep when soil is thoroughly warm.

Hybrids *p. 164   Pictured above*
Common garden canna. Grows 3–6 ft. high. Flowers in summer are up to 4 in. across, from whitish and yellow to red, spotted or particolored. Dwarf varieties (18 in. tall) are available. Zone 8.

Carissa
Ka-ris′sa
Apocynaceae. Dogbane family

Description
30 species of spiny evergreen shrubs, chiefly South African. *C. macrocarpa* is grown for ornament or hedges, more rarely for fruit.

How to Grow
Natal plum is easy to grow in warm, moist climates in full sun, though it can take shade. Tolerates drought near coast. Propagate by seeds or cuttings.

macrocarpa *p. 122*
Natal plum. (Also known as *C. grandiflora.*) A very bushy shrub to 15 ft., with plentiful spines. Oval leaves, 1–2½ in. long, polished bright green. Year-round flowers fragrant, star-shaped, white, nearly 2 in. wide. Red, egg-shaped berry, 1–2 in. long, can be eaten fresh or in sauce, tastes somewhat like a cranberry. Good screen or hedge. 'Fancy', to 6 ft., bears excellent fruit. 'Tuttle', to 3 ft., is a useful ground cover with heavy flower and fruit production. Zone 10.

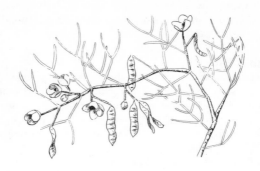

Cassia
Cash'i-a. Senna
Leguminosae. Pea family

Description
About 500 perennials, shrubs, and trees grown for their usually showy flowers. The species below are suitable in a shrub border or hedge or standing alone.

How to Grow
Very drought resistant, grow well in full sun and dry, well-drained, infertile soil. Do not overwater. Prune plants after flowers fade to prevent formation of seedpods.

artemisioides p. 123
Feathery cassia; wormwood senna. Compact evergreen shrub to 4 ft. Leaves silky gray with 6–8 needlelike 1-inch leaflets. Yellow flowers in 2–6 in. clusters from early spring to summer. Australia. Zones 9–10.

nemophila p. 123   *Pictured above*
Also known as *C. eremophila*. Similar to the above, but hardier and with green foliage.

Casuarina
Cas-you-a-ry'na
Casuarinaceae. Casuarina family

Description
Evergreen shrubs or trees, essentially leafless but with thin, jointed branches that create the effect of a pine. Flowers inconspicuous. Small cones are attractive.

How to Grow
Tough, hardy plants resist heat, drought, saline soil, wind.
Endure considerable frost. Good desert plants.

stricta p. 81
Mountain she-oak. To 35 ft. Narrow form and dark green
branchlets are attractive. Endures salt wind. South Australia.
Zone 9.

Ceanothus
See-a-no'thus
Rhamnaceae. Buckthorn family

Description
A large genus of very handsome North American shrubs, little
grown except in California (where they are called wild lilac
or buckbrush) because of their fussiness about temperature
and drainage. Leaves evergreen in most species. Small blue or
white flowers in showy, dense, branched clusters.

How to Grow
These plants prefer open sunlight and a light, porous soil. Too
much water can cause deadly root rot; keep them away from
sprinkler systems. Plants get rangy with age and are then best
replaced. Propagate by seeds, cuttings, or layering.

griseus horizontalis p. 192   *Pictured above*
'Yankee Point' Carmel creeper. 1½–2½ ft. high by 5–15 ft.
wide. Leaves are leathery, deep green, glossy, oval. Profuse
bright blue flowers in spring. An excellent ground cover; covers large areas. Zone 8.

× 'Julia Phelps' p. 124
Dense, broad, dark green shrub to 7 ft., with deep indigo-blue
flowers in spring. Zones 9–10.

× 'Ray Hartman'   *p. 124*
Tall shrub or small tree to 20 ft., with medium blue flowers.
Zones 9–10.

thyrsiflorus   *p. 125*
Blue blossom. Shrub or small tree to 30 ft. with light to medium blue flowers. 'Repens' is a dwarf, spreading form. Zones
8–10.

Cedrus
See'drus. Cedar
Pinaceae. Pine family

Description
Four species of handsome evergreens, the true cedars. All but
one are widely cultivated as screen and background trees, as
well as specimens for lawns and parks. Needles in clusters.
Erect cones have closely fitted scales. Somewhat resemble
larches in the arrangement of their needles.

How to Grow
Cedars need open spaces and ordinary good soil, preferably
not too moist. Container-grown transplants have the best
chances of success. Should not be exposed to drying winds in
summer or winter. No serious pests or diseases.

atlantica 'Glauca'   *p. 82   Pictured above*
Blue Atlas cedar. Handsome upright tree, 40–60 ft. (taller in
native habitat) with a main leader or trunk. Wide-spreading,
to about three-quarters of height. Short silvery blue needles.
Light brown cones 2–3 in. long. Needs plenty of space for
best landscape use. Tolerates drought. North Africa. Zones
6–9.

deodara
Deodar. Larger and faster growing than *C. atlantica* 'Glauca', to 80 ft. Needles grayish green. Branches sweep downward, then up. Tip of tree always nodding. India. Zones 6–10.

Centranthus
Sen-tran′thus
Valerianaceae. Valerian family

Description
A small group of mostly perennial herbs from the Mediterranean region. Dense clusters of small flowers.

How to Grow
Easy to grow; plants may self-sow abundantly. Sunny areas with well-drained soil are best; ideal sites include walls and limestone walks or outcroppings.

ruber p. 164 *Pictured above*
Red valerian; Jupiter's beard. Bushy, 1–3 ft high. Many small, fragrant flowers in late spring, early summer. A favorite garden plant. Also sold as *Valeriana rubra*, *V. coccinea*, or *Kentranthus*. Zone 5.

Ceratonia
Seh-ra-to′ni-a. Carob
Leguminosae. Pea family

Description
The single species is a broadleaf evergreen shrub or tree from the eastern Mediterranean, cultivated since antiquity for its

long, leathery pods known as St. John's bread. The sweet edible pulp surrounding the seeds is used as a substitute for chocolate. Normally shrubby and multistemmed, but easily trained into a single-stem tree. Heavy, wide-ranging root system can lift sidewalks.

How to Grow
Grows in full sun in any well-drained soil and tolerates drought. Water deeply but infrequently to avoid root rot. Can be grown as a hedge or a shade tree. To train as a tree, remove lower branches when the plant is young. Both male and female plants must be planted to ensure fruit.

siliqua p. 82
Carob. As a tree, rounded in form to 20–50 ft. high and wide. Wavy compound leaves of 4–8 broad, leathery leaflets, each 2–4 in. long. Clusters of tiny red flowers in spring. Dark brown pods, 4–12 in. long, form in fall. Zones 9–10.

Cercidium
Ser-sid'i-um. Palo verde
Leguminosae. Pea family

Description
Deciduous trees for desert regions. Leaves fall early, revealing leaf stalks and greenish branches. Deep roots make these trees drought resistant.

How to Grow
Water deeply but infrequently for best results, although established trees can get by without irrigation. Prune to shape.

floridum p. 83
Palo verde. (Also known as *C. torreyanum*.) Grows to 30 ft. tall and wide, has a fine show of bright yellow flowers in spring. Excellent tree for shade in desert. *C. microphyllum*, little-leaf palo verde, has paler flowers. *C. praecox* has lime-green bark. Native to the Southwest. Zones 8–10.

Cercis
Sir'sis. Redbud; Judas tree
Leguminosae. Pea family

Description
Very attractive shrubs or small deciduous trees. Simple, round-ish or heart-shaped leaves. Showy clusters of flowers, rose-pink, rose-purple, or white, in early spring, bloom mostly be-fore leaves expand. Fruit is a flat, thin pod.

How to Grow
Redbuds are easy to grow in open, sandy loam. They do not like heavy, moist sites and are hard to move when mature. In some parts of the country, a vascular wilt disease or a canker disease may be troublesome. Drought may increase chance of disease; mulch and irrigate during dry spells.

canadensis
Eastern redbud. Graceful small tree to 35 ft. with a fine show of rosy purple flowers in spring. 'Alba' has white flowers, 'Rubye Atkinson' pure pink, and 'Forest Pansy' has purple leaves. Eastern U.S. Zones 4–10.

occidentalis p. 125
Western redbud. Shrub or small tree to 10–15 ft. high and wide. Usually several trunks from the base. Profuse, small magenta flowers in early spring. Bluish green leaves turn light yellow or red in fall. Magenta seedpods start to form in sum-mer, turn reddish brown and remain on the branches all win-ter. California, Arizona. Zones 5–9.

Cercocarpus
Sir-ko-kar'pus
Rosaceae. Rose family

Description
Evergreen or deciduous shrubs or small trees with tiny flowers and small dry fruits with feathery tails. Several have handsome branch structures. Native to the West.

How to Grow
Plant from containers and water until established. Prune only to shape.

ledifolius p. 126
Curl-leaf mountain mahogany. Evergreen shrub to 12 ft., usually much lower. Narrow evergreen leaves have edges rolled under. Withstands intense cold, rocky soil. Zones 5–9.

Chaenomeles
Kee-nom'e-lees. Flowering quince
Rosaceae. Rose family

Description
Popular garden shrubs because of their beautiful early spring bloom. All are from East Asia. Hard, aromatic, quincelike fruits can be made into preserves. Shiny green leaves, handsome branching structure. Flowers, solitary or in small, close clusters, bloom before or with unfolding leaves.

How to Grow
Easy to grow in any soil with sun and average watering. May be chlorotic in alkaline soils. Widely used for hedges, though heavy clipping will reduce flowering.

speciosa p. 126
Many cultivars available. May be tall (6 ft. or more, with upright branches) or dwarf (2–3 ft., with spreading branches). Colors range from white through pink and orange to deepest red. All zones.

Chamaerops
Kam'ee-rops
Palmae. Palm family

Description
Single species is the sturdy fan palm, *C. humilis*. The only palm native to Europe, it forms clumps by making offsets from the base. Occasionally single-stem plants appear. Trunks arch outward, then up.

How to Grow
Slow-growing, needs sun and good drainage. Withstands drought, but water and fertilizer in summer will speed its growth. Excellent for containers or small gardens, hedges.

***humilis** p. 83 Pictured above*
European fan palm. To 20 ft. high and wide. Dramatic, sharply cut and angled leaves. Scars left when leaves fall off, making trunk ruggedly picturesque. One of the hardiest palms, it can survive occasional temperatures of near 0 degrees F. Mediterranean region. Zones 8–10.

Chilopsis
Ky-lop′sis. Desert willow
Bignoniaceae. Trumpet-creeper family

Description
Single species is a deciduous large shrub or small tree.

How to Grow
Grows easily in most soils with average or better drainage. Prune to shape while young. Dangling fruits can be removed in winter for neatness.

***linearis** p. 127*
Desert willow; flowering willow. Dark, shaggy trunk, long, narrow leaves that drop early. Grows rapidly to 25 ft. Trumpet-shaped flowers vary from white through pink and lavender, with purple markings. Long, thin seedpods follow. Native to the Southwest. Zones 9–10.

× *Chitalpa* p. 127
Ky-tal′pa. Bignoniaceae. Trumpet-creeper family

Description
A rare hybrid between genuses (*Chilopsis* and *Catalpa*) de-

veloped in the Soviet Union. Fast-growing deciduous tree to 30 ft., or large shrub. Narrow, bright green leaves to 4 in. long. Clusters of purple-striped pink flowers from early summer through fall.

How to Grow
Needs early shaping to form a single trunk. Tolerates drought but can take summer water. Fast-growing. Zones 7–10.

Chorisia
Ko-ris'i-a
Bombacaceae. Silk-cotton-tree family

Description
A small genus of South American deciduous trees, noted for large, highly ornamental flowers. Fan-shaped compound leaves. Fruit is a capsule; seeds have a silky floss.

How to Grow
Chorisias require excellent drainage and monthly deep watering. When trees are mature, reduce watering in late summer to encourage flowering.

speciosa p. 84
Floss silk tree. To 60 ft. Heavy trunk is green when young, gray later, studded with broad spines. Flowers nearly 3 in. wide, pink, purple, or white, appear profusely in fall just after leaves drop. New leaves sprout as flowers fade, so the tree is never completely bare. Brazil. Zones 9–10.

Chrysanthemum
Kris-san'the-mum
Compositae. Daisy family

Description
Many important garden plants, most from China, Japan, or Europe. Flowers are of all colors except blue and purple and range from immense to small and buttonlike.

How to Grow
Plant chrysanthemums in a sunny, well-drained spot. Shallow-rooted, they require moist soil and regular fertilization. Pinch

and remove soft growing tip of most species when 4–6 in. tall to encourage bushy growth and big flowers. Stop pinching in midsummer or when plants begin flowering. In cold-winter areas, mulch lightly or dig and store plants in a cold frame. Divide plants in spring, discard the older, woody stems, and replant the fleshy shoots.

coccineum p. 165
Pyrethrum; painted daisy. Very popular perennial, 1–3 ft. high, blooms in late spring. Leaves fernlike. Flower heads to 2½ in. wide, red, pink, lilac, or white, sometimes double. Prey to aphids and red spider mites. Cut stems to the ground after flowering to produce second bloom in late summer. Southwest Asia. Many named forms. Zone 4.

× *morifolium* p. 165
Florist's chrysanthemum. Perennial, originally 9–15 in. high, often grown today to 4 ft., pinched to form various shapes. Leaves grayish, hairy. Flower heads from 1–6 in. across; all colors but blue, and many forms, including single, double, pompon, and special ray-flower types such as quills and spiders. Susceptible to aphids and red spider mites. Cut back to 8 in. after bloom. Zone 5.

Cinnamomum
Sin-na-mo′mum
Lauraceae. Laurel family

Description
Aromatic evergreen trees, mostly from tropical Asia. Three species are widely grown as sources of camphor and cinnamon.

How to Grow
These trees do well in sandy loam or a variety of other soils. Thrive in hot summers. They grow slowly to moderately but are massive and oaklike at maturity and therefore not suitable for small spaces. No serious insect pests, but susceptible to verticillium wilt. Prune out affected branches, apply nitrogen fertilizer, and water deeply to improve vigor.

camphora p. 84
Camphor tree. To 40–50 ft. and wide-spreading. Bark is dark, almost black when wet. Shiny green foliage, new growth has tints of pink or red. Tapered leaves, to 5 in. long, are pale underneath. Tiny, fragrant yellow flowers in spring. Bruised

foliage is camphor-scented, and the wood is a commercial source of camphor. A stately ornamental or shade tree in southern California and the low and intermediate deserts. China and Japan. Zones 8–10.

Cistus
Sis′tus. Rockrose
Cistaceae. Rockrose family

Description
Mediterranean shrubs long known in Old World gardens. Fire retardant and drought resistant, they are valuable in dry areas of California. Leaves evergreen or nearly so, soft and hairy or shiny, aromatic, and resinous. Large 5-petaled flowers resemble single roses. Useful as bank and ground covers and in rock gardens.

How to Grow
Rockroses must have open sunlight and dry, slightly alkaline, well-drained soil. They will tolerate drought, heat (but not desert heat), poor soil, and salt spray, but not wet, cold winters. Propagate from seeds or cuttings. Established plants do not transplant easily. Prune out old stems after flowering.

hybridus
White rockrose. (Also known as *C. corbariensis.*) Spreading shrub to 5 ft. with gray-green leaves and white flowers, 1½ in. wide, in late spring. Zones 9–10.

ladanifer *p. 128   Pictured above*
Crimson-spot rockrose. To 5 ft., with dark green, fragrant leaves. White flowers, 3 in. wide, with a deep red spot at the base of each petal, in June and July. Portugal to France, west North Africa. Zones 9–10.

salviifolius p. 193
Sageleaf rockrose. Low, dense shrub to 2 ft. tall, 6 ft. wide, with gray-green leaves and, in late spring, white flowers with yellow basal spots. Useful as ground cover. Zones 9–10.

Citrus p. 85
Sit′rus
Rutaceae. Citrus family

Description
Evergreen trees or large shrubs with fragrant white flowers and aromatic, often delicious fruit. Few plants are more useful and attractive over so long a season. Trees come as standards (to 25 ft.) or on dwarfing rootstocks (slow growth to 12–15 ft.)

How to Grow
All citrus plants like good drainage, ample water, and some drying out between irrigations. They are heavy feeders and often need supplementary minerals, especially iron and zinc. They need little pruning but can be thinned, shaped, or even trained as espaliers. All are subject to a variety of pests (controllable) and virus diseases (incurable).

Citrus trees are much alike in appearance; their fruits are the chief marks of distinction. They differ considerably in hardiness. Limes and lemons are the most subject to frost; oranges, grapefruit, and mandarins (tangerines) are increasingly frost-tolerant. Kumquats (*Fortunella*) are even hardier.

Long, warm growing seasons are necessary to ripen fruits; grapefruit, especially, needs heat to develop sweetness, while limes and lemons need relatively little. Before selecting a citrus for home use, consult a knowledgeable nursery person or extension agent to find out what trees will do best in your garden. Zones 9–10.

Clematis
Klem′a-tis
Ranunculaceae. Buttercup family

Description
About 270 species of mostly woody, deciduous vines. Leaves usually compound, the leafstalk often curling like a tendril. Flowers often very showy, in white, yellow, pink, red, or purple, and intermediate shades. Some fruits have a plumed, showy "tail."

How to Grow
Grow on clematis trellis, fence, arbor, wall, tree stump, or other surface. Most species will scramble up through loose shrubs and small trees to sunlight. They prefer cool, rich, moist, well-drained soil. Add dolomitic lime, leaf mold, and sand when planting; never allow plants to become too dry. Provide a stable support for the brittle stems, which break easily in the wind. Grow best with leaves and flowers in full sun and roots in shade; mulch and underplant with a shallow-rooted ground cover or plant on north side of a low wall.

Spring-blooming types flower on previous year's growth; prune after flowering to preserve plant's general shape and remove dead wood and tangled stems. Summer-flowering kinds, including large-flowered hybrids, produce flowers on current year's wood, so prune in late winter or early spring. Young plants may be cut back to within a few inches of the ground or to 2–3 buds; established plants, to 12–18 in. Propagate species by seeds, hybrids by layering or by softwood cuttings. To control stem rot, remove affected parts of plant below ground level, then spray vine and planting area repeatedly with fungicide.

armandii
Fast-growing, vigorous evergreen vine to 25 ft. with large, shiny leaves. Large clusters of fragrant 2½-in. white flowers in earliest spring. Prune frequently to contain growth. China. Zones 7–10.

montana p. 209
Anemone clematis. Large deciduous vine with strong permanent woody structure. Heavy show of 2½-in. white flowers on old wood in early spring — prune after flowering. *C. m. rubens* has pink flowers. China. Zones 7–10.

paniculata p. 210
Sweet autumn clematis. (Also known as *C. dioscoreifolia*.) Tall deciduous vine with clouds of small, white, fragrant flowers in autumn. Japan. Zones 5–10.

Large-flowered Cultivars and Hybrids p. 209
Pictured above
These showy, colorful plants are the most popular hardy vines grown in the U.S. To 15 ft. Flowering times vary, but all produce flower clusters 4–8 in. wide, often in profusion. Colors range from white through pink and red to blue and purple. Prune in late winter. *C. jackmanii* has many velvety deep purple blooms in early summer; its cultivar 'Rubra' has pink flowers. *C. lawsoniana* 'Henryi' has pure white flowers, 8 in. wide, with dark stamens. *C.* 'Mrs. Cholmondeley' has pale lavender-blue flowers. *C.* 'The President' has purple flowers. All zone 5.

Cordyline
Kor-di-ly'ne
Agavaceae. Agave family

Description
Evergreen woody plants with sparsely branching stems, each branch ending in a cluster of swordlike leaves. Effect is something like that of a palm.

How to Grow
Species below is tolerant of many soils and water regimes, growing fastest in deep soil with ample water.

australis p. 85
Giant dracaena. To 30 ft., with narrow, 3-ft.-long leaves of

deep green. Big clusters of tiny white flowers in late spring. Tolerates drought; hardy to 15 degrees F. 'Atropurpurea' has bronzy purple leaves. New Zealand. Zones 8–10.

Coreopsis
Ko-ree-op′sis. Tickseed
Compositae. Daisy family

Description
About 100 species of handsome garden flowers, annuals and perennials, mostly North American. Profuse flowers, often yellow, on single stalks or clustered branches rising above foliage. Double varieties available. Among the most lasting of cut flowers.

How to Grow
Coreopsis is almost weedlike and very easy to grow in any ordinary, well-drained garden soil. Grow from seed or divide perennials in spring or fall.

auriculata 'Nana' *p. 166 Pictured above*
Dwarf eared coreopsis. Low-growing plant (6–9 in.), ideal for foreground in border. Yellow-orange flowers, 1–2 in. wide, bloom from spring to fall if deadheaded. Southeastern U.S. Zone 4.

verticillata p. 166
Threadleaf coreopsis. To 3 ft. with finely divided leaves and many yellow 2-in. flowers all summer and fall. Drought tolerant. 'Moonbeam', 1½–2 ft., has pale yellow flowers. Southeastern U.S. Zone 4.

Cortaderia
Kor-ta-deer'i-a. Pampas grass
Gramineae. Grass family

Description
About 24 species of tall, reedlike grasses from South America and New Zealand. Clump formers, with leaves clustered at base of stems. Flowers in large plumes.

How to Grow
Pampas grass grows best in fertile, well-drained soil in full sun but will tolerate drought. Propagate by division of the woody roots. Grow where it will not overwhelm smaller plantings. Occasionally remove dead material by hand from center of clump to improve appearance, or cut plant to the ground in late winter; handle razor-sharp leaf edges carefully.

selloana p. 167
Pampas grass. Stems 8–12 ft. high. Numerous long, narrow leaves. Female plants produce showy clusters of graceful, feathery, plumed spikes, 1–3 ft. long, silvery or pale pink. One of the finest ornamental grasses, of year-round interest. Zone 8.

Cotoneaster
Ko-to'nee-as-ter
Rosaceae. Rose family

Description
About 50 species of shrubs or small trees, many widely planted for their attractive habit and showy fruit. Native to Old World temperate zones. Some species evergreen. Flowers small, white or pinkish, blooming in early summer. Fruit is small, fleshy.

How to Grow

Cotoneasters prefer a sunny location and well-drained soil that is not overly acid. Prune lightly to maintain shape. They are subject to fire blight and, in dry summers, to spider mites. Although these conditions may be controlled by spraying, mass plantings may be at risk. Dwarf kinds do not thrive in low-desert heat.

adpressus p. 193

Creeping cotoneaster. Slow-growing deciduous shrub to 12 in. high, 6 ft. wide, with rooting stems. Leaves ½ in. long. Pinkish flowers in spring, red fruit. *C. a. praecox* is more vigorous, a little taller, with larger fruit. China. Zone 5.

dammeri p. 194   Pictured above

Bearberry cotoneaster. (Sometimes sold as C. *humifusus*.) Evergreen shrub to 12 in. high, with trailing branches that often root at the joints. Leaves 1 in. long, pale beneath. Flowers white, berries bright red. Similar forms are 'Coral Beauty', 'Lowfast', and 'Skogsholm'. China. Zone 5.

lacteus p. 128

Parney cotoneaster. Evergreen shrub to 12 ft. high, with arching branches. Leaves 1–3 in. long, hairy beneath. Flowers white, in clusters 2–3 in. across. Clusters of small, red fruit. Useful as a hedge or unclipped screen. China. Zone 7.

Cupaniopsis
Kew-pan-i-op'sis
Sapindaceae. Soapberry family

Description

About 55 species of woody plants, mostly from Australia and New Caledonia. The species below is a broadleaf evergreen grown as a shade tree in frost-free areas.

How to Grow

Tolerant of wet and salt, but susceptible to frost damage in colder areas of zone 9.

anacardioides p. 86

Carrot wood. Tree to 40 ft., not as wide. Leaves evergreen, compound, with 6–10 leathery leaflets, each about 4 in. long. Flowers inconspicuous. A relatively neat, clean tree casting fairly dense shade. Leathery yellow or orange fruits appear on mature trees in late spring, producing brief but abundant litter. Tree is deep rooting, suitable for lawns and near paving, but not drought tolerant. Tolerates wet conditions. Australia. Zone 10; semihardy in 9.

× *Cupressocyparis*
Kew-press-o-sip′ar-is. Leyland cypress
Cupressaceae. Cypress family

Description
A cross-genus hybrid found in the garden of C. J. Leyland in Wales in 1888, the offspring of *Chamaecyparis nootkatensis* and *Cupressus macrocarpa*.

How to Grow
Because the roots are stringy and difficult to ball and burlap, plant container-grown specimens. Almost any soil is acceptable except soggy, extremely dry, or highly alkaline soil. Plants need at least 75 percent full sun. Pruning is seldom necessary, other than to remove an occasional wayward branch; the tree responds well to shearing. Usually pest-free, but borers are sometimes troublesome.

leylandii p. 86
Leyland cypress. A narrowly conical tree reaching 100 ft. at maturity, narrower in youth than after 30–40 years. Feathery blue-green foliage on flat, spraylike branchlets. Small cones in fall. Often grows incredibly fast in youth. Excellent for screens, windbreaks, hedges, and large formal specimens. Cultivars include 'Leighton Green', with grayish green foliage; 'Castewellan', yellow; and 'Naylor's Blue', soft bluish green. Tolerates salt. Do not plant where cypress canker is a problem. Zones 6–10.

Cupressus
Kew-pres′sus. Cypress
Cupressaceae. Cypress family

Description
Magnificent coniferous evergreens, the true cypresses. Tiny, aromatic, scalelike leaves hug wiry branches. Globe-shaped

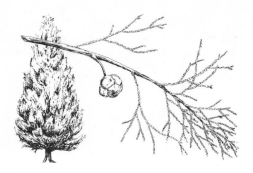

cones of woody scales. The 12 known species are mostly from the warmer parts of the Old World, a few from western North America. They make excellent accents, screens, and specimens.

How to Grow
Plant container-grown cypresses in full sun in well-drained soil. Irrigate during dry spells in the first few years; older trees are quite drought tolerant. Mulching is advisable. Prune unruly branches any time to maintain neatness; other pruning is unnecessary.

glabra p. 87 *Pictured above*
Smooth-barked Arizona cypress. Fast-growing to 40 ft., with smooth red bark and green to blue-green foliage. Excellent desert tree. Silvery and pyramidal forms are available. Zones 8–10.

sempervirens p. 87
Columnar Italian cypress. A narrowly upright cultivar of the ancient Mediterranean cypress. To 75 ft. Dark green leaves on erect branches, cones to 1½ in. in diameter. A strong formal element in the landscape, best used in rows or groups. Susceptible to mites. 'Glauca' has bluish foliage. Zones 8–10.

Dalea
Day'lee-ah
Leguminosae. Pea family

Description
Trees or shrubs with finely divided foliage, pealike flowers. Useful desert plants native to the Southwest.

How to Grow
All tolerate drought, but respond to occasional deep watering with rapid growth.

greggii p. 194
Trailing indigo bush. Trailing plant to 3 ft. wide with gray foliage and purple flowers in spring and early summer. Use as ground cover. Zones 9–10.

spinosa p. 88 *Pictured above*
Smoke tree. Nearly leafless small tree (to 12 ft.) with interesting interlaced gray branches; blue flowers in spring. May grow larger with ample water. Easy to grow from seed. Zones 9–10.

Dasylirion
Das-i-li′ri-on
Agavaceae. Agave family

Description
Short-trunked, stiff desert plants of Mexico and North America with long, narrow leaves used for thatching or baskets. Dense clusters of small whitish flowers on tall stalks.

How to Grow
These plants prefer full sun, heat, and sandy or rocky soils. Will stand some frost. Sometimes grown in pots or tubs.

wheeleri p. 167
Desert spoon. Spiky 3-ft. leaves make dense clumps that even-

tually form short trunks. Flower stalk can reach 15 ft. Cup-shaped ivory-covered bases of leaves broaden to form the "spoon," used in flower arrangements. Zones 7–9.

Delosperma
Dell-o-sper′ma. Ice plant
Aizoaceae. Carpetweed family

Description
About 140 species of small, dense, succulent perennials or small shrubs from South Africa. Small, fleshy leaves; daisylike flowers in spring. At home in rock gardens and as edging, they are much used as ground covers on slopes needing erosion control.

How to Grow
Plant in full sun and sandy, rich, well-drained soil. Ice plants tolerate drought once established but look better when watered during summer heat. Dry soil and temperatures above freezing are critical during the winter. Propagate from seeds or cuttings. Fertilize lightly when flower buds form.

cooperi p. 195
Hardy ice plant. Ground-hugging, spreading branches reach 6 in. high and 24 in. wide. Thick evergreen leaves are bright green. Flowers are purple. Zones 9–10.

nubigena
Close mat of 1-in.-long, cylindrical, fleshy leaves that turn red in winter cold. Bright yellow daisylike flowers in spring. Zones 5–10.

Dianthus
Dy-an′thus
Caryophyllaceae. Pink family

Description
About 300 species of annual or perennial herbs, mostly Eurasian. Some, such as sweet William, are important garden plants. Most form evergreen mats or tufts of foliage. Single or double flowers in a variety of colors are often fragrant.

How to Grow

Pinks are usually easy to grow in any ordinary garden soil that is extremely well drained. Most prefer full sun. Perennial plants are inclined to die out if left alone for 2 or 3 years, so keep a fresh stock coming along by division, layering, or cuttings, all easily managed as the plant roots freely. Cut off all faded flowers. In the mat-forming sorts, cut off all flowering stalks nearly to the base of the plant in fall. Most bloom in spring.

barbatus p. 168 *Pictured above*

Sweet William. Plants are 1–2 ft. high, with flat, broad leaves. Small red, rose-purple, white, or varicolored flowers, fragrant, in dense clusters 3–5 in. across; some forms are double-flowered. Most varieties biennial, although self-seeding makes them seem perennial. Sow seed in spring for bloom the following year. Prefers cool summers and mild winters. Europe. Zone 6.

plumarius p. 168

Grass pink. Perennial, makes excellent border edging. Loose mat of smooth, bluish gray foliage. Fragrant flowers 1½ in. across on stems 9–18 in. high, rose-pink to purplish, white, or variegated colors, petals fringed. Some forms double-flowered. Blooms June to October. Add lime to very acid soil and prune after flowering. Light mulch of evergreen branches reduces winter damage. Eurasia. Zone 4.

Dietes
Dy-ee'teez
Iridaceae. Iris family

Description
Irislike South African herbs. Evergreen, sword-shaped or narrower leaves rise from rootstocks or corms. Flowers are almost exactly like beardless iris.

How to Grow
African iris needs average, well-drained soil and full sun or light shade. Tolerates drought when established, does best with regular watering. Divide clumps in autumn or winter.

vegeta p. 169
African iris. Leaves, 2–4 ft. high, spread like a fan. Flowers white with yellow or brown spots and lavender shading, 2–2½ in. wide. Blooms last only a day, but plants rebloom over long season. Flower stalks are perennial; do not cut them off. *D. bicolor* is smaller, to 2 ft., with maroon-blotched yellow flowers. Stems not perennial and should be cut. Both zone 8.

Diospyros
Di-os'pi-ros
Ebenaceae. Ebony family

Description
Deciduous trees with inconspicuous flowers, fleshy fruits.

How to Grow
Plant bare-rooted or container-grown plants in winter. These trees need good drainage and a steady, though not heavy, water supply. Prune only to shape or remove dead branches.

kaki p. 88
Kaki; Japanese persimmon. To 30 ft. or more, wide-spreading. Glossy, attractive foliage turns yellow to red in fall. Showy, edible orange fruits ripen in November and December. Favored varieties include 'Hachiya', a shapely, round-headed tree, with big soft fruit that is puckery until dead ripe; and 'Fuyu', with hard fruit, sweet even while firm. May not fruit in desert areas. Zone 5.

Distictis
Dis-tick'tis
Bignoniaceae. Trumpet-creeper family

Description
A small genus of woody vines native to the West Indies and tropical America. Evergreen, compound leaves and tubular flowers.

How to Grow
Trumpet vine grows best in full sun or light shade in fertile soil. Increase by cuttings from side shoots in early summer.

buccinatoria p. 210   *Pictured above*
Blood-red trumpet vine. (Sometimes known as *Bignonia cherere*.) Handsome evergreen vine to 18 ft. high. Clusters of trumpet-shaped flowers, nearly 4 in. long, bright red, yellow at base and inside. Prized for foliage and long flowering period. Zone 9.

Dodonaea
Do-do-nee'a
Sapindaceae. Soapberry family

Description
Some 50 species of tropical trees and shrubs. Sometimes cultivated as ornamental or for medicinal use.

How to Grow
The species below is easy to grow, tolerating most soils, drought, heat, and wind.

viscosa **'Purpurea'** *p. 129*

Purple hop bush. Evergreen shrub or small tree to 15 ft. with many erect stems well clothed in narrow bronzy purple foliage. Insignificant flowers are followed by clusters of showy dry fruits, pinkish in color. Useful screen or tall hedge. New Zealand. A green form is native to Arizona. Zone 8.

Echium
Ek'i-um
Boraginaceae. Borage family

Description
More than 35 species of Eurasian biennials and perennials often grown as annuals. Broad leaves are rough and hairy. Funnel-shaped flowers, primarily blue, are on erect, one-sided spikes.

How to Grow
Most tolerate poor soil, drought, and sea wind, but not extreme heat. Grow readily from seed.

fastuosum *p. 169   Pictured above*

Pride of Madeira. Coarse, shrubby perennial with heavy branches 3–6 ft. high, thickly covered with long, narrow, hairy gray leaves. In spring each branch is tipped by a long, dense cluster of blue flowers. Remove spent flower spikes; prune to maintain bushy form. Zones 9–10.

Elaeagnus
Ee-lee-ag′nus
Elaeagnaceae. Oleaster family

Description
About 40 species of handsome shrubs and trees from the north temperate zone. Several are cultivated for their ornamental foliage covered with silvery scales and their decorative berrylike fruits, edible in some species. The tubular or bell-shaped flowers are small and not very showy but are fragrant. Can serve as windbreaks, hedges, and screens, and grow well in seashore gardens. They tolerate city conditions.

How to Grow
These plants are easy to grow in full sun and any reasonably well-drained soil. Tolerate adverse growing conditions as well as drought and wind. Let plants grow naturally or shear into formal hedges. Cut back side shoots in spring to encourage colorful new growth. Propagate from cuttings or seeds by layering.

angustifolia p. 89
Russian olive. Deciduous shrub or small tree, sometimes spiny, to 15–20 ft. high and wide in a rounded form. Twigs are silver; mature bark is brown and flaking. Narrow leaves, 2–3 in. long, are silvery underneath. Fragrant flowers, silvery or white outside and yellow inside, in spring. Sweet, mealy ½-in. fruits are yellow with silver scales. Eurasia. Zones 3–9.

pungens p. 129 *Pictured above*
Thorny elaeagnus. Usually spiny, spreading shrub to 15 ft. Evergreen leaves with wavy margins and silvery undersides. Very fragrant, drooping, silvery white flowers in fall. Fruit is brown, turning red. Forms with white or yellow variegation are widespread. East Asia. Zones 7–9.

Encelia
En-see′li-a
Compositae. Daisy family

Description
Low-branching shrubs or perennials with daisylike flowers, native to tropical Americas.

How to Grow
These plants will grow in almost any soil that is not boggy. Desert natives.

farinosa *p. 130*
Brittlebush; incienso. Shrub to 5 ft. with fuzzy gray leaves and sheaves of yellow flowers, 1 in. wide, in spring. Plant is aromatic. Native to the Southwest. Zones 8–9.

Eriobotrya
E-ri-o-bo′tri-a
Rosaceae. Rose family

Description
A small genus of Asiatic evergreen trees and shrubs. One species, the loquat, is grown as an ornamental tree with edible fruit. Large, toothed leaves. White flowers in woolly clusters.

How to Grow
Loquats seldom fruit north of the citrus-growing areas. Withstand temperatures of 10–15 degrees F, but fruit or blossoms in midwinter are damaged by a few degrees of frost. Plant in full sun, preferably in deep, well-drained soil, not in wet area, and mulch and water regularly. Once established, will endure considerable drought. Fire blight is a problem in some areas; consult local authorities for a suitable resistant cultivar for your area.

japonica *p. 89   Pictured above*
Loquat; Japanese plum; Japanese medlar. Tree to 30 ft., often
as wide as high. Nearly stalkless leaves are nearly 1 ft. long,
leathery and crisp, rusty-hairy beneath. Foliage alone is attractive enough to warrant landscape use. Clusters, 4–6 in.
long, of small, fragrant, white flowers in winter. Fleshy, plum-
shaped fruit, 1–2 in. long, in spring, agreeably acid, good for
eating raw and for making jelly. Fruit of some cultivars nearly
3 in. long. A form with variegated leaves is grown chiefly for
ornament. Central China. Zones 8–10.

Eriogonum
E-ri-og′o-num. Wild buckwheat
Polygonaceae. Knotweed family

Description
Annuals, perennials, and shrubs native to the western U.S.
Suitable for rock gardens or as a ground cover on dry banks.
Dried flowers are attractive in bouquets. Leaves in basal ro-
settes or on ends of branches; large, branched clusters of small
flowers in summer on almost leafless stalks.

How to Grow
Plant in full sun and loose, gravelly, well-drained soil. Once
established, these plants require little watering and withstand
wind well. Self-sow easily; remove fading flower clusters if
you do not want seedlings. Propagate by seeds or division.

fasciculatum *p. 130*
Shrub forming broad clumps to 3 ft. tall, 4 ft. across, with
narrow gray to gray-green leaves and clustered white to pinkish flowers. Lower-growing, greener 'Theodore Payne' is good
ground cover. Zones 8–10.

umbellatum *p. 170   Pictured above*
Sulphur-flower. Woody perennial with spreading branches
forms loose mat to 12 in. high and 3 ft. wide. Small green
leaves have woolly undersides; flowers are cream to bright
yellow in showy, dome-shaped clusters. Zones 4–10.

Erythrina
E-ri-thry′na. Coral tree
Leguminosae. Pea family

Description
About 100 species of handsome tropical shrubs and trees, both
broadleaf evergreens and deciduous plants. Leaves have 3
broad leaflets. Striking, pealike flowers in large racemes bloom
mostly before or after the leaves, not at the same time. Long,
woody pod.

How to Grow
Coral trees seem to have no special soil preferences other than
good drainage. Water regularly but infrequently during dry
spells. Full sun.

caffra
Kaffirboom coral tree. Broad, flat-topped tree to 40 ft., often
much broader than tall. Drops leaves in midwinter then produces clustered, deep orange-red flowers. New leaves follow
in earliest spring. Bare-branch silhouette is sculpturesque.
South Africa. Zones 9–10.

coralloides
Naked coral tree. Somewhat smaller than *E. caffra*. Red blos-
soms at ends of naked, strikingly twisted branches, March to
May. Leaves turn yellow before dropping in fall. Mexico.
Zones 9–10.

crista-gallii *p. 131   Pictured above*
Cockspur coral tree. Shrub or tree to 20 ft. Long, narrow clusters of deep pink to red flowers from spring through fall. Treelike where frosts are mild and infrequent; elsewhere a shrub producing new shoots from the base each year. Zones 8–10.

Eucalyptus
You-ka-lip'tus. Gum tree
Myrtaceae. Myrtle family

Description
Over 500 species of mostly aromatic evergreen trees, some gigantic, with striking flowers and foliage. Most are native to Australia. More than 70 species are grown in California, all prized for their freedom from pests and some as a source of nectar for bees. The fruits and leafy branches are often used in dried flower decorations. The following species are best for landscape use, though many species not described here are also good or excellent.

How to Grow
Eucalyptuses are easy to grow and do well in a variety of soils. Young trees grow very fast. Most are drought tolerant. Some need staking or pruning when young to strengthen trunks.

citriodora *p. 90*
Lemon-scented gum. Tree is 50–75 ft. high and slender. Bark smooth, cream-colored. Leaves lance-shaped, pendulous, strongly lemon-scented. Flowers and fruits unimportant. Adaptable to varying amounts of moisture in soil. Frost-tender. Australia. Zones 9–10.

forrestiana
Fuchsia eucalyptus. Shrub or, if pruned and staked, short tree

to 12 ft. Reddish branches and smooth, gray-brown trunk. Hanging, fuchsialike red flower blooms from time to time all year. Good for coast or dry areas. Western Australia. Zones 9–10.

microtheca
Coolibah. Tree to 35–40 ft., with one or several trunks. Dense blue-green foliage. Insignificant flowers and fruit. First-class desert tree. Zones 8–10.

nicholii *p. 90*
Narrow-leaved black peppermint. Tree to 40 ft. with narrow, drooping leaves on weeping branches. Leaves have strong peppermint scent. One of the better species for street or home garden use. Australia. Zones 9–10.

sideroxylon *p. 91   Pictured above*
Red ironbark. (Often sold as *E. s.* 'Rosea'.) To 80 ft. Rough, dark red or blackish bark doesn't shed. Narrow leaves, attractive flowers 1 in. wide, light pink, in hanging clusters 8–20 in. wide from fall to spring. The many forms may be shorter, upright, open, weeping, with darker green or silvery foliage, with red or rose flowers. Drought tolerant. Australia. Zones 9–10.

spathulata *p. 91*
Narrow-leafed gimlet. One of many eucalyptuses known as mallees, multistemmed small trees or large shrubs capable of sprouting from the base. To 20 ft., with several red-barked trunks and very narrow 2–3-in. leaves. Flowers yellow. Good desert plant. Zones 9–10.

Euonymus
You-on'i-mus. Spindle tree
Celastraceae. Spindle-tree family

Description
About 170 mostly Asian species of shrubs, vines, or trees, more than a dozen grown for their showy fruits, evergreen foliage, and pleasing form rather than for their inconspicuous flowers.

How to Grow
Not particular about soil. Euonymus grows equally well in sun or shade with moderate watering.

fortunei *p. 211*
Winter creeper. (Often sold as *E. radicans* or *E. fortunei radicans*.) A trailing or climbing evergreen vine. Allowed to sprawl, it will make a ground cover with branches rising to 12 in. from long, trailing stems. Given support of a tree or wall, it will climb. Smallish oval leaves, greenish white flowers, nearly round, pale pink fruit. Zone 4.

Some cultivars of *E. fortunei* are grown especially for ground cover. 'Colorata' (purple winter creeper) is a trailing shrub to 18 in. high; leaves turn deep purple in autumn and winter. 'Kewensis' (more correctly called 'Minima') is a fine-textured trailing form to 2 in. high, with small, narrow, whitish-veined leaves; it seldom fruits. Other cultivars, such as 'Emerald Gaiety' and 'Golden Prince', are grown as small, compact evergreen shrubs, often with variegated foliage.

Euryops
Eu-ry′ops
Compositae. Daisy family

Description
Shrubs with finely cut, evergreen leaves and yellow daisy flowers. Native to South Africa.

How to Grow
Plant from containers and water consistently until established, then deeply and infrequently. These shrubs are indifferent as to soil but need good drainage. Prune to control size. Propagate from cuttings.

pectinatus *p. 131   Pictured above*
Gray-leaved euryops. Dense, rounded shrub to 3 ft., with gray foliage and brilliant yellow daisies most of the year. Widely planted. Zones 9–10.

Fatsia
Fat'si-a
Araliaceae. Aralia family

Description
One species, an evergreen Japanese shrub or small tree, native to Japan. Large, tropical-looking lobed leaves are shiny and stiff. Small flowers in large, very showy, branched clusters.

How to Grow
Fatsia grows well in nearly every type of soil but prefers rich, sandy, slightly acid ones. Does best in full shade, with generous doses of fertilizer and water. Protect from winter sun and wind, which can cause marginal leaf burn. Propagate by semihard-wood cuttings.

japonica p. 132
Japanese aralia. To 10–12 ft. Leaf stalks 8–12 in. long, blades 9–15 in. wide. Whitish flower clusters to 18 in. long in fall. Tiny black fruit. (Often sold as *Aralia japonica*.) One form has variegated leaves. Zone 8.

Feijoa
Fa-jo'a
Myrtaceae. Myrtle family

Description
A small genus of evergreen South American shrubs or small trees. The species below is often grown for its delicious, white-fleshed fruit, but its flowers and gray-green foliage are also attractive. Considered the hardiest of the subtropical fruits.

How to Grow
This shrub does well in sandy, rich loam. Likes sun, is drought tolerant. Space 15–20 ft. apart. Can be pruned to almost any shape. Propagate from seeds, which germinate 2–3 weeks after sowing, or by cuttings made in July or August. Buy named varieties if possible; not all seedlings are self-fertile.

sellowiana p. 132
Pineapple guava. Shrub, to 20 ft. Leaves 2–3 in. long, white-felty beneath. Long-stalked flowers have many showy red stamens. Blooms in spring. Petals are edible. Grayish green berry, 2–3 in. long, larger in some varieties. Brazil, Argentina. Zone 8.

Festuca
Fess-too′ka. Fescue
Gramineae. Grass family

Description
Nearly 100 annual or perennial grasses, usually tufted; most from temperate regions, some found in pasture or lawn mixtures; the species below is grown as ornamental accent or at front of border.

How to Grow
Ornamental fescues prefer light, well-drained soil in full sun. They tolerate a little shade, but blue-gray species have best leaf color in full sun. Evergreen, but may be cut back when foliage becomes shabby. Propagate by division; plants benefit from division every few years.

ovina glauca p. 170
Blue fescue. Many stems, very fine, slender, tufted, 8–12 in. high, producing no stolons. Leaves silvery blue, rolled, thread-like, to 6 in. long. Flowering panicle. If plants die out in center, divide, reset, and cut back. Old and New Worlds, temperate regions. Zone 4.

Ficus
Fy′kus
Moraceae. Mulberry family

Description
More than 800 species of chiefly tropical trees, shrubs, and vines, including the common fig and many ornamentals. Minute flowers, fruit, are borne inside a closed, fleshy receptacle that is edible in the common fig but in few other species.

How to Grow
Figs are easy to grow if provided with good drainage and are free of pests except as noted below. Easily rooted from cuttings.

carica p. 92 *Pictured above*
Common fig. Deciduous tree, fast-growing to 30 ft.; can be kept smaller by pruning. Large, rather rough, bright green leaves are deeply lobed. Pale gray trunk is picturesque in age. Commonly grown dooryard kinds need no pollination. 'Smyrna' or 'Calimyrna' need male pollinators (caprifigs) and caprifig wasps to produce fruit; they are not often attempted by home gardeners. Favored varieties: 'Brown Turkey', brownish purple fruit; 'Genoa' and 'Kadota', white fruit; and 'Mission', purple-black fruit. 'Texas Everbearing', brownish purple fruit, is popular in desert regions. Mediterranean region. Zones 8–10.

microcarpa p. 92
Indian laurel; laurel fig. A tree to 40 ft., widely cultivated in parks and along streets where winters are warm. Bark smooth and grayish. Long, weeping branches; lower ones may be removed to display light gray trunk. Thick, elliptical leaves 2½–3½ in. long. Small, light green figs. Leaves, rosy-chartreuse when new, are produced throughout growing season; mature foliage is green. Foliage can be severely damaged by thrips, which are controllable (barely) by systemic insecticides. *F. rubiginosa*, the rustyleaf fig, is more resistant to thrips. Australia. Zone 10; semihardy in 9.

pumila p. 211
Creeping fig; climbing fig. Popular house or hanging basket plant in cold climates; where hardy, it is an outdoor vine clinging by sucker disks to 40 ft. high. Grows neatly and flat against walls. Small, very numerous leaves, larger on mature fruiting branches, which grow stiffly outward from the support. Pear-shaped yellowish fruit is not edible. Prune to keep young growth vigorous and to prevent development of coarse, mature leaves and branches, which detract from the trim effect. (Incorrectly known as *F. repens*.) East Asia. Zone 9.

Forestiera
Fo-res-ti-ee′ra
Oleaceae. Olive family

Description
About 20 species of deciduous and some evergreen trees or shrubs from North America, the West Indies, and South America. Inconspicuous flowers. Fruits are olive-sized, black or dark purple, inedible.

How to Grow
The species below thrives in full sun and sandy, dry, well-drained soil. Propagate from cuttings or by layering. Prune as needed each spring to shape the plant and control its size.

neomexicana p. 183
Desert olive; New Mexico privet. Weedy, rapid-growing deciduous shrub to 10 ft. high and wide. Leaves, 1½ in. long, open after flowers bloom in spring. Plant has little ornamental value but is useful for hedges or screening in harsh, dry climates. Native to the Southwest. Zones 5–10.

Fouquieria
Foo-kwee-ee′ri-a
Fouquieriaceae. Fouquieria family

Description
The species below is a cactuslike shrub with many stiff, narrow, erect, thorny stems arising from the base, to 10–20 ft. Leafless except following rains.

How to Grow
Ocotillo needs dry, well-drained soil, full sun. Roots easily from cuttings of almost any size.

splendens p. 133
Ocotillo; coach-whip. Narrow, whiplike, dark stems bear tiny roundish leaves, which soon drop. Clusters of showy red tubular flowers adorn tops of stems after summer rain. Good for hedges. Native to the Southwest. Zone 8.

Fragaria
Fra-gay′ri-a. Strawberry
Rosaceae. Rose family

Description
Low-growing perennial herbs known for their edible fruit; the species below is grown as an evergreen ground cover.

How to Grow
Beach strawberry grows well in full sun in most garden soils, particularly if slightly acid. Detach and plant the young plants that root at ends of runners. Needs annual mowing to reduce runners; water regularly in dry areas.

chiloensis p. 195   *Pictured above*
Beach strawberry. Low, bushy plant, 6–8 in. high, usually forms runners after fruit is set. Leaflets green and glossy above, pale bluish white beneath, tinted red in winter. White flowers in spring. Fruit edible but rarely seen. Coastal Alaska to California, South America. Zone 5.

Fraxinus
Frax′i-nus. Ash
Oleaceae. Olive family

Description
Some 65 species of mostly deciduous trees of the north temperate zone, several important as both ornamental and timber trees. Fast-growing but strong. Handsome rounded or upright trees with compound leaves. Flowers and fruit not showy.

How to Grow

Ash trees will grow in most ordinary garden soils except strongly alkaline; not suitable for very dry sites. They transplant easily; prune young trees early to a single trunk. Water deeply during drought to keep trees vigorous and reduce insect and disease problems. Self-sow easily. Selected named varieties do not set seed.

oxycarpa p. 93

Fine-textured foliage and modest size (to 30–35 ft.) make this a useful street or garden tree. 'Raywood' is seedless and has a fine deep purple fall color. Southern Europe to East Asia. Zone 6.

velutina p. 93 *Pictured above*

Arizona ash. Fast-growing, eventually to 50 ft., with somewhat smaller spread. Leaves turn yellow in fall. The species is rarely sold. Seedless varieties are recommended: 'Modesto', very widely grown, is excellent but often disfigured by anthracnose fungus after late-spring rains. 'Rio Grande', often called FanTex ash, has thicker, fleshier leaves and is especially useful in hot climates. Arizona, New Mexico. Zone 6.

Freesia

Free′zi-a
Iridaceae. Iris family

Description

Very fragrant and beautiful South American herbs with branching flower stems, deservedly popular, especially among florists, for their winter-blooming flowers. Freesias have been heavily hybridized, and there are many named forms. Narrow, sword-shaped leaves grow from bulblike corms. Tubular flowers, typically white or yellow, in spikes.

How to Grow

Freesias naturalize in California, sending up foliage when winter rains begin, blooming in earliest spring, then fading away. Plant in fall, 2 in. deep, in sunny area, well-drained soil. Need no summer water, but can tolerate it if drainage is excellent. Easy to grow from seed sown in midsummer, but seedlings tend to revert to creamy, yellow-marked *F. refracta*. Easily grown as pot plants indoors if kept cool until buds are well advanced.

× *hybrida*   p. 171

Horticultural hybrids, probably all derived from *F. refracta*. Perennial. Slender, usually branched stems, 1½–2 ft. high, carry spikes of funnel-shaped flowers with flaring mouths, to 2 in. long, in many colors including white and yellow, sometimes tinted or veined with pink, purple, blue, orange, or even brown. Creamy and yellow kinds have a delicious citrus fragrance; highly colored kinds have less scent. South Africa. Zone 9.

Fremontodendron

Free-mont-o-den′dron. Flannel bush
Sterculiaceae. Chocolate family

Description

Small genus of Californian evergreen shrubs or small trees with showy, saucerlike flowers on short stalks. Dark green, leathery leaves have soft covering on undersides.

How to Grow
These plants require well-drained soil and full sun. Completely drought tolerant; summer water can be fatal. They are excellent companions for ceanothus. Roots are shallow, so young plants need staking until they become established.

× **'California Glory'** *p. 134   Pictured above*
Fast growth to 20 ft. Huge spring display of 3-in. flowers, bright yellow, tinged red on the outside. 'Pacific Sunset' has somewhat larger flowers. Zone 9.

Gaillardia
Gay-lar'di-a
Compositae. Daisy family

Description
About 14 species of showy North American annual and perennial herbs. Low-growing with handsome daisylike flowers. Very popular garden plants.

How to Grow
Gaillardias prefer light, open soil and full sun. Propagated by seed or division, spring or fall. Bloom chiefly in summer. Good border plants and cut flowers.

grandiflora *p. 171*
Blanket flower. Perennial, 8–36 in. high. Leaves slightly hairy. Red and yellow flowers, 3–4 in. wide. Will not survive in heavy, wet soils during winter. Crown in center of plant often dies; dig and transplant new growth away from old crown. Often flowers in first year from seed. Zone 4.

Gardenia
Gar-dee'ni-a
Rubiaceae. Madder family

Description
About 200 species of tropical Old World shrubs and trees. Large, fragrant white flowers and glossy evergreen leaves.

How to Grow
Plant gardenias in moisture-retentive, acid soil to which peat or other organic matter has been added. Mulch to help retain

moisture and avoid injuring roots during cultivation. Best in partial shade. Water and feed regularly.

jasminoides p. 134 *Pictured above*
Gardenia; cape jasmine. Shrub to 2–5 ft. Thick, leathery, lance-shaped leaves, 3–4 in. long, occasionally variegated. Flowers 2–3½ in. wide, single or double, very fragrant. Blooms spring to summer. Popular cultivars include 'August Beauty', 4–6 ft. high, with double flowers from spring to fall; 'Mystery', 6–8 ft. high, double flowers; 'Radicans', 12-in.-high miniature with variegated leaves; and 'Veitchii', 3–4 ft. high, a very good bloomer from spring to fall. China. Zone 8.

Garrya
Ga′ri-a
Garryaceae. Silk tassel family

Description
About 15 species of North American evergreen shrubs with tassellike blossoms, male and female flowers borne on separate plants.

How to Grow
Buy male plants for their showier tassels. Will thrive in good garden soil with reasonable drainage. Full sun or shade. Can take summer drought when established, but tolerate summer water.

elliptica p. 135
Shrub to 10 ft., possibly small tree to 20 ft. Leaves dark green with wavy edges. Catkins silvery green, to 8 in. long on male plants in late winter. 'James Roof' a fine selection. Female

plants have shorter flower clusters, produce inedible fleshy purple fruits. Use as specimen, screen, or filler. California to southern Oregon. Zone 8.

fremontii
Smaller than *G. elliptica,* with lighter green foliage and shorter, yellowish or purplish catkins. Likes sun, takes drier conditions than *elliptica.* Zone 7.

Gazania
Ga-zay'ni-a
Compositae. Daisy family

Description
About 6 species of showy South African herbaceous perennials. A few have long been cultivated for their striking daisy flowers with yellow, golden, or white rays, often with dark spot at base. Flowers close at night or in cloudy weather. Hybrids come in many colors and are often multicolored. Good ground cover or edging plants.

How to Grow
Gazanias are well adapted to southwestern gardens and will endure for years if given excellent drainage. Start seeds indoors 6–8 weeks before last frost; set out in sunny, dry, well-drained soil after danger of frost is past. Or propagate selected forms by division or late-summer basal cuttings. Crowded plants may rot; best control is by thinning.

Hybrids
Clump-forming plants with evergreen foliage, whitish beneath, often deeply indented. Flowers on stems 6–10 in. long; peak of bloom is late spring and early summer. Many colors, white through pink to deep red, yellow, and orange. Seed-grown strains include 'Carnival', 'Chansonette', 'Sundance', and 'Sunshine'; the latter two have multicolored flower heads to 5 in. wide. Named forms propagated by division come in many colors as well, and a double yellow, 'Moonglow', remains open during cloudy weather. Hardy in mild-winter areas, where they bloom intermittently throughout year; grow as annuals elsewhere. Zones 8–9.

rigens leucolaena p. 196
Trailing gazania. Widely used as a ground cover. Trailing

stems spread rapidly, have silvery leaves and yellow, orange, bronze, or white flowers. Named selections sometimes available. Zones 8–9.

Geijera
Gee′je-ra
Rutaceae. Citrus family

Description
Evergreen shrubs or trees with alternate leaves dotted with oil glands; small white flowers in terminal clusters.

How to Grow
Species below is sold in containers. It requires only good drainage and reasonably good soil to thrive. Needs little pruning. Resists drought when established, but watering spurs growth.

parviflora p. 94
Australian willow. Tree to 30 ft. tall, 20 ft. wide. Graceful, upswept branches, very narrow, dark green drooping leaves. Flowers, fruit inconspicuous. Excellent street or garden tree; casts light shade, has well-behaved root system. Zone 9.

Gelsemium
Gel-see′mi-um
Loganiaceae. Buddleia family

Description
Two or three species of evergreen woody vines with funnel-shaped flowers, native to eastern Asia and eastern North America.

How to Grow
Species below needs fertile, well-drained soil in sun or light shade. Propagate by seeds or cuttings. Attractive on a trellis, fence, or lamp post, or as a ground cover. Somewhat drought tolerant, best when watered.

sempervirens p. 212
Carolina, or yellow, jessamine or jasmine. (True jasmine is *Jasminum.*) Climbs 10–20 ft. high. Shiny, oblong leaves, 2–4 in. long. Dense clusters of bright yellow flowers, very fragrant, in spring. There is a double-flowered form. All parts of plant, including the nectar, are poisonous. Southeastern U.S. Zone 7.

Gerbera
Ger'ber-ra
Compositae. Daisy family

Description
About 40 species of South African or Asiatic herbs; only the one below is of garden interest.

How to Grow
Provide good, well-drained soil in sun or light shade. Water deeply and let soil dry out somewhat before watering again. Plant so that crown is not buried and keep soil from washing over it. Fertilize frequently. Divide crowded plants in earliest spring.

jamesonii p. 172
Transvaal daisy. Leaves somewhat resemble sturdy dandelion leaves, in slow-spreading clumps. Solitary daisy flowers, 4 in. or more across, on 18-in. stems. Flowers are single, duplex (two rows of ray flowers), or double, and may be nearly white to yellow, pink, or red. Superb cut flowers. South Africa. Zone 9, but hardy in cold frames in colder regions.

Ginkgo
Gink′o; jink′o. Maidenhair tree
Ginkgoaceae. Ginkgo family

Description
A remarkable deciduous Chinese tree, the only surviving species and only genus of a nearly extinct family. All cultivated specimens have been grown from trees preserved around Chinese temples. Young trees are often ungainly, with clumsy branching, but older trees have dignified appearance. One of the finest street and specimen trees in the temperate world.

How to Grow
Plant only male trees to avoid the foul-smelling fruit of the female tree. Ginkgoes require full sun; otherwise very tolerant of soil conditions and air pollution. Water in dry seasons when young. Prune young trees when dormant to control unruly branches. Practically immune to all pests and tolerate street conditions very well.

biloba *p. 94* *Pictured above*
Ginkgo; maidenhair tree. To 70–80 ft. Fan-shaped leaves, 2½–3½ in. wide, resemble a segment of a maidenhair fern frond. Foliage turns soft yellow in autumn; most leaves fall at one time, as if by command. Small yellow fruits are foul smelling, but kernel is edible. 'Autumn Gold' is more spreading than the species and has rich yellow fall foliage. Several narrowly upright cultivars are excellent choices for street plantings. China. Zones 5–9; semihardy in 4.

Hedera
Hed'er-a. Ivy
Araliaceae. Aralia family

Description
Perennial evergreen woody vines from northern Eurasia and
North Africa. They climb by aerial rootlets that cling easily
to brick or masonry, less easily to wood. Grown for handsome
foliage. Only mature specimens flower.

How to Grow
Ivies thrive in rich, moist soil. They grow well in shade; full
sun will scorch some varieties. Propagate from cuttings of
young growth rooted in sand, light soil mix, or water, or by
layering. Prune heavily or shear for desired habit and compact
growth. Vines readily cover any rough surface and will hide
chain-link fence, but do not twine and must be woven into
the links. Ivies make a good ground cover under trees where
grass cannot be maintained, but should be kept from climbing
into trees. Deep roots help control soil erosion on banks.

canariensis p. 212
Algerian ivy. Leaves to 8 in. wide are larger, glossier than
English ivy, more widely spaced along stems, more shallowly
lobed. Needs more water than English ivy. Fast-growing. 'Variegata' has leaves edged with creamy white; cannot take desert
sun. Both are used as wall or ground covers. North Africa.
Zone 9.

helix p. 213 *Pictured above*
English ivy; evergreen ivy. Creeping or climbing to 50 ft. high,
often completely covering walls. Leaves dark green above,
yellowish green beneath, 2–5 in. long. Flowers green, incon-

spicuous. Black fruit is tiny, nearly round. Popular varieties include 'Baltica', hardy, with medium-size triangular leaves and prominent white veins; 'Buttercup', with brighter green leaves; 'Glacier' and 'Gold Heart', both variegated forms; the widely planted, vigorous 'Hibernica', with glossy leaves; 'Ivalace', a bushy spreader for small areas; and 'Thorndale', said to be hardy to −20 degrees. All zone 6.

Hemerocallis
Hem-er-o-kal′lis. Daylily
Liliaceae. Lily family

Description
Very popular perennial plants from central Europe to China and Japan. About 15 species and almost countless hybrids of all sizes and many flower colors. Narrow, sword-shaped leaves arise from tuberous roots. Numerous distinctive, lilylike flowers on often branched stems; each flower lasts only a day.

Excellent for many situations: in borders, along fences or driveways, under high-branching trees that give light, dappled shade. Miniature varieties are suited to rock gardens. Leaves provide handsome garden background before and after flowers.

How to Grow
Daylilies are tolerant of many conditions and soils. They grow best in sun, in moist but well-drained soil. Plant divisions in spring or fall; divide crowded clumps at same time.

Hybrids *p. 172   Pictured above*
Daylily. Attractive deciduous or evergreen leaves from less than 1 ft. to 2½–3½ ft. high. Flowers 2–6 in. across on stems to 6 ft. high, in every color except blue and true white. Cultivars available that flower in spring, summer, or fall; some are repeat bloomers. Zone 5.

Hesperaloe
Hes-per-a′lo
Agavaceae. Agave family

Description
Small genus of evergreen, perennial desert plants native from Texas to Mexico. Dense rosettes of narrow, 4-ft. leaves resemble delicate yucca or coarse grass. Long, airy clusters of flowers arise from clump.

How to Grow
Red yucca grows in any well-drained soil. It resists drought but tolerates summer water.

parviflora p. 173
Red yucca. Long, branched flower stalks arise from clump in spring and summer. Flowers tubular, deep pink to rose-red, 1 in. long, on stalks 3–4 ft. high. Good container plant. Texas. Zone 5.

Heteromeles
Het-er-om′e-leez
Rosaceae. Rose family

Description
Single species in genus. Evergreen, red-berried shrub or small tree native to California.

How to Grow
Plant from containers or grow from seed. Toyon tolerates much drought when established, also tolerates summer water. Watch for fire blight. Sun or part shade. Good for screens, banks, erosion control.

arbutifolia p. 135
Toyon; Christmas berry. Grows as dense shrub to 10 ft. or small tree to 25 ft., depending on climate, water supply, and pruning. Leathery, dark green, toothed leaves set off clusters of white flowers in late spring. Heavy crop of clustered red fruit in fall or winter. Attracts birds and bees. Zone 8.

Heuchera
Hew'ker-a. Alumroot. Coral bells
Saxifragaceae. Saxifrage family

Description
About 40 species of attractive North American perennial
herbs. Low clumps of roundish leaves; long stalks arise from
stout rootstock, crowned most of summer with narrow cluster
of small bell- or saucer-shaped flowers.

How to Grow
Coral bells are well suited to sunny or partly shaded border.
They require fertile, well-drained soil with lots of humus. In
winter, good drainage is very important; may need mulching.
In hot climates, grow best in filtered shade. Grow from divisions or seed in spring; divide every 3–4 years, discarding old,
woody rootstocks.

sanguinea p. 173 *Pictured above*
Coral bells. Best known and easiest to grow. Tidy rosettes of
small leaves, stems 1–2 ft. high. Small, bell-shaped red flowers.
Most coral bells are cultivars or hybrids of this species. There
are pink and white varieties, and a mixture may be grown
from seed. Native to the Southwest. Zone 4.

Hypericum
Hy-per'i-cum. St.-John's-wort
Hypericaceae. St.-John's-wort family

Description
About 300 species of perennials and shrubs, nearly all from
the north temperate zone. Pleasing foliage, handsome flowers.

How to Grow
These plants prefer well-drained, not too fertile soil in sun or partial shade. Will tolerate dry soil but grow best with adequate moisture. Propagate by seeds, cuttings, and, in low-growing kinds, by divisions and rooting stems.

calycinum p. 136
Aaron's-beard; rose-of-Sharon. Small, spreading evergreen shrub, to 12 in. high, grown as ground cover; good in sun or shade, sandy soil. Oblong leaves, 3–4 in. long, are pale beneath. Bright yellow flowers to 3 in. wide in summer. Southeastern Europe and Asia Minor. Zone 5.

Iberis
Eye-beer'is
Cruciferae. Mustard family

Description
About 30 species, mostly Mediterranean, of free-blooming annuals and perennials used as edgings, in rock gardens, as ground covers, and for cutting.

How to Grow
Perennial species are easily propagated by division or cuttings. They will stop flowering if too dry. In cold and windy climates, mulch perennials lightly to protect foliage from browning. Sow seed of annuals in fall (mild areas) or early spring.

sempervirens p. 174
Candytuft. Perennial. Narrow, shiny, dark green leaves are usually evergreen; grows to 12 in. high and wide. Flowers white, 1½ in. across, in long, finger-shaped spikes, early spring to June, or in November in mild areas. Prune stems after flowering to stimulate new growth and promote reblooming. Zone 4.

Ilex
Eye'lecks. Holly
Aquifoliaceae. Holly family

Description
Extremely valuable, mostly evergreen trees and shrubs. About 400 species, widely scattered in temperate and tropical regions,

grown for their attractive leaves, showy, berrylike fruits (on females only), and pleasing shapes.

How to Grow
Deciduous hollies are easy to grow in any good garden soil and present no difficulties in transplanting. Evergreen kinds are slower growing and more difficult to establish. Prefer good garden soil, slightly acidic, tolerate sun, need ample water and good drainage. Keep balled-and-burlapped or container-grown plants moist until planting; water freely the first year or so. Plant male and female plants together to ensure a crop of berries. Many are useful as hedges. Pruning young plants will force them to put out extra stems.

× *altaclarensis* 'Wilsonii' *p. 95*
Wilson holly. Evergreen tree to 30 ft.; usually kept to 10–15 ft. as a shrub. Leathery green leaves, 5 in. long and 3 in. wide. Very vigorous grower, lots of berries. Tolerates wind, sun, shade, most soils. Somewhat drought tolerant. Zone 8.

cornuta *p. 136   Pictured above*
Chinese holly. Dense-branched evergreen shrub, usually 8–15 ft. high. Lustrous, spiny leaves, large red berries produced without fertilization (no need for male trees). 'Burfordii', a female form, usually to 10 ft., has bright green, wedge-shaped leaves with only a few spines at the tip; also available in a compact form. 'Rotunda' is a dwarf male form to 18 in. Eastern China. Zone 7.

vomitoria *p. 137*
Yaupon. Evergreen shrub or small tree, to 15–25 ft. Narrow, oblong, dark green leaves. Tiny scarlet berries require no pollinator. Many cultivars. Tolerates salt spray and alkaline soils. Southeastern U.S. Zone 7.

Iris
Eye′ris
Iridaceae. Iris family

Description
Over 150 perennial species mostly from the north temperate zone, with thousands of horticultural varieties. Narrow sword-shaped or grasslike leaves rise from stout rhizomes or bulbous rootstocks. The showy flowers vary in color and form; most bloom in spring and early summer.

How to Grow
Care varies greatly from species to species. Most need sun, but some tolerate shade. Plant rhizome-producing irises with the rhizome showing or barely covered and the fan of leaves pointing in the direction you want the plant to grow. Irises rarely need mulching. Propagate species by seed and hybrids by division.

kaempferi p. 174   *Pictured above*
Japanese iris. (Also sold as *I. ensata*.) Handsome sword-shaped leaves with prominent midrib. Stems 2–3 ft. high bear very large flowers in white, blue, purple, or red-violet, often marked with a contrasting color. Water-loving: plant where they will be constantly moist. Will not tolerate hot, dry conditions or alkaline soils or water. Zone 5.

Louisiana Iris
Group of hybrids based on species native to Louisiana bayous. They resemble Japanese iris and need similar treatment, but have somewhat smaller flowers and a wide range of colors, from white and yellow through pink and purple to red and blue. Zone 5.

Pacific Coast Iris
Group of species and their hybrids native to the Pacific Coast and adapted to mild-winter, dry-summer climates. Plants grow to 2 ft. and come in blue, purple, yellow, and a wide range of mixtures. In warmer-summer areas they need light shade, infrequent summer water.

Bearded Iris
Complex group of hybrids divided into many height classes. Best known are tall-bearded, with branched clusters of flowers to 4 ft. tall, and flowers to 6 in. wide in all the colors of the rainbow and more (Iris was the Greek goddess of the rainbow). Varieties are too numerous to mention, and dozens of new ones appear each year. One of the cornerstones of the perennial border, excellent as cut flowers. Zone 4.

Jacaranda
Jack-a-ran'da
Bignoniaceae. Trumpet-creeper family

Description
More than 50 deciduous, tropical American shrubs and trees. The species below is one of the most widely planted of all tropical ornamental trees, highly valued for its beautiful clusters of wisteria-colored blooms.

How to Grow
Plant in frost-free areas, or after frost danger is past, in springtime. Stake and prune young trees to establish a main trunk. Jacarandas do best in sandy soil but tolerate other soils if not extreme. Water infrequently but deeply; too much water encourages lush, tender growth. In zone 9, often grows as a shrub, dying back after frost, then sprouting multiple stems.

mimosifolia p. 95
Jacaranda. Tree to 50 ft. high, wide-spreading, holding its leaves until early in spring. Hairy, fernlike leaves are delicately textured. Clusters nearly 8 in. long of tubular, 2-in.-long, striking bluish lavender flowers. Usually blooms in spring on bare trees, but may overlap with young foliage; sporadic bloom in fall. Rounded, flattened woody seed capsules in fall can be used in arrangements. Brazil. Zone 10; semihardy in 9.

Juniperus
Jew-nip'er-us. Juniper
Cupressaceae. Cypress family

Description
About 70 species of evergreen plants, ranging from low, prostrate shrubs to tall, slender trees — ideal for almost all landscape uses. Twigs clothed with needle-shaped or scalelike foliage, inconspicuous flowers, berrylike fruit. Throughout Northern Hemisphere, from the Arctic to the subtropics.

How to Grow
Junipers are tolerant of all southwestern soils but will suffer from root rot if kept constantly moist. Perform best in full sun, though in hot areas may benefit from some shade.

chinensis p. 196
Chinese juniper. Species varies from low, almost prostrate shrubs to trees 60 ft. high. *J. c. sargentii* (Sargent juniper) is a prostrate shrub to 18 in. high and 8–10 ft. wide, main branches prostrate, twigs ascending. Crushed foliage has odor of camphor. Fruit purplish brown. Zone 5. 'San Jose' is a deep green shrub 2 ft. tall, 6 ft. wide with heavy horizontal branches. Numerous ground cover and shrubby varieties exist.

chinensis 'Torulosa' p. 137
Hollywood juniper. Big shrub or small tree to 15 ft. with picturesquely twisted branches in flame effect.

conferta p. 197
Shore juniper. Handsome prostrate shrub to 18 in. high; good seashore plant. New growth is light green, later becoming blue-green. 'Blue Pacific' is more heat tolerant. Fruit black with powdery coating. Zone 6.

horizontalis p. 197   *Pictured above*
Creeping junipers. Prostrate shrubs with long, spreading branches. Blue fruit, sometimes with powdery bloom. Grow well in sandy, rocky soil. 'Bar Harbor' forms a dense mat to 12 in. high. Steel-blue foliage turns silvery purple in winter. 'Plumosa' has ascending branches to 18 in. high with feathery light green foliage, tinged purplish in winter. 'Wiltonii' has prostrate branches forming a silver-blue carpet 6 in. high; trails nicely over a wall or large rock. All zone 3.

Justicia
Jus-tiss'i-a
Acanthaceae. Acanthus family

Description
Subtr pical herbs or shrubs with showy flowers, a few native to the deserts of California and Arizona.

How to Grow
The species below likes full sun and is very drought tolerant. Regrows quickly after freezing to the ground.

californica p. 138   *Pictured above*
Chuparosa. Shrub to 5 ft. Arching branches with tiny leaves. Bright red tubular flowers in April and May. Zone 5.

Kniphofia
Nip-ho'fi-a
Liliaceae. Lily family

Description
About 65 species of African herbaceous perennials, called torch lily, flame flower, or poker-plant. Long, linear leaves

from the base. Flowers rise in long red or yellow clusters above leaves; bloom from early summer to frost.

How to Grow
Kniphofias are easy and persistent in most of the Southwest. Cut flower stalks after bloom, remove old leaves in fall. In winter, mulch heavily with hay or similar material to keep moisture out of crown and to prevent freezing. At highest elevations it is safest to overwinter plants in boxes of soil in a cold but frost-free cellar. Propagate by division, offsets, and seed.

uvaria p. 175
Red-hot poker; torch lily. 2–6 ft. high. Spikes of drooping, red and yellow flowers on erect stalks. Cultivars are yellow, orange, scarlet, or coral. South Africa. Zone 5.

Koelreuteria
Kel-roo-teer′i-a. Golden-rain tree
Sapindaceae. Soapberry family

Description
A small genus of deciduous Asiatic trees often planted for their yellow, summer-blooming flower clusters and lanternlike seed-pods in fall. Deep, noninvasive roots; annuals and perennials can be planted beneath them.

How to Grow
Golden-rain trees are better suited to open sun than shade. Young plants may be harmed by winter temperatures, but mature trees withstand drought and grow well in acid to slightly alkaline soils. Stake and prune young trees to promote high branching, and prune out weaker, crowded branches periodically.

paniculata p. 96
Tough, hardy tree to 30–35 ft. with equal spread. Compound leaves with featherlike arrangement of leaflets. Flower clusters in summer, tan to brown "lanterns" in fall. Zone 5. *K. bipinnata,* with twice-compound leaves, larger flower clusters, and flame-colored lanterns, is taller, less hardy. Zone 8.

Lampranthus
Lam-pran'thus
Aizoaceae. Carpetweed family

Description
About 160 species of South African subshrubs. The plants
below are perennial succulents known as ice plants, grown
mostly in California as bedding or bank covers. Upright or
trailing, woody at base, with fleshy leaves and flowers in late
winter or spring.

How to Grow
Ice plants prefer well-drained soil that is not too rich, in full
sun. Drought tolerant once established. Propagate by seeds or
cuttings. Cut back lightly to remove fruit after bloom.

spectabilis *p. 198   Pictured above*
Trailing ice plant. To 12 in. high, sprawls to 2 ft. Gray-green,
fleshy leaves. Many 2-in.-wide flowers, March–May, in bril-
liant yellow, orange, pink, or purple, or in combinations.
Other ice plants include *L. aurantiacus,* to 15 in. tall, flowers
February–May; *L. aureus,* to 2 ft.; *L. filicaulis,* fine foliage,
slow-spreading; *L. productus,* to 15 in., much bloom January–
April. South Africa. Zone 9.

Lantana
Lan-tan'a
Verbenaceae. Verbena family

Description
Very ornamental tropical or subtropical vining shrubs. Small
flowers in dense spikes or heads.

How to Grow
Softwood cuttings root easily. Lantanas tolerate most soils. Prefer warm weather; drought tolerant once established. When growing them as perennials, prune hard in spring to prevent woodiness and remove frost damage.

camara p. 138
To 4 ft., occasionally prickly. Rough, dark green leaves, 2–6 in. long. Small flowers in clusters 1–2 in. wide above leaves; yellow at first, then orange or red, sometimes all three colors in a single cluster. Blooms year-round. Foliage scent may seem unpleasant. Numerous named hybrids in pink, yellow, cream, red, and blends of these, some dwarf, some tall. Tropical America. Zone 9.

montevidensis p. 198 *Pictured above*
Weeping lantana. (Sometimes sold as *L. sellowiana*.) Vinelike shrub trailing to 3 ft. long and 18 in. high. Leaves dark green and purplish, 1 in. long. Flowers pink-lilac, in clusters 1 in. wide. Perennial grown as half-hardy annual in colder areas. Long flowering period in frost-free areas makes it valuable as a bank cover or for cascading over a wall. Good hanging basket plant. South America. Zone 9.

Larrea
Lar're-a
Zygophyllaceae. Caltrop family

Description
Five or six evergreen aromatic desert shrubs with tiny leaves and small yellow flowers. The species below is widespread in southwestern deserts.

How to Grow
Creosote bush is easiest to grow in desert, full sun. It survives without water but is more dense and attractive if irrigated.

tridentata p. 139
Creosote bush. Open, gaunt shrub with odor of creosote. Smallish leaves are leathery, dark green, gummy. Small yellow flowers much of the year. Under cultivation it becomes dense and leafy; can be used as a screen or clipped hedge. Native to the Southwest. Zone 7.

Laurus
Law'rus. Laurel
Lauraceae. Laurel family

Description
A small but important genus of Mediterranean evergreen trees. Two species; the one cultivated is probably the true laurel of history and poetry.

How to Grow
Laurel will stand considerable frost but is not reliably hardy north of zone 8. Plant in well-drained, ordinary soil. Water young trees in dry spells; they will endure quite a bit of drought once established. A site with afternoon shade is best in very hot climates.

nobilis p. 96
Laurel; bay; sweet bay. Tree to 40 ft. with broadly triangular profile. Leaves elliptical to lance-shaped, to 4 in. long, dark green, aromatic, used in cooking. Clusters of small, inconspicuous, yellowish green flowers. Fruit a small black or purple berry. Grows slowly, takes many years to produce a specimen tree. Can be sheared as a hedge or topiary and is a good indoor-outdoor container plant in cold regions. (Sweet bay is also a common name for *Magnolia virginiana*.) Zones 8–10.

Lavandula
La-van'dew-la. Lavender
Labiatae. Mint family

Description
Old World herbs or shrubs, evergreen. Narrow, gray-green, aromatic leaves. Lavender or dark purple flowers, crowded on spikes atop long stalks, are used for perfumes, sachets.

How to Grow
Plant in sunny areas with well-drained, sandy soil. Soil that is too fertile will reduce hardiness. Lavenders need little water or feeding. Mulch in winter. In spring, prune back old wood; prune after bloom to keep plants from sprawling.

angustifolia p. 139 *Pictured above*
English lavender. 1–3 ft. high. Lance-shaped leaves. Small lavender flowers on spikes 18–24 in. long in July and August. Good for hedges in mild climates. Dwarf varieties and varieties with deep purple flowers are available. *L. latifolia*, spike lavender, is similar but with coarser foliage and flower spikes frequently branched. Both zones 5–6.

dentata
French lavender. To 3 ft. tall, with gray, toothed foliage and spikes of purple flowers topped with a tuft of purple bracts. There is a green-leafed form. Blooms much of the year. Zone 9.

stoechas p. 140
Spanish lavender. Resembles French lavender, but leaves are not toothed. Deep purple flowers on short spikes crowned by large purple bracts, in early summer. Zone 9.

Leptospermum
Lep-to-sper′mum. Tea tree
Myrtaceae. Myrtle family

Description
More than 40 species of Australasian shrubs and trees. Several widely cultivated in mild climates for their spring display of long, graceful, drooping branches of numerous white, pink, or red flowers, shaped like tiny single roses. Branches crowded with small, rigid, often pricklelike leaves.

How to Grow
Easy to grow in full sun and well-drained, acid to neutral soil. Water generously when newly planted; fairly drought tolerant once established. Prune back to side branches in early spring to shape the plants.

laevigatum p. 140
Australian tea tree. Large shrub or, with training, a tree to 30 ft. Small, oval, gray-green leaves. If untrained, it will sprawl and twist in picturesque fashion, with contorted trunk and weeping branches. Staked, it becomes a single-trunk tree with a broad canopy. Can also be clipped as formal hedge. Zone 9.

scoparium
New Zealand tea tree. Shrub to 10 ft. Erect branches densely clad with narrow dark to reddish green leaves. Flowers white to deep red, single to double, very profuse. Many named varieties, including dwarf and sprawling, ground-cover kinds. Zone 9.

Leucophyllum
Loo-ko-fill′um
Scrophulariaceae. Snapdragon family

Description
A small genus of showy evergreen shrubs from Texas, New Mexico, and adjacent Mexico, used often for hedges.

How to Grow
Leucophyllum grows well in hot, dry, windy areas. Tolerates alkalinity if the soil is well drained. Needs heat to flower.

frutescens *p. 141*
Texas ranger; barometer bush. Compact shrub to 6–8 ft. Smallish, oblong, gray leaves with silvery white undersides. Small, bell-shaped, violet-purple flowers in summer. There are green- and gray-leafed forms and a compact form. Zone 9.

Liatris
Ly′a-tris
Compositae. Daisy family

Description
About 40 species of rather coarse, weedy North American herbs with very showy flower spikes.

How to Grow
Liatris is easy to grow in open sun and light soil. It tolerates heat, cold, poor soil. Divide tuberous rootstocks to propagate.

spicata *p. 175*
Gay-feather. Perennial. Narrow, very leafy stems, 4–6 ft. high. Small purple or white flowers in narrow, dense spikes 6–12 in. long. Fairly drought tolerant. 'Kobold' is 18–24 in. high, with dark purple flowers. Zone 4.

Lilium
Lil′ee-um
Liliaceae. Lily family

Description
Longtime favorite garden perennials. Erect stems grow from scaly bulbs, topped by one to many showy flowers in all colors but blue.

How to Grow

Culture varies somewhat with kind, but generally all lilies like well-drained soil, year-round moisture, mulch or shade over the roots, and sun on their heads. Plant bulbs in fall or spring, setting them roughly 3 times their diameter in depth. Propagate by division of bulbs or by seed (slow and difficult in some species). Protect against aphids, which spread a virus disease.

candidum *p. 176 Pictured above*
Madonna lily. The lily of Christian legend. Native to dry, hot regions of the Mediterranean. Unlike most lilies, it should be planted in late summer or early fall about 1 in. deep. Rosette of leaves stands over winter, then grows to 3–4 ft., producing as many as 20 pure white, fragrant flowers, 6 in. wide. Zone 5.

Hybrids

There are dozens of species of lilies, but the principal interest today is in hybrids, generally less fussy than the species. Most widely planted and earliest to bloom are the Asiatic Hybrids, with fine displays of upward- or outward-facing flowers in orange, red, yellow, white, or pink, often with contrasting spots or central blotches. Most grow 3–4 ft. Fiesta and Harlequin strains have nodding flowers and are slightly taller. Oriental Hybrids have very large flowers, bowl-shaped to flat or sharply recurved, in white, pink, or red, usually with conspicuous red dots and a delicious fragrance. They bloom in late summer. Zone 4.

Limonium
Ly-mo'ni-um. Sea lavender, sea pink
Plumbaginaceae. Plumbago family

Description

About 150 species of mainly annual or perennial herbs. Clouds of tiny flowers on many-branched stems above low clumps of often tufted foliage. Flowers, mostly lavender, rose-pink, or bluish, sometimes yellow or white, hold color for long periods and are often used in dried bouquets. All bloom in summer or early autumn.

How to Grow

Easy to grow, preferably in full sun in somewhat sandy, moist soil. Perennials are easily increased by division, moderately drought tolerant when established. Grow annuals from seed.

perezii *p. 176*
Sea lavender. (Often sold as *Statice perezii*.) A large perennial
with leathery leaves to 1 ft. long, and tall, open, airy clusters
of blue and white flowers. Likely to freeze out in heavy frosts
but can come back from the root. Grows quickly from seed,
can naturalize along coast. Canary Islands. Zones 9–10.

Linum
Ly'num. Flax
Linaceae. Flax family

Description
Nearly 200 species of rather slender annual or perennial herbs.
Common flax yields linseed oil and linen; other species are
grown only for ornament. Narrow leaves, erect, branching
stems bearing many 5-petaled flowers from late spring to summer or fall.

How to Grow
Flax is easy to grow in full sun and well-drained soil. Drought
resistant. Propagate by seed, division or cuttings.

perenne *p. 177*
Perennial blue flax. Vigorous plant, to 1–2 ft. Clear, sky-blue
flowers to 1 in. across. Europe. Zone 5. *L. lewisii,* native to
the American West, is now considered a somewhat more ro-
bust variety of common flax.

Liquidambar
Lik-wid-am'bar. Sweet gum
Hamamelidaceae. Witch-hazel family

Description
Few deciduous trees turn such a gorgeous fall color as the
native sweet gum, the only commonly cultivated species of
this small genus. It has maplelike leaves, male flowers in racemes or branching clusters, female in globose heads. Attractive, spiny, ball-shaped fruit.

How to Grow
Plant balled or container-grown plants in good, moist, acid
soil. Mulch and water deeply during drought; sweet gum is

more tolerant of poor drainage than of dryness. Choose sunny site away from walks and patios because the hard, round fruits may turn ankles.

styraciflua p. 97 *Pictured above*

Sweet gum. An extremely handsome tree, to 75 ft., taller than wide, its foliage brilliant yellow, scarlet, or purple in the fall. Twigs and young branches sometimes corky-winged. Clusters of small flowers are inconspicuous. Cultivars selected for fall color are 'Palo Alto', orange red to bright red; 'Burgundy', deep red leaves that hang on long into winter; and 'Festival', yellow, pink, red, orange, and green. North America. Zones 7–10.

Liriope
Li-ri'o-pe. Lily turf
Liliaceae. Lily family

Description
Asiatic herbs. Clumps of grasslike leaves often form thick mats. Spikes of white, blue, or violet flowers. Ornamental berrylike fruit. Good for ground cover, border, or rock garden.

How to Grow
Plant lily turf in fertile, moist soil amended with organic matter, in shade inland or full sun on coast. In cold-winter areas, foliage may become tattered or brown, but roots will probably survive. Mow foliage to ground to promote new growth. Increase by division.

muscari p. 199   *Pictured above*
Blue lily turf. To 18 in. high. Tiny flowers lilac-purple to white. Clumps of arching, straplike leaves. Good ground cover. Forms with white- or yellow-variegated leaves are available. Prey to slugs and snails. Cultivars include 'Majestic', 'Silvery Sunproof', 'Variegata'. Japan, China. Zone 6.

spicata p. 199
Creeping lily turf. Narrow grasslike leaves to 18 in. long, with minute teeth on margins. Tiny flowers, pale lilac to nearly white, in lax, open clusters. There is a striped-leaf form. China, Vietnam. Zone 5.

Lonicera
Lon-iss′er-ra. Honeysuckle
Caprifoliaceae. Honeysuckle family

Description
More than 150 species of shrubs and woody climbers found throughout the Northern Hemisphere. Tall forms are useful in shrub borders; some of the lower ones are grown in rock gardens. The often showy flowers are abundant and sometimes sweetly scented. The fruits, white, yellow, orange, red, blue, or black, are quite ornamental and a favorite food for birds.

How to Grow
Honeysuckles thrive in almost any location, do best in loamy, reasonably moist soil. Prune just after flowering. Propagate by seeds or cuttings.

× *heckrottii* p. 213
Goldflame honeysuckle. Attractive deciduous or semideciduous shrub to 12 ft. high, with spreading, sometimes twining branches. Leaves 1–2½ in. long, whitish beneath, blue-green above. Tubular flowers, 1½ in. long, in terminal clusters, coral-purple outside, yellow within. Long-blooming, late spring and summer. Zone 4.

japonica 'Halliana'

Hall's honeysuckle. Vigorous, evergreen (half-evergreen in coldest climates) climber, 20–30 ft. high, with slender, hairy branches. Leaves 1–3 in. long, usually downy on undersides. White, sweet-scented flowers fade to yellow, 1–1½ in. long, blooming in late spring. Fruit black. Can become a nuisance if neglected; prune hard if necessary. A useful bank or fence cover when controlled. Drought tolerant. East Asia. Zone 5.

Macfadyena
Mac-fad′ye-na
Bignoniaceae. Trumpet-creeper family

Description
Small genus of tropical American vines with clawlike tendrils and bright yellow, trumpet-shaped flowers.

How to Grow
These vines grow in ordinary soil; need little water once established. Cut back occasional out-of-bounds growth to encourage bushiness at the base.

unguis-cati p. 214
Cat's-claw. Quick-climbing vine to 30–40 ft. Bright green leaves, each consisting of 2 leaflets and a tendril with 3 claws. Clings to any surface, endures strong light and heat. Bright yellow early-spring flowers are 2 in. long. Useful as wall cover. Mexico. Zones 9–10.

Magnolia
Mag-no′li-a
Magnoliaceae. Magnolia family

Description
About 85 species of North American, West Indian, Mexican, and Asiatic evergreen or deciduous trees and shrubs. Several are among the most beautiful spring-flowering ornamental trees. Species and varieties can be chosen to produce flowers from early spring to midsummer and even into late summer. Fruit ripens late summer to early fall in the form of long, often colorful, conelike formations that split at maturity, exposing scarlet seeds.

How to Grow

Plant balled-and-burlapped or container-grown plants in spring in acid to nearly neutral soil, deep and moist. Cover root zone with mulch and avoid disturbing the fleshy roots even by planting bulbs. Avoid transplanting established plants. Irrigate during drought. Prune after flowering for form or maintenance only. Magnolias seldom have serious pests.

grandiflora p. 97   Pictured above

Southern magnolia; bull bay. A large evergreen tree of noble proportions, to 80 ft. Branchlets and buds are rusty-woolly when young. Large, leathery leaves are shiny above and rusty-woolly beneath. Large cup-shaped, creamy white, richly fragrant flowers emerge in spring from great silky-hairy buds. Fruit 4 in. long. Many cultivars, including the smaller 'San Marino' and 'St. Mary'. North Carolina to Florida and Texas. Zones 7–9; semihardy in 6.

Mahonia

Ma-ho′ni-a
Berberidaceae. Barberry family

Description

About 100 species of American and Asian evergreen, thornless shrubs. Their attractive foliage and form make them valuable as border and foundation plantings. Leaves often turn purplish in autumn. Long, dense clusters of yellow flowers. Dark blue or red berries, usually covered with a powdery bloom.

How to Grow

Easy to grow, mahonias are usually disease resistant, drought tolerant. Plant in sunny or shaded well-drained soil. Prune only to remove excess or out-of-scale stems.

aquifolium

Oregon grape. Shrub or erect growth to 6 ft., spreading slowly by underground stems. Shiny, leathery, dark green leaves have up to 9 spine-edged leaflets. Spikes of yellow flowers in spring give way to dark blue edible (sour) fruit. Leaves turn bronze or purple-red in cold winters. 'Compacta' grows 2 ft. tall. Zone 5. *M. pinnata* is similar, but with taller stems, spinier leaves, greater drought resistance. Zone 9.

nevinii p. 141   Pictured above

Nevin mahonia. Grows 3 to 10 ft. tall with many erect stems bearing gray leaves. Short clusters of yellow flowers followed by red fruits. Tolerates heat, sun, shade. Needs little water once established. Southern California. Zone 9.

repens p. 200

Creeping mahonia. Shrub with underground rooting stems, rarely more than 12 in. high. Leathery, spiny compound leaves, dull bluish green above, powdery white below. Yellow flowers in April and June. Black berries. Zone 5 (zone 6, with winter protection).

Maytenus
May-tee′nus
Celastraceae. Spindle-tree family

Description
Large genus of evergreen trees or shrubs; only the one below is of horticultural interest.

How to Grow
Mayten trees need average soil with good drainage. Avoid digging around the roots, which sucker if disturbed. Grow as

a multitrunk tree or remove side growth and stake into standard form. Moderately drought tolerant when established, but looks best when watered.

boaria p. 98
Mayten tree. Broad, spreading tree to 30 ft. or more. Pendulous branches clothed with narrow, deep green leaves. Effect is that of a delicate, evergreen weeping willow. Shape tends to vary in seed-grown plants. 'Green Showers', grown from cuttings, is a good form. Chile. Zones 9–10.

Melaleuca
Mel-a-lew'ka. Bottle-brush; tea tree
Myrtaceae. Myrtle family

Description
More than 100 species of Australian broadleaf evergreen trees and shrubs, closely related to the genus *Callistemon,* which is also called bottle-brush. The trees are grown for their striking flowers, foliage, and bark. Spikes or heads of pink, lavender, red, white, or yellow flowers. The protruding, prominent stamens resemble bottle brushes. Woody seed capsules are often rather decorative.

How to Grow
These trees will grow in almost any soil and will endure heat, wind, and drought. Young trunks are flexible; stake the first season. Prune at any time to keep vigorous branches in check.

linariifolia p. 98
Flaxleaf paperbark. An umbrella-shaped tree to 30 ft. White bark is soft and thick, shreds into paper-thin flakes. Stiff, needlelike leaves, 1¼ in. long, bright green. In late spring, white flowers in spikes 2 in. long give the appearance of fluffy snow on the branches. Tolerates drought. Suffers from ocean winds; does best inland. Australia. Zone 10; semihardy in 9.

quinquenervia
Cajeput tree. (Often sold as *M. leucadendron.*) Single or many-stemmed tree to 20–40 ft. Thick, spongy bark peels off in strips, tan to nearly white. Leaves 2–4 in. long. Flowers white, pink, or purplish, not so numerous as in *M. linariifolia.* Tender to hard frost, but tolerates sea winds. Excellent seashore tree. Australia. Zone 10.

Melampodium
Mel-am-po'di-um
Compositae. Daisy family

Description
Perennial herbs with daisylike flowers, native to the Southwest and tropical America.

How to Grow
These plants will tolerate much heat and drought but need sun and good drainage. Trim back straggly growth in fall.

leucanthum p. 177
Blackfoot daisy. Compact clumps of gray foliage to 1 ft. tall and wide are topped by a profusion of small, white, yellow-centered flowers for much of the year in warmest desert climates, spring and summer elsewhere. Native to the Southwest. Zones 6–10.

Miscanthus
Mis-kan'thus
Gramineae. Grass family

Description
About 20 species of tall, perennial, Old World grasses, mostly clump-forming, including some popular ornamental grasses cultivated in the U.S. Leaf blades have distinct white midrib and rough margins, feathery flowers.

How to Grow
Miscanthus grows best in full sun or light shade in well-cultivated, fertile garden soil that is kept moist but not soggy during growing season. Propagate in spring by dividing the woody roots, using a saw if clumps are sizable. Cut foliage down in late winter. Effective as specimens; taller species are useful for screening.

sinensis p. 178 *Pictured above*
Japanese silver grass. Arching leaves, 2–3 ft. long, 1 in. wide, usually in heavy clumps, 4–8 ft. high. Beautiful long feathery plumes of flowers in autumn. Species and its many varieties suitable for waterside plantings. Choose cultivars for leaf color, pattern, and flower color. 'Gracillimus' (maiden grass) to 5 ft., is fine-textured, with graceful, upright, arching habit; leaves buff-colored with curled tips in autumn. 'Silver Feather' is similar to the species but has showy silver plumes and blooms somewhat earlier. Excellent for backlighting effect. 'Variegatus' (variegated silver grass) is graceful, upright, and open, to 5 ft.; narrow leaves with creamy stripes, buff-colored in winter. Holds shape well through winter. 'Zebrinus' (zebra grass), to 7 ft., medium-textured, upright, narrow form; leaves have horizontal yellow bands, turn buff-colored with rust-orange tips in winter. East Asia. All zone 5.

Muhlenbergia
Mew-len-bear'gee-uh
Gramineae. Grass family

Description
About 125 species of grasses of low to medium height, some cultivated as ornamentals.

How to Grow
Plant in ordinary soil and full sun. Use mass plantings to control erosion on slopes. Drought tolerant and pest-free.

dumosa p. 178
Giant mullee. Clump-forming perennial grass with arching leaves 2–3 ft. long. Slender flower heads on upright stalks in summer and fall. Dried flowers and old leaves are attractive through the winter, well suited to informal desert gardens. Dwarf mullee, *M. rigens,* is similar but shorter; leaves form tufts to 18 in. tall. Both native to Mexico. Zone 7.

Myoporum
My-o-pore'um
Myoporaceae. Myoporum family

Description
About 30 species of shrubs and trees, principally from Aus-

tralia and the Pacific region. All have evergreen leaves, small white or pinkish flowers, and small, fleshy fruits.

How to Grow
Species vary widely in cultural needs. See below.

laetum
Small tree or large shrub, fast-growing to 30 ft., with dense, round head of dark green, glossy, rubbery leaves dotted with translucent glands. Flowers ½ in. wide, white, dotted with purple, followed by poisonous purple fruit. Tender to hard frost, but tolerates sea winds and is an excellent beach plant. Much used for dense screen along highways. Roots are aggressive. New Zealand. Zone 10.

'Pacificum'
Apparently a hybrid. Bright green leaves on a sprawling plant 2 ft. tall, several yards across. Drought resistant near ocean; needs irrigation inland. Zone 10.

parvifolium *p. 200*
Low shrub with trailing branches a few inches tall, several yards wide, with narrow, bright green leaves, white flowers, and inconspicuous purple fruits. Quick ground cover that can endure much drought but performs better with occasional water. 'Putah Creek' and 'Davis' are similar varieties selected for uniformity. Australia. Zone 10.

Myrtus
Mir'tus. Myrtle
Myrtaceae. Myrtle family

Description
About 16 species of tropical or subtropical shrubs or trees. One species is widely grown for its handsome evergreen foliage easily trained for hedges.

How to Grow
Myrtle grows well in sun or partial shade in well-drained soil. It tolerates heat and drought. Propagate by semihardwood cuttings under glass or by seeds.

communis *p. 142*
True myrtle. Aromatic evergreen shrub, 3–15 ft. high. Shiny green leaves 1–2 in. long. Small flowers, white or pinkish, in

summer. Small bluish black or white berries. 'Compacta'
grows slower to 2–3 ft.; useful for edgings. Mediterranean
and western Asia. Zone 9.

Nandina
Nan-dy′na
Berberidaceae. Barberry family

Description
A single species of evergreen shrub, native to China and Japan,
grown often in the Southwest for its columnar form, bright
red berries, and brilliant fall foliage.

How to Grow
Nandina grows well in any soil but prefers a reasonably moist
site; it will die if not watered regularly. Tolerates shade. North
of zone 7, plant in a protected place; if the top is winter-killed,
the roots may survive, especially if well mulched.

domestica p. 142
Heavenly bamboo; nandina. Attractive shrub, 6–8 ft. high.
Smallish, narrow leaflets. Handsome 1-ft.-long clusters of
white flowers in spring. Small red fruit is very handsome when
ripe. 'Nana' and 'Nana Purpurea' are 1-ft. dwarfs; can be lacy
or coarse. 'Compacta' is 4–5 ft. tall. 'Harbour Dwarf', 1½ ft.
tall, spreads fast by underground stems, is a choice ground
cover. Zone 7.

Nerium
Neer′i-um. Oleander
Apocynaceae. Dogbane family

Description
Widely cultivated evergreen shrubs or trees from the tropics,
especially useful in the Southwest because they tolerate heat,
drought, and salt. Narrow, thick, leathery leaves. Clusters of
showy flowers.

How to Grow
Plant oleander in any well-drained soil in a hot, sunny location.
Prune in early spring for best shape. All parts of the plant are

poisonous, so keep children and pets from eating them and do not burn clippings.

oleander *p. 143   Pictured above*
Common oleander; rose-bay. Shrub or small tree, 8–20 ft. high. Narrow leaves, 4–10 in. long, dark green above, paler and with a prominent midrib beneath. Flowers are yellowish, red, white or pink, 2 or more in. wide, 4–5 in a cluster; double in some cultivars, sometimes fragrant. Useful for borders, screens, along roads or walks. The Petite series grows 3–4 ft. tall and comes in white ('Casablanca'), dark red ('Algiers'), and pink ('Tangier'); all are somewhat less frost hardy than standard oleanders. Zones 8–10.

Oenothera
Ee-no-thee'ra; ee-noth'er-ra
Onagraceae. Evening primrose family

Description
Evening primroses and their day-blooming relatives, the sun-drops. Some 80 species of herbs, all American. Very showy

flowers, mostly yellow, but some species white or rose. All
bloom in summer.

How to Grow
Primroses are easy to grow in sunny sites in sandy or loamy
soil. Increase by division.

berlandieri p. 201 Pictured above
Showy primrose. Day-blooming perennial. Stems 6–18 in. tall,
erect or spreading. Flowers nearly 2 in. wide, white or pink.
Needs little care once established. Plant where spreading will
not be troublesome. Native to the Southwest. Zone 5.

missouriensis p. 179
Missouri primrose; Ozark sundrops. Perennial. Trailing
branches nearly 1 ft. long. Yellow flowers, 4–5 in. across, open
in the evening and remain open until the end of the next day.
Tolerates poor soil and sunny, dry sites; may rot in wet soil.
A garden favorite. Zone 5.

Olea
O'li-a. Olive
Oleaceae. Olive family

Description
Evergreen shrubs and trees of the Old World. One of the 20
species has been cultivated since antiquity for its fruit, the
olive. Soft-textured and picturesque in the landscape.

How to Grow
Plant in full sun in well-drained soil; there is little else to worry
about. Some authorities claim olive trees are more attractive
in outline if soil is dry and nutrient-poor. Trees may sucker
from the base. To obtain a tree form, select one trunk or
several, and diligently remove all sucker growth and lower
branches from the trunk. Pruning in early summer will reduce
resprouting. Problems are scale insects, easily controlled with
dormant oil spray, and olive gall; prune off galls or infected
branches and disinfect pruners after each cut.

europaea p. 99
Olive. Ruggedly picturesque tree to 30 ft., often long lived.
Thornless branches. Leaves 1–3 in. long, green above, silvery
and somewhat scurfy beneath, giving a pleasant willowlike
effect. Flowers are small, white, fragrant, in small clusters.

Fruit is the edible olive, 1½ in. long, green changing to purplish black. Fruit stains walks, driveways, patios. The fruitless cultivar 'Swan Hill' is best for landscape use. Native to hottest parts of Mediterranean region. Zone 9; semihardy in 8.

Olneya
Ol-nay'a
Leguminosae. Pea family

Description
Single species is the tree described below.

How to Grow
Needs only occasional water once established. Best in deep soil with some subsoil moisture.

tesota p. 99
Desert ironwood. Evergreen, gray-green leaves divided into 8–24 leaflets, each leaf with a pair of thorns at the base. Little lavender flowers appear in summer, followed by seedpods. Thrives in desert heat. Loses leaves in hard frost. Native to the Southwest. Zone 9.

Ophiopogon
O-fi-o-po'gon. Lily-turf, Mondo grass
Liliaceae. Lily family

Description
The few species are all natives of East Asia. Thick, grasslike foliage with clusters of small flowers. Used as ground cover. Similar to *Liriope,* but has blue instead of black fruit.

How to Grow
Mondo grass grows well in ordinary garden soil in sun or shade. Propagate by division. If foliage becomes shabby in winter, cut back hard in early spring. Best used under trees or as border edging. Slugs can be a problem.

japonicus p. 201 *Pictured above*
Mondo grass. Good sod-forming ground cover, to 12 in. high. Leaves dark green, 8–16 in. long. Tiny, light lilac flowers, pea-size blue fruit. 'Nana', sometimes called 'Kyoto Dwarf', is about half the size. Zone 7.

Opuntia
O-pun'ti-a; o-pun'shi-a. Prickly pear
Cactaceae. Cactus family

Description
About 300 species of cacti, from New England to Tierra del Fuego. Two general types are cultivated: those with flat or broad joints (some known as tuna) and those with cylindrical or round joints (some known as cholla). Some are prostrate or clambering without a trunk; others, mostly tropical, are treelike. The small leaves are usually deciduous. Flowers generally large, showy. Berries are edible in many species.

How to Grow
Full sun and well-drained, sandy soil are ideal. Moist soil may cause root rot. Very drought tolerant. Small red-brown hairs on the surface of the joints lodge easily under the skin; handle with care.

ficus-indica p. 179
Prickly pear, tuna. Treelike stem to 15 ft. bears broad, thick, gray-green pads 1½ ft. long with few spines but abundant short, irritating, clustered hairs. Yellow flowers, 4 in. wide,

followed by red or yellow edible, seedy fruits with a somewhat melonlike flavor. Beware irritating hair when handling fruit. Zones 9–10.

microdasys *p. 180   Pictured above*
Bunny ears. To 2 ft. tall, 4–5 ft. wide. Thin, roundish pads; 2 often grow from another, like rabbit ears. Many bunched, golden-yellow hairs dot surface of pads. Yellow flowers followed by red fruit. Texas, New Mexico. Zones 9–10.

violacea '**Santa-Rita**' *p. 180*
Dollar cactus. Nearly round, 8-inch pads with few or no spines, yellow flowers, brownish to pink fruit. Texas, New Mexico, Arizona. Zones 9–10.

Osmanthus
Oz-man'thus
Oleaceae. Olive family

Description
Some 30 or 40 species of evergreen shrubs or small trees, primarily from Asia and Polynesia. Attractive, leathery foliage. Flowers often very fragrant but not showy.

How to Grow
Easy to grow in acid or neutral soil in partial shade or full sun. Use for hedges or espaliers or grow in containers. Propagate by late-summer cuttings of semihardwood, rooted under glass.

fragrans *p. 143   Pictured above*
Fragrant tea olive. Shrub or small tree, to 25 ft. Oval leaves, 2–4 in. long. Small white flowers are very fragrant; heavy bloom in spring and summer, intermittent throughout rest of year in mild-winter areas. 'Aurantiacus' has pale orange flow-

ers of even stronger fragrance, concentrated in autumn. South-east Asia. Zone 8.

heterophyllus 'Ilicifolius'

Shrub to 20 ft. with strongly toothed leaves like those of holly. Creamy, fragrant flowers. 'Variegatus' grows slowly to 5 ft., has white leaf margins. Japan. Zones 6–10.

Osteospermum
Os-ti-o-sper'mum
Compositae. Daisy family

Description
About 70 species of annual or perennial herbs or shrubs, mostly native to South Africa. Daisylike flowers in a variety of colors on long stems; open only in sunlight.

How to Grow
Plant these daisies in spring or fall in sun in any good garden soil except heavy clay. Pinch tips of young plants for bushy form. Cut back old sprawling branches to encourage flowering and keep plants tidy. They perform best with moderate water but will tolerate drought. Increase by seeds, cuttings, or, in some types, by layering. Use in borders or on slopes.

fruticosum   *p. 202*   *Pictured above*

Trailing African daisy; freeway daisy. Trailing plant to 12 in. high and 3 ft. wide. Stems root as they spread. Leaves variable, usually oval with a few teeth. Flowers 2 in. wide, lilac fading to white, are profuse in late winter and early spring, sporadic throughout the year. Several forms have purple, pink, or white flowers. Zone 9.

Parkinsonia
Par-kin-so'ni-a
Leguminosae. Pea family

Description
Desert shrubs or small trees with green branches, yellow flowers.

How to Grow
Trees need little or no supplementary water once established. They tolerate a wide variety of soils. Require staking and shaping when young.

aculeata p. 100
Jerusalem thorn; Mexican palo verde. Picturesque deciduous tree to 20–30 ft., with green bark, spiny twigs. Open growth habit gives sparse, filtered shade. Leaves, to 9 in. long, have many minute leaflets that soon fall. Long clusters of yellow flowers in spring and intermittently through the year. Zones 8–10.

Parthenocissus
Par-then-o-sis'sus
Vitaceae. Grape family

Description
Deciduous woody climbers from East Asia and North America, grown chiefly for their foliage, some brilliantly colored in autumn.

How to Grow
Boston ivy is not particular about soil but grows more vigorously in fairly moist loam in sun or light shade. Clinging tendrils can be a nuisance to remove from wood siding.

tricuspidata p. 214
Boston ivy; Japanese ivy. Climbs to 60 ft. high and clings firmly. Large, shiny leaves either 3-lobed or divided into 3 leaflets. Semi-evergreen in mild-winter areas. Insignificant flowers in summer, then blue-black fruit. Foliage brilliant scarlet in autumn. An outstanding wall cover, with leaves overlapping like shingles. (Formerly known as *Ampelopsis tricuspidata*.) 'Veitchii' has smaller leaves that are purple when young. China, Japan. Zone 5.

Passiflora
Pass-i-flo'ra. Passion-flower
Passifloraceae. Passion-flower family

Description
Tendril-climbing vines; most of the 400 species are native to the New World. Many species and hybrids, with strikingly handsome flowers ranging from white and lavender to pink, red, and purple. Some have edible fruit.

How to Grow
Best in light, evenly moist soil and full sun. Increase by cuttings of ripe wood. May die to the ground in winter; mulching aids survival and resprouting. The vine is vigorous; prune it to prevent a tangle. Useful for a fence or trellis or rambling over shrubs. Also suited to greenhouse culture.

× *alatocaerulea* p. 215
(Also known as *P. pfordtii*.) Rapid growth to 20 ft. or more. Leaves 3-lobed, dark green. Flowers to 4 in. wide, white blended pink and lavender, with white-and-blue-banded corona. No fruit. Zones 8–10.

Pelargonium
Pel-ar-go'ni-um. Garden geranium; stork's-bill geranium
Geraniaceae. Geranium family

Description
A large genus of mostly South African evergreen perennials of diverse habit. Stems can be trailing, herbaceous, or woody. Clusters of showy flowers, from pure white to pink, crimson, and bright scarlet, grow on leafless stalks.

How to Grow

All garden geraniums do well in pots. Outdoors, plant in good, fast-draining soil, in full sun near coast, light shade where summers are hot. Geraniums need regular watering and little feeding. Deadhead for increased bloom. Pinch growing tips for bushy growth. Increase by tip cuttings.

× *hortorum* p. 181   *Pictured above*

Zonal geranium. Grows 1–3 ft. high, often much taller in mildest climates and with some support. Flowers 2–2½ in. wide in flat-topped or rounded clusters, red, salmon-pink, white, coral, peach, or bicolored, some with double blossoms. Zones 9–10.

peltatum

Ivy geranium. Smaller leaves than above, bright green and smooth, trailing stems to 3 ft. long. Single or double flowers are white, pink, lavender, or red; some have strong white markings. Excellent hanging basket plant or, in mildest climates, a brilliant ground cover.

Pennisetum

Pen-i-see′tum
Gramineae. Grass family

Description

About 80 species of chiefly tropical annual or perennial grasses, a handful grown for ornament. Flat, narrow leaf blades are sometimes colored. Flowers in spikes, sometimes plumed.

How to Grow

These grasses grow best in fertile soil in full sun. Hardy perennial types can be increased by spring division. Annuals and perennials may be started from seeds.

setaceum p. 181

Fountain grass. Perennial grown as an annual. Graceful clump of arching, narrow leaves 15–20 in. long, green, bronze, or reddish purple. Feathery flower spikes rise to 3 ft. The species is a freely seeding weed. Grow the nonseeding cultivars 'Cupreum' and 'Atropurpurea'. Africa. Zone 8.

Penstemon
Pen-stee'mon. Beardtongue
Scrophulariaceae. Snapdragon family

Description
250 species of perennial herbs (rarely shrubs), chiefly from the western U.S. Showy, tubular flowers bloom in summer.

How to Grow
The many species come from different habitats and require different conditions; one constant is good drainage. Propagate from seed or cuttings. Few are long-lived.

barbatus p. 182   *Pictured above*
Beardlip penstemon. Grows 2–3 ft. high. Red flowers with bearded lower lip are 1 in. long, in spikes. Selections include 'Rose Elf', rose colored, and 'Prairie Fire', scarlet. Mountains of Colorado, Utah, and Mexico. Zone 4.

eatonii p. 182
Similar to *P. barbatus* in color. Native to desert regions and quite heat and drought tolerant. Zone 7.

heterophyllus purdyi 'Blue Bedder' p. 183
Sprawling plant to 2 ft. tall and wide. Pure blue flowers open from pinkish blue buds; April–July. California. Zones 9–10.

Perovskia
Per-ov'ski-a. Russian sage
Labiatae. Mint family

Description
A small Central Asian genus of salvialike herbs or subshrubs;
one is grown for ornament.

How to Grow
Russian sage is easy to grow in full sun and well-drained soil.
Plants in shade will sprawl. Propagate by summer cuttings.
Cut it to the ground each spring to promote strength and good
flowers.

atriplicifolia *p. 144*
Azure sage. Shrubby perennial, 3–5 ft. high. Bruised foliage
smells like sage. Lance-shaped leaves covered with gray-white
hairs. Spikes of tiny tubular blue flowers in September. (This
plant is now considered a hybrid, not the species.) Western
Asia. Zones 5–6.

Philodendron
Fill-o-den'dron
Araceae. Arum family

Description
Tropical herbs, sometimes gigantic, climbing or shrubby in
habit, with large, glossy evergreen leaves in a variety of shapes,
and callalike flowers.

How to Grow
Most philodendrons are house plants, but the following species
is hardy where frosts are not severe. It needs rich soil, ample
water, and some shade in hottest regions.

selloum p. 144   *Pictured above*
Split-leaf philodendron. Giant shrubby plant with deeply cut leaves to 3 ft. long. Good for jungle effects. When formed, flowers are pale green. Brazil. Zones 9–10.

Phlomis
Flo'mis. Jerusalem sage
Labiatae. Mint family

Description
About 100 species of strong-growing perennial herbs or subshrubs of the Mediterranean region east to China. Grown for their flowers.

How to Grow
Jerusalem sage is easily propagated by seeds, cuttings, or division of tubers. Grow in full sun in well-drained sandy loam with low fertility. Cut back after bloom to prevent ranginess.

fruticosa p. 183
Jerusalem sage. Stout, sparsely branching to 4 ft., with 6-in. gray-green fuzzy leaves and whorls of small yellow flowers at intervals along the upper third of the stems. Can bloom several times if watered in summer. Mediterranean. Zone 5.

Phoenix
Fee'nix
Palmae. Palm family

Description
An important genus of feather palms, including the date palm and several others widely grown ornamentally. There are 20 known African and Asiatic species, and 5 are horticulturally important. Trunks are often spineless, except for the spinelike lower segments on leaves of some species. Leaflets or segments long and narrow. The date palm has male and female flowers on different plants.

How to Grow
Plant from a container in any season, preferably summer, when new roots are formed, in sun and in rich, well-drained soil.

Irrigate regularly during dry weather, but do not overwater. Hose down leaves occasionally to discourage aphids. Old leaves dry and hang for a considerable time; remove them to improve appearance.

canariensis p. 100
Canary Islands date palm. Handsome plant, 50–60 ft. high at maturity. Impressive arching leaves, 15–20 ft. long, with numerous narrow leaflets or segments, the lower ones spiny, standing at different angles from the main leaf stalk. Flowers are insignificant. Clusters, 6–8 ft. long, often drooping, of small, yellowish red, egg-shaped fruit in fall to winter. A deservedly popular palm, hardier than many others, much used for avenue planting in California and Canary Islands. Zones 9–10.

dactylifera
Date palm. Widely grown for fruit in the hottest deserts. Sometimes used in landscaping, especially for parks and golf courses. Grows to 80 ft. and makes offsets at the base. Asia, Africa. Zones 9–10.

Phormium
For'mi-um. New Zealand flax
Agavaceae. Agave family

Description
Two species of large herbs grown for ornament in California; one grown for fiber in its native New Zealand. Flowering stalks rise above big clumps of very tough, long, sword-shaped leaves. Clusters of modest tubular flowers are striking in silhouette.

How to Grow
These plants are easy to grow in sun or partial shade. They are not fussy about water — will tolerate a lot or a little. Increase by dividing roots. Grow as specimens in garden or container. Give plants plenty of space in borders. Remove withered leaves, spent flower stalks.

tenax p. 145
New Zealand flax; flax lily. 8–15 ft. high. Striking leaves up to 9 ft. long, 5 in. wide, leathery, usually red-margined, and shreddy at tip. Flowers dull red, 2 in. long, in a cluster well above foliage. 'Variegatum' has yellow and green leaves;

'Bronze', brownish red. A host of new selections from New Zealand are smaller (3–5 ft. tall), and leaves are variously marked with yellow, pink, red, or bronze. Look for 'Maori Sunrise', 'Apricot Queen', and others. Zone 9.

Photinia
Fo-tin′i-a
Rosaceae. Rose family

Description
40 species of deciduous or evergreen shrubs or trees from northern Asia with attractive foliage, white flowers, and red fruit. The leaves of deciduous species turn red and scarlet in the fall; evergreens have handsome, shiny foliage that is red at first.

How to Grow
Photinias like a sunny location and well-drained loamy soil. Water them often.

× *fraseri* p. 145 *Pictured above*
Fraser photinia. Evergreen shrub, to 15 ft., sometimes trained as tree. Leaves elliptical, 3–5 in. long. New growth is red. Flowers in 3–5 in. clusters. Useful as a hedge or screen. Mildew resistant. Zone 8.

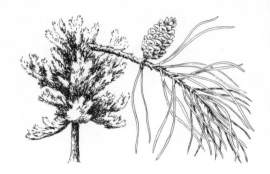

Pinus
Py′nus. Pine
Pinaceae. Pine family

Description
Magnificent evergreen trees of outstanding value for ornamental use and timber. Almost all of the approximately 90 species are from the north temperate zone. In nearly all pines, the trunk, barring injury or special pruning, is continuous and has whorls or tiers of branches bearing clusters of needlelike leaves. The pines listed below are readily available, easy to grow, and make handsome screen or ornamental plantings.

How to Grow
Most pines will grow quite well in rather light soil. Drainage is important; few succeed in wet soil. Drying summer winds and warm winter sun are more damaging than dry soil. The roots cannot stand long exposure to air, so transplant trees with a ball of earth. Prune by removing leading branches back to side branches or to main trunks. Expanding buds form long candles in spring; snapping off part of a candle will reduce the length of the ensuing branch by the same ratio. Improve the shape of young pines by this method.

edulis p. 101
Piñon; nut pine. Picturesque small, round or flat, horizontal branching tree with short, dark green needles in bundles of 2. (Other species have 1, 3, or 4 needles to a bundle.) Seeds are edible. Native to the Southwest. Zones 4–10.

eldarica p. 101
Afghanistan pine. Resembles *P. halepensis,* below, but darker green, more symmetrical, better adapted to desert heat and wind. Zones 7–10.

halepensis p. 102 *Pictured above*
Aleppo pine. Upright open tree, to 60 ft. Light green needles, 3–4 in. long, in bundles of 2, rarely 3. Cones 3 in. long. Tolerant of drought, heat, wind, and salt. (More attractive pines are available for good growing conditions.) Mediterranean region. Zones 8–10.

pinea p. 102
Italian stone pine. Young trees bushy, mature trees flat-topped, to 80 ft. — too large for most gardens. Dark green to gray-green needles, 5–8 in. long, in bundles of 2. Cones 4–6 in. long. Mediterranean region. Zone 9.

thunbergiana p. 103
Japanese black pine. Irregularly picturesque in outline, to 90 ft., usually much shorter. Dark green needles 3–5 in. long or more, in bundles of 2. Cones 2–3 in. long. One of the most satisfactory of cultivated pines, especially in exposed, windswept places along the seacoast. Excellent for training into sculptured forms. Japan. Zones 5–9.

Pistacia
Pis-tash'i-a. Pistachio
Anacardiaceae. Sumac family

Description
Aromatic shrubs or trees, deciduous and evergreen; most of the 10 species are Eurasian. (*P. vera* is the source of pistachio nuts.)

How to Grow
Plant balled or container-grown trees in full sun. Pistachios grow best in good, well-drained soil but will do quite well in poor; dry soil. Withstand wind and drought and have no serious pests. May need early pruning to develop a symmetrical, rounded shape.

chinensis p. 103
Chinese pistache. Rounded shade tree to 60 ft. Handsome lance-shaped, deciduous leaflets, red (sometimes yellow) in the fall, even in semidesert conditions. In fall, small, flattened fruit on female trees is scarlet at first, ultimately purplish. Excellent for lawn or street planting. China. Zones 7–9.

Pittosporum
Pit-toss'por-um
Pittosporaceae. Pittosporum family

Description
More than 100 species of chiefly Australasian evergreen shrubs and trees. Handsome foliage and form; some have attractive flowers and fruit.

How to Grow
Easy to grow in a variety of soils. Pittosporums adapt especially well to sandy soils and hot, dry locations but can also stand shade. Watch for aphids and scale insects.

crassifolium p. 146
To 25 ft., but easily kept to 5 ft. with pruning. Rather small, nearly round, gray-green leaves. Tiny, dark red flowers. Withstands sea winds. Excellent screen or hedge. New Zealand. Zones 9–10.

eugenioides p. 104
To 40 ft. as tree, but usually clipped into a hedge 4–10 ft. tall. Leaves yellowish to bright green, shiny, with wavy edges. Fragrant yellow flowers appear if plants are not closely sheared. New Zealand. Zones 9–10.

tobira p. 146 *Pictured above*
Japanese pittosporum. Shrub to 15 ft., lower with pruning. Useful for informal hedges. Thick, leathery leaves, 3–4 in. long, on brittle twigs. Clusters, 2–3 in. wide, of small, fragrant, greenish white to lemon-yellow flowers in early spring. Small, densely hairy fruit. 'Wheeler's Dwarf' makes a cushion 1 to 2 ft. tall and wide. 'Variegata', to 6 ft., has gray-green leaves with creamy edges. China and Japan. Zone 9.

undulatum p. 104

Victorian box. Broadleaf evergreen tree, 30–40 ft. high. Narrow, shiny green leaves, 4–6 in. long, with wavy margins. Clusters of small, fragrant, white flowers in spring. Small, orange fruit is messy on walks. An attractive tree for lawn and street planting or may be sheared regularly as a screen. Australia. Zones 9–10.

Platanus
Pla'ta-nus. Plane tree
Platanaceae. Sycamore family

Description
Large deciduous trees with lobed leaves and inconspicuous flowers followed by ball-shaped seed clusters. Older, dark bark flakes off to reveal pale, smooth inner bark. Branches of mature trees make striking silhouettes.

How to Grow
All species grow easily in ordinary, well-drained soil. Moderately drought tolerant, but do best with deep watering in summer. Withstand city air pollution and hard pruning but are subject to anthracnose blight in wet springs.

× *acerifolia*
London plane. Excellent street tree to 40 ft. high and wide, often pruned hard to stubby branches (pollarded) to restrict size and control form. Seed balls hang singly. Zone 5.

racemosa p. 105 *Pictured above*
California sycamore. Fast-growing tree to 100 ft. Deeply lobed maplelike leaves, nearly white bark, seed balls strung in clusters. Grows near watercourses in much of California. Zone 6. *P. wrightii* is a somewhat smaller species from Arizona canyons. Zone 7.

Podocarpus
Po-do-kar′pus
Podocarpaceae. Podocarpus family

Description
Some 75 species of handsome evergreen trees or shrubs, mostly from the mountain areas of the Southern Hemisphere northward to the West Indies and Japan. A few are grown in California for their handsome foliage and form.

How to Grow
Easy to grow in reasonably good, well-drained soil. Will thrive in full sun, but prefer light shade in hottest regions. Best with regular watering. Few pests. Prune to shape or control size.

gracilior p. 105
Fern pine. If grown from seed, young plants are upright with bright green needles; become broad-branched with short, gray-green needles in maturity. If grown from cuttings (sometimes sold as *P. elongatus*), plants have short needles and tend to be vinelike. Stake to grow as a tree, or grow as espalier or vine. Africa. Zones 9–10.

macrophyllus
Yew pine. Slow-growing shrub or tree to 50 ft. Narrow, dark green leaves to 4 in. long. Resembles yew. *P. m. maki* is shrubbier, with dense, erect growth. Fine container plant. China. Zone 7.

Populus
Pop′you-lus. Poplar; aspen; cottonwood
Salicaceae. Willow family

Description
About 30 to 40 species of deciduous trees widely distributed across the Northern Hemisphere. Flowers appear in catkins before the broad leaves open.

How to Grow
Fast-growing trees of easiest culture, withstanding heat, wind, and cold. Need some water, but often are all too efficient at finding it; deep roots can invade septic tanks, drain fields, or sewer lines.

alba p. 106
White poplar. To 50 ft. Leaves bright green above, nearly white underneath; shimmer in the slightest breeze. Dense growth makes it a good screen or windbreak. 'Pyramidalis' (usually called *P. bolleana*) is narrow and erect. Both sucker freely from the roots. Eurasia. Zone 5.

fremontii p. 106
Western cottonwood. Familiar on desert watercourses. To 60 ft. or more, with broad, irregular head. Bright yellowish green leaves turn gold in fall. Female trees generate masses of cottony seeds — a nuisance. Plant male trees grown from cuttings. May need regular watering in desert areas. Native to the Southwest. Zone 8.

Prosopis
Pro-soap'is. Mesquite
Leguminosae. Pea family

Description
About 25 species of tropical or subtropical thorny trees or shrubs. With proper care, they can be effective as a screen or windbreak or as shade trees for arid areas.

How to Grow
Shrubs are drought tolerant when young. They need deep soil and regular watering to take tree form but tolerate drought thereafter. Remove lower branches for headroom as trees develop.

glandulosa p. 107
Mesquite; honey mesquite; western honey mesquite. Deciduous shrub or small tree, to 30 ft. high, the crown spreading an equal distance or more. Twigs with sharp thorns 1–2 in. long, especially on young plants. Bright green feathery leaflets. Tiny, yellowish green flowers in short, dense spikes; attractive to bees. Blooms spring to summer. Flat seedpods 2–6 in. long in winter. Plants offered as Chilean mesquite are fast-growing and may be deciduous or evergreen. Native to the Southwest. Zones 7–9.

Prunus
Proo′nus
Rosaceae. Rose family

Description
More than 400 species of deciduous and broadleaf evergreen shrubs and trees, nearly all from the north temperate zone, a few south to the Andes. Includes plums, cherries, apricots, peaches, and almonds as well as Japanese flowering cherries and many other superb flowering shrubs and trees with generally inedible fruit.

How to Grow
Trees in this genus need full sun and reasonably moist, well-drained soil. Stress of any sort increases susceptibility to various insects and diseases; plants are short-lived (about 30 years) unless coddled. Spread organic mulch to the drip line and water deeply and regularly during drought. Prune weak or crossing branches in early spring. Watch for insect and disease problems and treat them promptly.

× *blireiana*
Blireiana plum. Deciduous tree to 20–25 ft. with very early, double, pink flowers and purple leaves that turn bronzy green in summer. No fruit. Zone 4.

campanulata
Taiwan cherry. Ornamental. Especially adapted to southern California conditions. Early-blooming flowers are deep purple-pink. Taiwan, southern Japan. Zone 7.

caroliniana *p. 147   Pictured above*
Carolina laurel cherry. Ornamental evergreen shrub or tree to 30 ft. or more, easily maintained at 10–20 ft. Dense, shiny

green foliage sets off small spikes of tiny white flowers. Small black fruits follow. Clip as a hedge or screen, or shape into a small to medium shade tree. Zone 7.

cerasifera p. 107

Cherry plum, flowering plum. Deciduous tree to 30 ft. Species has white flowers; red or yellow 1-in. fruit is bland and sweet. Many varieties are grown for ornament. Purple-leafed forms include 'Atropurpurea' ('Pissardii'), 'Hollywood', 'Newport', and 'Thundercloud'. Zone 5.

lyonii p. 108

Catalina cherry. Evergreen shrub or tree to 45 ft., easily pruned to a 10–20 ft. hedge or screen. Glossy, smooth-edged, dark green leaves set off 6-in. spikes of small white flowers. Edible, thin-fleshed, 1-in. black cherries follow. *P. ilicifolia*, hollyleaf cherry, is similar but has spine-edged leaves. Hybrids of the two with intermediate characteristics are common. Entirely drought resistant once established. Needs good drainage. California. Zone 7.

mume p. 108

Flowering apricot. Deciduous tree of slow, picturesque growth to 20 ft. Very early flowers with spicy scent, in white ('Rosemary Clarke'), pink ('Dawn', 'Peggy Clarke', 'W. B. Clarke'), or red ('Bonita'). China, Japan. Zone 5.

persica

Flowering peach. Small deciduous tree resembling common peach in every detail except for fruit production and quality. Requires heavy annual pruning and spraying for fungus-caused peach leaf curl. Flowers may be single or double, white, pink, red, or particolored. Prune while trees are in full bloom and use cut branches for arrangements. Leave 6-in. stubs to produce next year's flowering wood. Zone 4.

Punica
Pew'ni-ka. Pomegranate
Punicaceae. Pomegranate family

Description

Two species of deciduous shrubs or trees. The one below is widely grown for its bright orange flowers, vivid fall color, and edible fruit.

How to Grow

Plant pomegranates in deep, fertile loam soil in full sun for the most flowers and fruit. Prune, if necessary, during the winter since blossoms form on new growth. Can withstand much heat, drought when established. Propagate by cuttings or seeds.

granatum p. 147

Pomegranate. Asiatic shrub or small tree, to 10–20 ft. Narrow, shiny green leaves turn bright yellow in fall. Branches are often spine-tipped. Orange-red flowers in midspring. Fruit 2–5 in. in diameter with crimson, slightly acid flesh. Useful for hedges. Zone 8. Fruiting varieties are 'Wonderful' (most common) and 'Sweet' (yellow-skinned, pink-fleshed). 'Nana' (to 3 ft.) and 'Chico' (1½ ft.) are grown for flowers or as edgings. Zone 7.

Pyracantha

Py-ra-kan′tha. Firethorn
Rosaceae. Rose family

Description

A small genus of Asiatic evergreen, thorny shrubs closely related to cotoneaster. Most are grown for their fine foliage and bright red or orange fruits that persist in winter. Small white flowers bloom in spring.

How to Grow

Plant in full sun in well-drained soil for best fruiting. Long thorns make pyracanthas useful as hedges but painful to prune, so place them where they will have room to spread. If pruning is necessary, remember that flowers and fruit form on the previous summer's wood. Fire blight can be troublesome. Pyracantha nomenclature is confusing — many named "varieties" have no botanical standing — so we have grouped them by height and given names that you are likely to find at a nursery.

Tall Varieties *p. 148*
Useful as a screen, impenetrable hedge, or espalier against wall
or fence. Hardiest tall kinds are 'Mohave' (orange-red berries,
12–15 ft.) and *P. coccinea* 'Lalandei' (orange berries, rounded
form, 8–10 ft.). Zone 6. 'Cherri Berri', 'Graberi', and 'Victory'
have deep red fruit. Zone 7.

Low Varieties
'Santa Cruz' and 'Walderi' are widely used as ground covers.
Low-growing and spreading, they can be kept at 2–3 ft. by
cutting out the occasional upright branch. Zone 7.

Pyrus
Py'rus. Pear
Rosaceae. Rose family

Description
About 20 species of mostly deciduous trees and shrubs native
to Eurasia and Africa. A few species are among the most
beautiful spring-flowering deciduous trees.

How to Grow
Pear trees are easily transplanted in spring if bare-rooted or
balled; container-grown plants can be set out any time. Most
soils are adequate except wet, very dry, and highly alkaline
ones. Pears can tolerate heavier soils than most fruit trees. Full
sun is paramount. Irrigate young plants in dry spells. Established trees will tolerate moderate drought. Prune in late winter
or early spring to protect against the spread of fire blight;
remove damaged, diseased, or crowded branches, making cuts
several inches below point of apparent damage and sterilizing
pruning tool between cuts.

calleryana 'Bradford' *p. 109*
Bradford pear. The species is usually no taller than 30 ft.,
broadly triangular in outline, showy when in bloom. (The
cultivar 'Bradford' was selected in 1918.) Glossy green leaves
turn scarlet to purple in fall. Small clusters of profuse white
flowers in very early spring. Small, inedible fruit is not messy.
Resistant to fire blight. Old trees tend to split in storms. Newer
cultivars are less subject to breakage: 'Aristocrat' is narrower
and more erect; 'Capital' and 'Whitehouse' are narrowly erect.
China. Zones 5–9.

Quercus
Kwer'kus. Oak
Fagaceae. Beech family

Description
About 450 species, nearly all from the north temperate zone, including fine hardwood timber trees and many beautiful species for planting on lawns, parks, and streets. Most species in the United States are deciduous (the genus is mostly evergreen), but many hold their withered leaves over most of the winter. (Only those whose leaves stay green through the winter are designated as evergreen in the list below.)

How to Grow
Oaks grow best in rich, deep soil without hardpan; plant in full sun, though most will tolerate light partial shade. Mulch, but do not disturb the root zone, which may reach 3 times the branch spread. Trenching, grade changes, or soil compaction in the root zone can seriously harm or kill the tree.

agrifolia p. 109   *Pictured above*
Coast live oak. Broad-topped evergreen tree to 70 ft., with heavy, spreading limbs and smooth- to spine-edged leaves 1–3 in. long. Old leaves drop in spring as new leaves appear. Native to California's coast ranges, where old specimens are much cherished. Heavy irrigation of old trees near the junction of soil and trunk nearly always causes crown rot or oak-root fungus, which will kill the tree. Trees purchased from a nursery can tolerate garden watering. Oak moth larvae may be a disfiguring pest in some years. Trees can be restricted in size by pruning. Zones 8–10.

Other California live oaks are *Q. engelmannii*, mesa oak, from southern California, and *Q. wislizenii*, interior live oak, native to much of interior California, including lower elevations of the Sierra Nevada. Their differences are not obvious to most people, and the trees, cherished where they are found, are not much planted. *Q. ilex,* holly oak, a Mediterranean native, is similar in appearance and fairly widely available. *Q. virginiana,* southern live oak, native to the southeastern U.S., is an attractive and useful tree, especially in hot-summer climates. Zones 8–10.

coccinea p. 110
Scarlet oak. Upright, roughly cylindrical tree, 50–80 ft. high. Deciduous leaves are 4–6 in. long, shining green, sharply and deeply lobed; turn brilliant scarlet in the fall. Similar to pin oak, *Q. palustris,* but more tolerant of alkaline soils. Prefers a light, sandy loam. Transplant when small for best results. Eastern North America. Zones 5–9.

suber p. 110
Cork oak. Round-headed tree to 60 ft. with equal spread. Bark thick and corky, lending a picturesque, rugged appearance. Evergreen leaves to 3 in. long are coarsely toothed; shiny green above, gray-felty beneath. Drought resistant when established. Not hardy below 0 degrees F. Europe, North Africa. Zones 7–9.

Rhaphiolepis
Ra-fi-ol′e-pis
Rosaceae. Rose family

Description
Handsome Asiatic evergreen shrubs widely planted in warm areas for their leathery green foliage, showy flower clusters, and usefulness in borders and hedges and as ground covers.

How to Grow
All species are easy to grow in a variety of soils in full sun or

partial shade. Though they will stand some frost, they cannot be grown safely north of zone 8. Propagate by seeds or hard-wood cuttings under glass.

indica Pictured above
Indian hawthorn. To 5 ft. Pointed leaves, 2–3 in. long. Loose clusters of small pinkish white flowers in fall or winter to spring. Tolerates drought. A number of widely grown cultivars have flowers that range from pure white to deep pink. Heights range from 2–6 ft. China. Zone 8.

umbellata p. 148
Yeddo Rhaphiolepis. Roundish leaves set off white flowers. Plant can grow to 6 ft., possibly to 10. Japan. Zone 8.

Rhus
Roos. Sumac
Anacardiaceae. Sumac family

Description
About 150 species of deciduous or evergreen shrubs and trees, widely scattered. Those cultivated are of great decorative value in fall, when their foliage turns a more brilliant red than that of almost any other shrub or tree. Clusters of small, red, berrylike fruits are also attractive.

How to Grow
Easy to grow in any garden soil or even in dry sand or on rocky hillsides. Transplanting is not difficult, nor is raising plants from seeds or root cuttings.

glabra
Smooth sumac. Deciduous shrub or small tree to 20 ft. Fernlike leaves have deeply toothed leaflets. 'Laciniata' is even more fernlike, with more deeply cut leaflets. Inconspicuous conelike flower clusters are followed by long-lasting, erect bunches of red berries. Fall foliage is brilliant yellow, orange, and scarlet. Plant spreads by underground stems. Eastern North America. Zone 4.

lancea p. 111
African sumac. Evergreen tree to 25 ft. high and wide. Trunk is dark red, branching open; outer branchlets droop. Leaves have 3 narrow leaflets. General effect is airy and graceful.

Tolerates intense summer heat and endures either drought or summer irrigation. South Africa. Zones 9–10.

ovata p. 149
Sugar bush. Smooth, evergreen shrub from southwestern deserts, 5–10 ft. high, with simple, oval leaves, 1–3 in. long. Short, dense spikes of greenish white flowers in spring. Hairy, dark red fruit. Zone 9.

typhina p. 149
Staghorn sumac. Similar to *R. glabra,* but larger, and branches covered with short hairs, which give a velvety finish. North America. Zone 4.

Robinia
Ro-bin'i-a. Locust
Leguminosae. Pea family

Description
A small genus of deciduous trees and shrubs native to North and Central America. Feathery compound leaves and drooping clusters of white, rose, or pink pealike flowers, resembling those of wisteria. Branches are often thorny, brittle, and easily broken.

How to Grow
Grow locusts in full sun in any well-drained soil. They tolerate poor soil and are well adapted to heat and drought. Prune the shrubby forms in early spring to shape them and control their size.

× *ambigua p. 111*
A number of hybrids bear this name. 'Idahoensis' reaches 40 ft. and has drooping clusters of deep purplish pink flowers. 'Purple Robe' has flowers of darker color. Zone 4.

pseudoacacia
Black locust. Open, sparsely branched tree to 70 ft. with deeply furrowed dark bark and clusters of white fragrant flowers. Native to eastern U.S., but common in much of the West. Zone 4.

Rosa
Ro′za. Rose
Rosaceae. Rose family

Description
About 200 species of prickly shrubs or vines grown throughout the region (and everywhere else) for their beautiful, often fragrant flowers, which range from small 5-petaled wild types to extravagant, many-petaled hybrids.

How to Grow
Roses grow well in fertile, well-drained soil free of tree roots. They need at least 6 hours of sun daily. Most species roses require no special care and seem to have fewer insect problems than many modern roses, though they can be bothered by aphids, mites, and Japanese beetles. Black spot, powdery mildew, and canker are common diseases. Species roses are good for borders or for naturalizing. When secured, the long canes of some species suit them for covering fences and trellises. Others, left unsupported, make good ground covers.

banksiae *p. 215*   *Pictured above*
Lady Banks' rose; banksia rose. More like a vine than a shrub, this rose is long-lived and easy to grow. Long, vigorous canes make it outstanding for fences or arbors, or for cascading from trees. Climbing, evergreen, 15–30 ft. high, with a few thorns or none. Profuse clusters of smallish flowers in spring. Disease resistant. Single white and yellow forms exist, but the commonest are 'Alba Plena', double white with the fragrance of violets, and 'Lutea', double yellow. China. Zone 7.

'Climbing Peace' *p. 150*
For information on growing this and other garden roses and

on selecting from the vast assemblage of Hybrid Teas, Floribundas, Grandifloras, and Climbers, consult *Taylor's Guide to Roses.*

Rosmarinus
Ros-ma-ry'nus. Rosemary
Labiatae. Mint family

Description
A few species of evergreen shrubs, native to the Mediterranean region, one widely cultivated as a culinary and sweet herb; also an attractive ornamental plant.

How to Grow
Rosemary tolerates hot sun and poor soil, but good drainage is essential; it grows best in soil that is not too rich. Water to establish and as needed in desert areas; needs little water elsewhere. Prune after flowering to improve form and prevent excessive woodiness.

officinalis 'Prostratus' *p. 202*
Trailing rosemary. Trailing branches spread to 4 ft. wide and mound to 2 ft. high. Leaves aromatic, glossy, dark green on upper side, white beneath. Small, light blue flowers in winter, spring, and sometimes fall. Popular in the Southwest as ground cover or for cascading over walls. Zone 7.

Salvia
Sal'vi-a. Sage
Labiatae. Mint family

Description
About 750 species of annual, biennial, or perennial herbs, subshrubs, and shrubs distributed throughout the tropical and temperate world. The leaves of some species are used for seasoning. Tubular flowers in whorls, sometimes spikes.

How to Grow
The salvias below are easy to grow in full sun or partial shade and average to dry, well-drained soil.

clevelandii
Shrub to 4 ft., often wider, with gray-green leaves and blue flowers in spring and summer. Entire plant has a strong, pleasant fragrance. Southern California. Zones 9–10.

farinacea *p. 184   Pictured above*
Mealy-cup sage. Perennial grown as annual in colder regions. Mound to 3 ft. of gray-green leaves, 4 in. long. Many-whorled spikes of small violet-blue flowers. White-flowered varieties exist. Flower stalks sometimes bluish. Texas, New Mexico. Zone 8.

greggii *p. 150*
Evergreen shrub to 4 ft., with small green leaves and open clusters of red flowers in spring and summer; fall and winter in low desert. There are pink, coral, salmon, purplish red, and white varieties. Texas, Mexico. Zone 8.

leucantha *p. 151*
Mexican bush sage. Shrub of spreading habit to 3–4 ft., with gray-green leaves and long, slender, velvety purplish pink spikes displaying small white flowers. Summer, fall bloom. Zone 8.

Santolina
San-to-ly′na
Compositae. Daisy family

Description
Evergreen, aromatic subshrubs, most of the 8 species native to the Mediterranean region. Handsome foliage and many small flowers; good as ground covers or low hedges.

How to Grow
All species grow best in full sun and well-drained soil. Drought resistant.

chamaecyparissus p. 203
Lavender cotton. Silvery gray evergreen, 1–2 ft. high. Leaves cut into very narrow segments. Unclipped plants produce single yellow flowers on 6-in. stalks in summer. Prune to prevent plants from becoming ragged. Mediterranean region. Zone 4.

Sapium
Say'pi-um
Euphorbiaceae. Spurge family

Description
About 100 species of tropical trees with milky, poisonous sap. The deciduous species below is commonly grown as a shade or screen tree with handsome fruit and fall color.

How to Grow
The species below grows rapidly when young in dry or wet, acid or alkaline soil. Requires full sun and cannot withstand temperatures of 0 degrees F. Insects and diseases are not problems. Prone to multiple trunks and suckering, but easy to train to single trunk.

sebiferum p. 112
Chinese tallow tree; popcorn tree. To 50 ft. high, usually lower. Roundish, pointed leaves 1–3 in. long on red-tipped stalks. Casts light shade, allowing grass and other plants to grow underneath. Fall color varies from orange through red to purple on different specimens. Flowers are not showy. Small, decorative fruit has white seeds (hence the name popcorn tree), whose waxy covering yields a tallowlike substance used for soap and candles. South China, Japan. Zones 8–9.

Schinus
Sky'nus
Anacardiaceae. Sumac family

Description
About 28 species of chiefly South American resinous trees; those commonly grown are broadleaf evergreens planted for

shade. When dried, the reddish, berrylike fruits constitute the pink peppercorns of the spice trade. Some people may be allergic to them or to the pollen.

How to Grow
These trees are easy to grow in almost any soil. Young plants may need pruning to encourage a tree shape.

molle p. 112
California pepper tree. To 40 ft. with heavy, contorted trunk, wide-spreading branches. Drooping, willowy branchlets carry delicate, fernlike foliage. Clusters of small white flowers in summer. Open clusters of pink berries dangle from female trees. Tolerates drought and heat. Much loved for grace and "old mission" look, but many deplore its greedy root system. Peru. Zones 9–10.

terebinthifolius p. 113
Brazilian pepper tree. Differs from the above in its dense, nearly globular growth, coarser foliage. Female trees bear clusters of bright red berries. Considered an invasive pest in Florida, it is a valued shade or ornamental tree in the Southwest. Brazil. Zone 10.

Sedum
See'dum. Stonecrop
Crassulaceae. Stonecrop family

Description
About 600 species of low-growing, chiefly perennial herbs, found throughout the Northern Hemisphere. Succulent foliage and small flowers in white, yellow, pink, red, or rarely blue.

How to Grow
Sedums are particularly adapted to the rock garden, but a few

species can be used in flower borders or as ground covers. Easy to grow in well-drained, average soil in sun or partial shade. Good drainage is essential, particularly in winter. Easily propagated by cuttings at almost any time.

× **'Autumn Joy'** *p. 184*   *Pictured above*
Autumn Joy sedum. Perennial to 2 ft. high. Leaves scattered along succulent stems. Small pink to rusty red flowers in clusters that resemble broccoli heads. Dormant in winter. Zone 4.

spurium *p. 203*
Two-row stonecrop. Trailing perennial with small, evergreen, succulent leaves that turn from green to bronze in winter. Clustered pink flowers in summer. 'Dragon's Blood' has darker leaves, red flowers. Zone 4.

Senecio
Sen-ee′si-o. Groundsel; ragwort
Compositae. Daisy family

Description
More than 2,000 species of perennials, shrubs, vines, and small trees found throughout the world. Some are grown for their daisylike flowers, others for their foliage.

How to Grow
The species described below is very drought resistant. Grows best in warm to hot climates. Space 12 in. apart in full sun or light shade and sandy, light, well-drained soil. Fertilize at planting time. If plants become leggy, cut them back.

cineraria *p. 185*
Dusty miller. Spreading, shrubby perennial to 2½ ft. high. Attractive leaves are thick, woolly, whitish. Clusters of small yellow or cream-colored flowers bloom at any time. Other plants with white, gray, or silver foliage are also known as dusty miller, but this is one of the more common species. Mediterranean. Zone 5.

Simmondsia
Sim-mond'si-a
Buxaceae Box family

Description
One species, an evergreen shrub native to the warmer, drier parts of Arizona, California, and Mexico.

How to Grow
Goat nut needs little water (if any) once established. It requires good drainage and soil free of verticillium wilt and Texas root-rot fungi.

chinensis p. 151
Goat nut; jojoba. Stiff shrub to 6–7 ft., often lower, with dull gray-green narrow leaves. Inconspicuous male and female flowers borne on separate plants. Pollinated flowers develop small nutlike edible fruit that yields jojoba oil. Grown for oil or as hedge or edging plants. Zone 10.

Solanum
So-lay'num
Solanaceae. Nightshade family

Description
Annuals, perennials, shrubs, and vines. More than 1,500 species, with conspicuous wheel-shaped flowers, usually 5-pointed, in blue, yellow, or white. The genus includes potato and eggplant, as well as many ornamentals.

How to Grow
The species below thrives in sun or light shade in any well-drained soil. Prune often to avoid overgrowth and tangling.

jasminoides *p. 216*
Potato vine. Fast-growing, twining vine to 25–30 ft. Dark green leaves are evergreen but may drop in unusual cold. Clusters of smallish white flowers appear over most of the year. Brazil. Zones 9–10.

Sophora
So-for′ra
Leguminosae. Pea family

Description
Handsome, profusely flowering shrubs or trees; most of the 50 species are Asiatic broadleaf evergreens, but a few are native to North America.

How to Grow
These plants do well in most soils. They require little care except training while young, good drainage, and sunshine.

japonica *p. 113   Pictured above*
Pagoda tree; Japanese pagoda tree; Chinese scholar tree. Excellent shade tree. Spreading, round-headed, 40–70 ft. high, sometimes more. Numerous narrow leaflets. Small, yellowish white flowers in long, loose clusters, very showy in late summer. Pods 2–4 in. long. Tolerates city conditions. Requires some protection from cold when young, but hardy once established. 'Regent' grows faster, has better foliage, and blooms at an earlier age. China, Korea. Zones 5–8.

secundiflora *p. 152*
Mescal bean; Texas mountain laurel. Evergreen shrub or small, slow-growing tree to 25 ft. Small, shiny leaflets. Violet-blue flowers in spring, in drooping clusters like wisteria, strong fragrance. Seedpods open to show bright red, highly poisonous

seeds. Needs little water once established, but grows faster with adequate irrigation. Native to the Southwest. Zones 9–10.

Stachys
Stack'iss. Betony; woundwort
Labiatae. Mint family

Description
About 300 species of annual or perennial herbs distributed throughout the world, but chiefly in the temperate zones. Species below grown as border edging or as ground cover beneath high-branching trees.

How to Grow
Easy to grow in average, well-drained soil in full sun. Propagate by seeds in early spring or by division in early spring or fall.

byzantina p. 185
Lamb's-ears. (Also sold as *S. lanata* and *S. olympica*.) Perennial to 18 in. high. Leaves and stems covered with soft, white, woolly hairs. Small purple flowers in dense whorls. Tolerates dry soil. Cultivar 'Silver Carpet' does not produce flowers. Caucasus and Iran. Zone 5.

Syringa
Sir-ring'ga. Lilac
Oleaceae. Olive family

Description
A large group of decorative deciduous shrubs and trees from the Old World. Lilacs have long been popular for their fragrant late-spring blossoms in white, pink, lavender, or purple.

How to Grow
Lilacs will grow in any well-drained soil, but should be fertilized every 2 years. Remove old blossoms as soon as they fade. Prune any time during winter, removing all weak wood that does not bear large flower buds or that still carries last year's fruit. Doing this every 3 years will produce a regular

sequence of bloom. The first year the quantity will be reduced, but each cluster will be very large. The second season there will be more and larger flowers, and the third year still more clusters, but smaller than those produced the first year. If quality of bloom is more important than quantity, prune more lightly every 2 years.

vulgaris *p. 152   Pictured above*
Common lilac. Handsome, widely cultivated shrub to 15 ft., sometimes becoming a small tree. Heart-shaped to oval leaves, 2–6 in. long. Flower clusters 6–8 in. long, very fragrant, in May. There are many forms, with white, pink, blue, or purple flowers. Lilacs are often not successful where winters are warm. A series called Descanso Hybrids was developed in southern California to overcome this fault. 'Lavender Lady' and 'White Angel' are best known. Southeastern Europe. Zone 4.

Tabebuia
Ta-be-bew'i-a
Bignoniaceae. Trumpet-creeper family

Description
Deciduous or evergreen trees from tropical America. Leaves usually compound, with leaflets spread like fingers of a hand. Large clusters of trumpet-shaped, showy flowers.

How to Grow
Provide good drainage and ample water for fast growth. Once established, these trees can get along with little water. Shape to a single trunk while young or grow as a multiple-trunk tree.

chrysotricha p. 114
Golden trumpet tree. Spreading tree, fast-growing to 25 ft.
Leaflets drop for a short time in spring when heaviest bloom
appears. Bright yellow, 3–4 in. flowers come in big, rounded
clusters. Brazil. Zone 10.

Tecoma
Teck-o′ma
Bignoniaceae. Trumpet-creeper family

Description
Several species of shrubs or small trees with trumpet-shaped
flowers, native to tropical and subtropical America. Many
vines now listed under other genera were once treated as *Tecoma* and are still often sold as such.

How to Grow
The species below does best with heat, ample water, and deep
soil. Freezes back to the ground in hard frost but recovers fast.
In frost-free areas it can be staked and pruned to tree form.

stans p. 153
Yellowbells; yellow elder; yellow bignonia. Dense, large bush
to 20 ft. Leaves have toothed leaflets. Flowers are bright yellow, 2 in. wide, bell-shaped, in large clusters from early summer to midwinter. Good desert plant. Zones 9–10.

Trachelospermum
Tra-kell-o-sper′mum
Apocynaceae. Dogbane family

Description
About 20 species of Indo-Malayan or Chinese woody vines,
most with showy flowers.

How to Grow
Star jasmine grows in a variety of soils with average watering
but is slow to become established. Give some shade in hot
areas. Provide support when planting and train it on a post,
wall, or trellis. Prune older plants occasionally to prevent excessive woodiness. Can also be grown as a ground cover if

growing tips are occasionally pinched out to encourage branching.

jasminoides p. 204   *Pictured above*
Star jasmine; confederate jasmine. Slow-growing, twining vine, to 30 ft. or more. Evergreen, oval leaves, 2–4 in. long. Flowers white, starlike, resembling a pinwheel, to 1 in. wide, sweetly fragrant, in small clusters. China. Zones 9–10.

Tristania
Tris-tay'ni-a
Myrtaceae. Myrtle family

Description
About 20 species of chiefly Australasian broadleaf evergreen trees and shrubs. Those below grown for attractive evergreen foliage and colorful shedding bark.

How to Grow
These plants grow best in fairly good soil with deep weekly watering in dry spells. (Strongly alkaline soil may cause foliar chlorosis.) Endure drought when well established.

conferta p. 114
Brisbane box. Tree to 50 ft., somewhat resembling a eucalyptus. Reddish brown, shedding bark. Leaves 3–6 in. long, often grouped at ends of twigs. Small, white, fluffy flowers, mostly in small clusters, in summer. Australia. Zones 9–10.

laurina
Large, slow-growing, dense shrub, eventually a small tree.

Glossy green, 4-in., narrowish leaves and clusters of small yellow flowers. Dark red bark peels to show smooth white inner bark. Handsome screen plant or lawn tree, either single- or multiple-trunked. Zones 9–10.

Ulmus
Ul′mus. Elm
Ulmaceae. Elm family

Description
Some 18 species, mostly deciduous, all from the north temperate zone of North America, Europe, and Asia. Excellent shade trees, broadly upright, high-branching, creating a canopy of dappled shade.

How to Grow
Elms are easy to transplant and grow in a wide variety of soils except wet and very dry. They need more or less full sun. Prune young trees to minimize narrow crotches, which are likely to split in later years. The species below is resistant but not necessarily immune to Dutch elm disease, which has decimated *U. americana,* the beautiful American elm. Good cultural conditions improve resistance to disease.

parvifolia p. 115   Pictured above
Chinese elm; lacebark elm. Spreading small tree, usually not more than 60 ft. high and inclined to forking. Quickly makes a broad shade tree; give it room to spread. The attractively mottled bark sheds to make multicolored patterns, better in some trees than others. Leaves may turn yellowish or reddish purple in fall. Flowers in small clusters in late summer are not ornamental. Small, slightly ornamental fruit in fall. 'Brea' (erect, large-leafed), 'Drake' (small-leafed, somewhat weeping), and 'True Green' are usually evergreen in zones 9 and 10. China, Japan. Zones 5–10.

Ungnadia
Ung-nay'dia
Sapindaceae. Soapberry family

Description
The species below, which grows along limestone bluffs in Texas, New Mexico, and Mexico, is the only one in the genus.

How to Grow
Mexican buckeye tolerates dry soil and drought. Plant in full sun or partial shade.

speciosa *p. 153*
Mexican buckeye. Shrub or small tree to 30 ft. Deciduous compound leaves, attractive pink flowers in clusters before leaves open in spring. Buckeye-like nuts in fall. Grow as a specimen tree or in mixed hedge. Zone 7.

Verbena
Ver-bee'na. Vervain
Verbenaceae. Verbena family

Description
About 200 species of tender or hardy annual or perennial herbs, mostly native to the Americas.

How to Grow
Verbenas are useful in sunny, well-drained borders. They thrive in heat, tend to rot in heavy, poorly drained, or wet soils.

bipinnatifida *p. 204*
Sprawling perennial ground cover with finely cut foliage and roundish heads of flowers in summer. In coldest areas plants may die out but will self-sow. Western U.S. Zone 4.

hybrida
Garden verbena. Tender perennial grown as an annual in cold-winter climates. Less than 1 ft. tall, can spread to 3 ft. Easy to grow from seed, it is available in white, red, blue, pink, purple, and mixes. Attractive individual plants can be propagated from cuttings. Give good air circulation and avoid wetting foliage to fend off mildew. Zones 9–10 as perennial.

peruviana

Peruvian verbena. Prostrate perennial a few inches tall, 2 ft. or more across. Flat-topped flower clusters are brilliant scarlet in the species. Garden varieties include pink, white, and purplish rose. South America. Zones 9–10. Grow as an annual elsewhere.

Viburnum
Vy-bur'num
Caprifoliaceae. Honeysuckle family

Description
Some 225 species of chiefly deciduous shrubs and small trees, many cultivated for their attractive spring flower clusters and their often showy fruits.

How to Grow
Viburnums, generally easy to grow, prefer moist, well-drained, slightly acid soil. Prune after flowering if necessary.

× *carlcephalum* p. 154
Fragrant snowball. Deciduous shrub, 8–10 ft. tall and half as wide. Smallish, dull gray-green leaves, fuzzy on undersides. Dense clusters of waxy white, fragrant flowers in spring. No fruit. Zone 4.

japonicum
Evergreen shrub or small tree with leathery, shiny, 6-in. leaves. White flowers in clusters in late spring; scarlet fruit. Use as filler or background, provide some shade in hottest areas. Japan. Zones 7–10.

suspensum p. 154
Sandankwa viburnum. Evergreen shrub, 6–12 ft. high. Oval

leaves, 3–4 in. long. Dense clusters of fragrant, pinkish flowers, 1½ in. wide. Fruit red, or black when mature. Tolerates drought. Ryukyu Islands. Zone 9.

tinus *p. 155* *Pictured above*
Laurustinus. Handsome evergreen shrub, 7–10 ft. high. Dark green leaves, 2–3 in. long. Flower clusters 3 in. wide, often faintly pinkish, unpleasantly scented, bloom from winter to spring. Fruit metallic blue, turning black. Several horticultural forms, one with variegated leaves. Useful as a hedge. Mediterranean region. Zone 7.

Vinca
Ving'ka
Apocynaceae. Dogbane family

Description
About 12 species of evergreen, erect or trailing perennial herbs or vinelike shrubs, native to the Old World. Excellent ground covers.

How to Grow
Vincas make a thick carpet in moderately fertile garden soil. They tolerate full sun but grow best in light shade. May be sheared annually to encourage dense growth.

major *p. 205* *Pictured above*
Big periwinkle. Trailing stems are thin and wiry, mounding to 18 in. high, usually lower. Shiny, dark green, heart-shaped leaves; blue flowers, 1–2 in. wide. 'Variegata' has yellowish white leaf margins. Much used as an annual in window boxes in cold climates, ground cover in warmer areas. Less cold-hardy and more open in growth habit than *V. minor*. A ramp-

ant grower, it can smother more fragile neighbors. Europe. Zone 7.

minor
Periwinkle; creeping myrtle. Trailing, hardy, to 10 in. high, rooting stems thin and wiry. Dark green, broadly lance-shaped leaves to 2 in. long. Small, light blue flowers. Good plant for shady places. 'Bowles' Variety' has large, bright blue flowers in profusion. Europe. Zone 5.

Vitex
Vy'tex
Verbenaceae. Verbena family

Description
About 270 species of ornamental trees or shrubs found chiefly in the tropical and warmer regions of the world.

How to Grow
Plant in any good garden soil. Performs best in hot-summer climates.

agnus-castus *p. 115*
Chaste tree. Deciduous shrub or small tree, 7–20 ft. high. Lance-shaped, dark green leaflets covered with short gray hairs on the underside; pleasantly scented when bruised. Flowers fragrant, lilac-blue, in dense, showy spikes 1 ft. long in summer. 'Alba', a white form with larger leaves, is one of the best of the cultivated forms. 'Latifolia' has shorter, broader leaves. Southern Europe. Zone 7.

Wisteria
Wis-tair'i-a
Leguminosae. Pea family

Description
Beautiful woody vines, 2 species native to the U.S., the other 5 Asiatic, widely grown for their profuse bloom.

How to Grow
Wisterias grow best in fertile, well-drained soil. They tolerate

some shade, but flower best in full sun. Slow to become established, so provide extra fertilizer and water when young; older plants flower better without supplements. May be trained as a single or multistemmed vine over a porch, trellis, or dead tree. May also be grown as a small weeping tree or as a ground cover. Wisterias require several years to reach blooming stage. Mature plants can be encouraged to set buds by proper pruning techniques. Discourage excessive vegetative growth by pruning roots and fertilizing with phosphate to promote flowering; avoid nitrogen fertilizers.

floribunda
Japanese wisteria. Resembles the above, but flower clusters are longer, and flowers open more gradually from base to tip of cluster. There are white, near pink, and double purple forms. 'Longissima' has extra long (to 40 in.), light lavender-blue clusters. Japan. Zone 4.

sinensis *p. 216* *Pictured above*
Chinese wisteria. Climbs to 40 ft. high. Numerous leaflets, 2–4 in. long. Foot-long clusters of fragrant, bluish violet flowers in spring before leaves open fully. Pods densely velvety. 'Alba' is a white-flowered form. China. Zone 4.

Xylosma
Zy-los′ma
Flacourtiaceae. Indian plum family

Description
More than 100 species of tropical shrubs and trees, some grown for their shiny, yellow-green foliage. The small flowers are inconspicuous.

How to Grow

Xylosma is easy to grow in full sun or partial shade in most soils. Looks best with occasional watering but tolerates heat and drought. It responds well to pruning and can be trained into an espalier.

congestum p. 155

Xylosma. A shrub 8–10 ft. high and wide. Unpruned, the main stem zigzags as it grows, and the side branches arch or droop. Oval evergreen leaves, 3½-in. long, are bronzy when young and a beautiful, glossy, light yellowish green when mature. Survives moderate light frost although it may lose its leaves. Useful hedge or screen plant. 'Compacta' is smaller, less willowy. China. Zones 9–10.

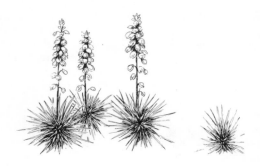

Yucca

Yuck′a

Agavaceae. Agave family

Description

About 40 species of chiefly Mexican semidesert plants, a few cultivated for their striking flower clusters.

How to Grow

All do best in well-drained sandy loam in full sun. They are propagated by seeds or offsets.

elata p. 186

Soaptree yucca. Single or branched trunks to 20 ft. carry rosettes of 4-ft., swordlike leaves. White flowers in long spikes in summer. Native to the Southwest. Zones 8–10.

whipplei p. 186   *Pictured above*

Our Lord's candle. Stemless rosette of stiff, spine-tipped, gray-green leaves, 1½ ft. long. Heavy, branching flower clusters to 10 ft. or more carry multitudinous white, bell-shaped flowers.

Rosettes die after bloom; they may or may not produce offsets. California, Baja California. Zones 6–10.

Zauschneria
Zaush-near'i-a
Onagraceae. Evening primrose family

Description
These perennials spread by underground runners or by seed. Narrow green or gray-green leaves and brilliant scarlet flowers in late summer.

How to Grow
All can tolerate poor, dry soil and still produce showy bloom late in the season. They tend to be untidy when not in bloom and may be somewhat invasive.

californica p. 187
California fuchsia. Erect or leaning stems form patches of fine-textured foliage topped with fiery red, tubular, 2-in.-long flowers. Hardy anywhere, but evergreen only where winters are mild. The subspecies *Z. c. latifolia* makes 6-in.-tall spreading mats, with flowers much like those of the species. It is dormant in winter.

Zinnia
Zin'i-a
Compositae. Daisy family

Description
Annual or perennial plants, each flower stalk with a single, showy flower. The common garden zinnia (*Z. elegans*) is typical, though exaggerated in cultivated forms.

How to Grow
The plant below needs sun and good drainage. Once established, it can survive with little water, but irrigation gives longer, more profuse bloom.

grandiflora p. 187
Perennial to 10 in. tall, somewhat broader, with narrow leaves and yellow flower heads 1½ in. across. Colorado to Texas. Zone 4.

Appendices

Pests and Diseases

Pests and diseases are unavoidable in the garden. But only a very small percentage of the organisms — animals, insects, bacteria, fungi — that pass through or live there cause any damage to plants or inconvenience to gardeners. Most are innocuous, and some are even beneficial. Yet when we set out, for instance, to eradicate an infestation of aphids with toxic pesticides, we unintentionally eradicate helpful and harmless creatures as well.

Today's gardeners, confronted with a pest problem, are far less willing than their predecessors to wage war with an arsenal of chemicals. Instead of a battle, they seek a partnership, attempting to nudge the ecosystem rather than bludgeon it. They take preventative measures, then deploy "soft" controls, such as soaps, oils, and beneficial organisms, before turning to biotoxic materials, such as carbaryl, malathion, and Diazinon, as a last resort.

Here we will introduce the types of pests and briefly outline this "least toxic" approach to controlling them. Because pest problems can be difficult to diagnose, and the selection of controls can be confusing, we strongly encourage you to consult with a knowledgeable person at a local nursery, or a cooperative extension agent, or an expert at a nearby college or university.

What Are Garden Pests?

There are, generally speaking, four categories of garden pests: insects and mites, nematodes, diseases, and environmental problems.

Insects and mites

Insects and mites are categorized according to how they damage plants. Chewers (grasshoppers, caterpillars, and beetles, for instance) chomp away on leaves and stems. Tunnelers, such as leafminers, make tunnels inside leaves. Borers chew their way through the insides of branches and stems. Aphids, scales, and mealybugs suck the juice from plants, as do spider mites.

Nematodes
These microscopic roundworms live in soil. Of the many kinds, most are harmless to plants. A few are beneficial, parasitizing certain garden pests; a few more are themselves pests, colonizing and damaging the roots of desirable plants.

Plant diseases
Diseases, typically caused by viruses, bacteria, or fungi, appear on plants as leaf spots, blights, mildews, or wilts. Leaf spots, which may be black, brown, purple, or orange, often defoliate plants. Blights can suddenly wither entire stems, shoots, and branches, or they may appear as leaf spots. Mildews usually form grayish, powdery layers on the surfaces of plants, distorting and destroying leaves and flowers. Wilts induce entire plants suddenly to shrivel and die. They usually enter plants from the soil.

Environmental problems
Winter cold, summer heat and drought, salt spray, air pollution, nutrient deficiencies, poor drainage, high winds, and lawn mower injury can all make plants suffer. To avoid problems, try to provide the conditions each plant prefers.

A number of animals can create problems for gardeners in the Southwest — deer, squirrels, moles, and gophers, and environmental stress can exacerbate these problems. Drought and lack of forage can push deer, for example, into populated areas where they might not otherwise go.

Managing Pests

Don't wait until an insect or disease problem forces you to take action. The following preventive measures will help you maintain a natural balance in the garden and keep problems from getting out of hand.

Plant mostly pest-free, adapted plants
Select plants that are well adapted to your climate and specific site and that are known to be pest-free. By relying mostly on these plants, which include many native and exotic plants from similar climates, you eliminate many pest problems at the outset. Many of us, of course, are fond of certain plants — fruit trees, roses, orchids — despite their susceptibility to pests

and disease. Learn about their specific problems and keep an eye on them.

Keep plants healthy

Healthy, vigorous plants are less prone to pest attack than weak, struggling plants. In fact, many insects and diseases are programmed by nature to colonize weak plants. A gardener's efforts to counteract such pests must focus on reestablishing the vigor of the plant.

Be a good garden housekeeper

Cultivate the soil often to expose insect eggs and larvae and disease-causing organisms; sunlight and wind may desiccate and kill many of them. Also destroy diseased or infested plants and plant parts as well as pest-harboring weeds.

Use physical barriers

Insect traps, sticky barriers, and fabric or plastic plant covers can reduce damage caused by pests, often substantially.

Control ants

Ants live in many gardens, often with no ill effects. However, they are known to spread and protect many plant-damaging insects, such as aphids and scale, as well as to discourage the natural predators of those pests.

Tolerate a few pests

Part of the art of pest management is knowing when to intervene. In some cases there is no need to act at the first sign of a pest. By giving nature a chance to restore its own balance, you avoid the possibility of upsetting the balance further and creating more problems.

Most plants in most situations can live with a few pests. If, for some specific reason, you require perfect foliage or a perfect flower, treat those plants separately and as needed. A garden free of all insects is also free of those that are beneficial; a few pests are necessary so that your garden will have a healthy number of beneficial insects.

Controls

When you must intervene to protect a plant, use the most benign, "softest" control measures first. None promises total eradication, but they will augment nature's efforts in your behalf.

Biological measures include beneficial microorganisms (such as *Bacillus thuringiensis*) and insects (such as the green lacewing) and chemicals (such as pheromones) that affect insect behavior. Sulfur and horticultural soaps and oils are inorganic insecticides. Sulfur controls mites and some diseases. Soaps are effective against many kinds of soft-bodied insects. Oils coat the insects, smothering them. Botanical insecticides are derived from plant substances. Two common ones are pyrethrin, which is extracted from a kind of daisy, and rotenone, which is extracted from many types of legume.

If these soft measures fail, or none is available for your problem, consider synthetic insecticides, such as Diazinon and malathion, carefully. Be certain that you've correctly identified the insect or disease. Then be sure to use a chemical that is known to be effective. Always follow the label's cautions and directions to the letter. If you are uncertain about the pest or the control, consult with a knowledgeable person before taking action.

Sources of Seeds
and Plants

Gardeners in the Southwest can buy from many nurseries that specialize in regional plants. We encourage you to seek out local nurseries where the staff will be familiar with the plants and problems of your area. Some of the nurseries listed below sell only through the mail; others sell on site. Some have display gardens open to the public. Some sell a wide range of plants, and others are more specialized. We have indicated this information in each entry (see the key), but you should call the nursery to confirm it before ordering plants or making a trip there.

Key:
[S]: seeds
[P]: plants
MO: mail order
Nu: on-site sale
Gdn: display garden
appt: some restriction, call for appointment

Arizona

B&B Cactus Farm, Inc. [P]
11550 E. Speedway Blvd.
Tucson, AZ 85748
602 721-4687
Cactuses and succulents for the Southwest
Catalog: free
MO, Nu, Gdn

Desert Enterprises [S]
P.O. Box 23
Morristown, AZ 85342
602 388-2448

Wildflowers, cacti, desert shrubs, trees, native grasses
Catalog: free
Phone orders only

Hubbs Brothers Seed Company [S]
40 N. 56th St.
Phoenix, AZ 85034
602 267-8132
Native seeds from Sonoran and Mohave deserts
Catalog: free
MO, retail store

Southern California

Abbey Garden [P]
4620 Carpinteria Ave.
Carpinteria, CA 93013
805 684-5112
Cacti and succulents
Catalog: $2
MO, Nu, Gdn

Buena Creek Gardens [P]
418 Buena Creek Road
San Marcos, CA 92069
619 744-2810
Daylilies, iris, perennials, drought-tolerant and subtropical plants
Nu, Gdn

Clyde Robin Seed Co., Inc. [S]
P.O. Box 2366
Castro Valley, CA 94546
415 785-0425
California natives, wildflowers, shrubs, trees
Catalog: free
MO

Greenlee Nursery [P,S]
301 E. Franklin Ave.
Pomona, CA 91766
714 629-9045
Ornamental grasses
Catalog: $5 (free price list)
MO, Nu (appt)

Las Pilitas Nursery [P,S]
Star Route, Box 23X
Las Pilitas Rd.
Santa Margarita, CA 93453
805 438-5992
California native plants
Catalog: $4 (free price list)
MO, Nu (appt), Gdn (appt)

Mockingbird Nursery [P]
1670 Jackson St.
Riverside, CA 92504
714 780-3571
California native plants
Catalog: free
Nu (appt)

Moon Mountain Wildflowers [S]
P.O. Box 34
864 Nappa Ave.
Morro Bay, CA 93442
California natives and others
Catalog: $2
MO

Pacific Tree Farms [P]
4301 Lynwood Dr.
Chula Vista, CA 91910
619 422-2400
New and rare plants and trees, subtropical fruits
Catalog: $2
MO, Nu, Gdn

Plants for Dry Places [P,S]
33336 Mission Trail
Lake Elsinore, CA 92530
714 674-4620
Natives, drought-tolerant plants
Nu, Gdn

Rogers Gardens [P,S]
2301 San Joaquin Hills Rd.
Corona del Mar, CA 92625
714 640-5800
Many demonstration gardens
Nu, Gdn

Stallings Ranch Nursery [P]
910 Encinitas Blvd.
Encinitas, CA 92024
619 753-3079
Many tropical and subtropical plants
Catalog: $3
MO, Nu

Theodore Payne Foundation for Wildflowers and Native Plants [P,S]
10459 Tuxford St.
Sun Valley, CA 91352
818 768-1802
California wildflowers and native plants; regional gardening books
Catalog: $2
MO (seed only), Nu, Gdn

Tropic World Nursery [P]
26437 N. Centre City Parkway
Escondido, CA 92026
619 746-6108
Cacti, succulents, roses, and more
Nu, Gdn

Van Ness Water Gardens [P]
2460 N. Euclid
Upland, CA 91786-1199
714 982-2425
Water gardening plants and supplies
Catalog: $3
MO, Nu, Gdn

Weber Nursery [P]
237 Seeman Drive
Encinitas, CA 92024
619 753-1661
California natives
Nu, Gdn

Wildwood Nursery [P,S]
3975 Emerald Ave. (in La Verne)
P.O. Box 1334
Claremont, CA 91711
714 593-4093 or 621-2112
California natives, drought-tolerant plants
Catalog: $1
MO, Nu, Gdn

New Mexico

Agua Fria Nursery [P]
1409 Agua Fria St.
Santa Fe, NM 87501
505 983-4831
Native plants, wildflowers, perennials
Nu

Bernardo Beach Native Plant Farm [P,S]
520 Montano Rd. N.W.
Albuquerque, NM 87107
505 345-6248
Southwestern native plants
Catalog: $1
Nu

Desert Moon Nursery [P]
P.O. Box 600
Veguita, NM 87062
505 864-0614
Natives, drought-tolerant plants
Catalog: $1
MO, Nu (appt), Gdn (appt)

Desert Nursery [P]
1301 S. Copper
Deming, NM 88030
505 546-6264
Cacti, succulents
Catalog: free with stamp
MO, Nu, Gdn

Mesa Garden [P,S]
P.O. Box 72
Belen, NM 87002
505 864-3131
Cacti, succulents
Catalog: two first-class stamps
MO, Nu (appt), Gdn (appt)

Plants of the Southwest [P,S]
930 Baca St.
Santa Fe, NM 87501
505 983-1548
Plants for water-saving gardens
Catalog: $1.50
MO, Nu

Texas

Womack's Nursery Co. [P]
Rte. 1, Box 80
Highway 6 between De Leon and Gorman
De Leon, TX 76444-9660
817 893-6497
Fruit, nut, and shade trees for the Southwest; shrubs, roses, grapes, berries
Catalog: free
MO (no California sales), Nu

Yucca Do Nursery [P]
P.O. Box 655
Waller, TX 77484
409 826-6363
Native Texas plants and their Mexican and Asian counterparts
Catalog: $3
MO

Public Gardens

One of the best ways to learn about plants and garden design is to see superb gardens firsthand. Here is a selection from the many excellent public gardens in the Southwest. Be sure to phone or write ahead for opening times, admission fees, and travel directions.

Arizona

The Arboretum at Flagstaff
South Woody Mountain Rd.
P.O. Box 670
Flagstaff, AZ 86002
602 774-1441
200 acres, demonstration gardens, research on water-efficient plants

Arizona-Sonora Desert Museum
2021 N. Kinney Rd.
Tucson, AZ 85743
602 883-2702 or 883-1380
186 acres, native plants in natural habitats, demonstration garden

Boyce Thompson Southwestern Arboretum
P.O. Box AB
Superior, AZ 85273
602 689-2811 or 689-2723
35 acres, arid-land plants, demonstration gardens

Desert Botanical Garden
1201 N. Galvin Parkway
Phoenix, AZ 85008
602 941-2867
145 acres, many displays, demonstration gardens

Tohono Chul Park
7366 N. Paseo del Norte
Tucson, AZ 85704
602 575-8468, 602 742-6455
36 acres, demonstration gardens

Tucson Botanical Gardens
2150 N. Alvernon Way
Tucson, AZ 85712
602 326-9255, 602 326-9686
5 acres, many small gardens, xeriscape garden

Southern California

Balboa Park
City of San Diego Parks and Recreation Central Division
Balboa Park Management Center
San Diego, CA 92101
619 239-0512
1,200 acres, many gardens

Descanso Gardens
1418 Descanso Drive
La Canada, CA 91011
818 952-4400 or 952-4401
165 acres, camellia heaven, other displays

Desert Water Agency Demonstration Gardens
1200 Gene Autry Trail S.
P.O. Box 1710
Palm Springs, CA 92263
619 323-4971
15 acres, test and demonstration gardens

Huntington Library, Art Collections and Botanical Gardens
1151 Oxford Rd.
San Marino, CA 91108
818 405-2141
150 acres, 15 different types of gardens

Landscapes Southern California Style
450 Alessandro Blvd.
P.O. Box 5286
Riverside, CA 92517-5286
714 780-4170, 714 780-4177
1 acre, water-efficient demonstration garden

The Living Desert
47900 Portola Ave.
Palm Desert, CA 92260
619 346-5694
1,200 acres, including many demonstration gardens

Los Angeles County Arboretum
301 North Baldwin Ave.
Arcadia, CA 91007
213 681-8411
127 acres, many displays, demonstration gardens

Lummis Home State Historical Monument
200 E. Avenue 43
Los Angeles, CA 90031
213 222-0546
2 acres, low-water, low-maintenance garden

Quail Botanical Gardens
230 Quail Gardens Dr.
Encinitas, CA 92024
619 436-3036
30 acres, many gardens including native demonstration garden

Rancho Santa Ana Botanic Garden
1500 N. College Ave.
Claremont, CA 91711
714 625-8767
85 acres, California native plants, demonstration gardens

Santa Barbara Botanic Garden
1212 Mission Canyon Road
Santa Barbara, CA 93105
805 682-4726
65 acres, California native plants, demonstration garden

South Coast Botanical Garden
26300 Crenshaw Blvd.
Palos Verdes Peninsula, CA 90274
213 544-6815
87 acres, many gardens, demonstration gardens

Theodore Payne Foundation for Wildflowers and Native Plants
10459 Tuxford St.
Sun Valley, CA 91352
818 768-1802
21 acres of gardens and a retail nursery

Nevada

Desert Demonstration Garden
3701 Alta Dr.

c/o Las Vegas Valley Water District
3700 West Charleston
Las Vegas, NV 89153
702 258-3205
2½ acres, low-water demonstration garden

Ethel M Botanic Garden
2 Cactus Garden Dr.
Henderson, NV 89014
702 458-8864
2 acres, dry-climate garden

University of Nevada Las Vegas Arboretum
4505 Maryland Parkway
Las Vegas, NV 89154
702 739-3392
On-campus displays and xeriscape demonstration garden

New Mexico

Albuquerque Garden Center
10120 Lomas Blvd. N.E.
P.O. Box 3065
Albuquerque, NM 87190
505 296-6020
Landscaped garden, many services for gardeners

Albuquerque Xeriscape Garden
Osuna and Wyoming N.E.
Albuquerque, NM
505 857-8650
Demonstration garden

Bosque del Apache National Wildlife Refuge Visitor's Center
P.O. Box 1246
Socorro, NM 87801
505 835-1828
Landscape with native plants

Living Desert Zoological & Botanical State Park
1504 Skyline Dr.
Carlsbad, NM 88220
505 887-5516 ·
Chihuahuan Desert plants in native setting

Texas

Cactus Gardens
Judge Roy Bean Visitor's Center
Langtry, TX
915 291-3340
Native trees, shrubs, cacti

Chamizal National Memorial
800 South San Marcial St.
El Paso, TX 79905
915 534-6668
549 acres, traditional Spanish colonial garden

Chihuahua Desert Visitor's Center
P.O. Box 1334
Texas Highway 118 (north of Alpine)
Alpine, TX 79831
915 837-8370
Desert gardens

Texas A & M Experiment Station
1380 A & M Circle
El Paso, TX 79927
915 859-9111
Xeriscape garden

Wilderness Park Museum
4301 Woodrow Bean–Transmountain Road
El Paso, TX 79924
915 755-4332
Chihuahuan Desert garden

References

Happily, the number of books about regional gardening has increased in recent years. The advantage of a regional approach is that you share with the author climate and growing conditions as well as the gardening bug. The following books are, with a few exceptions, regional in scope. Available in bookstores, mail-order catalogs, or the library, they will make a valuable supplement to your basic gardening texts. In addition, contact your state extension service for a list of the many informative books and pamphlets they publish.

Barton, Barbara J. *Gardening by Mail: A Source Book*. Boston: Houghton Mifflin, 1990.

Connelly, Kevin. *Gardener's Guide to California Wildflowers*. Sun Valley, Calif.: Theodore Payne Foundation (10459 Tuxford St., Sun Valley, 91325), 1991.

Dinchak, Ronald K. *An Illustrated Guide to Landscape Shrubs of Southern Arizona*. Mesa, Ariz.: 3D Publishers (1738 S. Cholla Ave., Mesa 85202).

———. *An Illustrated Guide to Landscape Trees of Southern Arizona*. Mesa, Ariz.: 3D Publishers (1738 S. Cholla Ave., Mesa 85202).

Dourley, John, and Lee Lenz. *California Native Trees and Shrubs for Garden and Environmental Use in Southern California and Adjacent Areas*. Claremont, Calif.: Rancho Santa Ana Botanic Garden, 1981.

Duffield, Mary R., and Warren D. Jones. *Plants for Dry Climates: How to Select, Grow and Enjoy*. Los Angeles: HP Books, 1981.

Johnson, Eric. *Landscaping to Save Water in the Desert*. Palm Desert, Calif.: Eric A. Johnson (74-228 Angels Camp Rd., Palm Desert 91325), 1989.

Johnson, Eric A., and Scott Millard. *Beautiful Gardens: Guide to Over 80 Botanical Gardens, Arboretums and More in Southern California and the Southwest*. Tucson, Ariz.: Ironwood Press (2968 W. Ina Rd., #285, Tucson 85741), 1991.

Keator, Glenn. *Complete Garden Guide to the Native Perennials of California*. San Francisco: Chronicle Books, 1990.

McPherson, E. Gregory, and Charles M. Sacamano. *Southwestern Landscaping That Saves Energy and Water,* Extension Publication 8929. Tucson, Ariz.: Office of Agricultural Sciences Communications (715 N. Park Ave., Tucson 85719).

Natural Vegetation Committee-SCSA, Arizona chapter. *Landscaping with Native Arizona Plants*. Tucson, Ariz.: University of Arizona Press, 1985.

Nokes, Jill. *How to Grow Native Plants of Texas and the Southwest*. Houston: Pacesetter Press, 1986.

Ortho Books. *Gardening in Dry Climates*. San Ramon, Calif.: Ortho Books, 1989.

Perry, Bob. *Trees and Shrubs for Dry California Landscapes*. Claremont, Calif.: Land Design Publications (P.O. Box 68, Claremont 91711), 1981.

Phillips, Judith. *Southwestern Landscaping with Native Plants*. Santa Fe, N.M.: Museum of New Mexico Press, 1987.

Schmidt, Marjorie G. *Growing California Native Plants*. Berkeley: University of California Press, 1980.

Smaus, Robert. *Los Angeles Times California Gardening*. New York: Harry Abrams, 1983.

———. *Los Angeles Times Planning and Planting the Garden*. New York: Harry Abrams, 1990.

Sunset Magazine. *Sunset's New Western Garden Book*. Menlo Park, Calif.: Sunset-Lane, 1988.

———. *Waterwise Gardening: Beautiful Gardens with Less Water*. Menlo Park, Calif.: Sunset-Lane, 1989.

Taylor's Guide to Water Saving Gardening. Boston: Houghton Mifflin, 1990.

Wasowski, Sally, and Julie Ryan. *Landscaping with Native Texas Plants*. Houston: Texas Monthly Press, 1985.

Wasowski, Sally, and Andy Wasowski. *Native Texas Plants: Landscaping Region by Region*. Houston: Pacesetter Press, 1988.

Photo Credits

John E. Bryan, Inc.
95B, 104B

Rita Buchanan
97B, 105B, 120B, 121A, 123B, 138A, 138B, 139A, 169B, 176A, 180A, 183B, 204B, 208B

Gay Bumgarner: PHOTO/NATS
109A

David Cavagnaro
80A, 84B, 88A, 88B, 93B, 110B, 125A, 127A, 131A, 134A, 135B, 140A, 152A, 161A, 170B, 198B, 200B, 214B

Michael A. Dirr
81B, 86B, 101B

John E. Elsley
194A

Thomas E. Eltzroth
78A, 81A, 82B, 85A, 86A, 90A, 90B, 91A, 92A, 93A, 94A, 95A, 98A, 102A, 103A, 105A, 108A, 111A, 112A, 114B, 115A, 119B, 121B, 122B, 123A, 124A, 129A, 132B, 137B, 147A, 153A, 155B, 162A, 163A, 173B, 177B, 179B, 195B, 196A, 202B, 205A, 210B, 212A

Derek Fell
78B, 96A, 97A, 109B, 110A, 113A, 115B, 116, 143A, 144A, 145B, 149B, 175A, 190B, 191A, 192A, 198A

Charles Marden Fitch
142A, 147B, 148B, 150A, 170A, 196B, 202A, 204A, 211B

Pamela Harper
79B, 80B, 83B, 85B, 87A, 89B, 96B, 100A, 101A, 102B, 104A, 106A, 107B, 108B, 112B, 119A, 122A, 124B, 125B, 128A, 128B, 129B, 131B, 132A, 133B, 134B, 136A, 139B, 140B,

141B, 143B, 144B, 145A, 146A, 146B, 148A, 149A, 150B, 151A, 152B, 153B, 154A, 154B, 155A, 158A, 158B, 159A, 162B, 163B, 165B, 166A, 167B, 168B, 169A, 171B, 172A, 172B, 174A, 174B, 176B, 177A, 179A, 181A, 181B, 182A, 184A, 185A, 185B, 187A, 192B, 193B, 197A, 197B, 199A, 199B, 201A, 201B, 208A, 209A, 212B, 215A, 215B, 216A, 216B

Robert E. Heapes
195A

Saxon Holt
135A, 180B, 183A, 186B, 188, 193A

Horticultural Photography, Corvallis, Oregon
79A, 84A, 87B, 98B, 99A, 100B, 103B, 190A

Philip E. Keenan
94B

Robert E. Lyons: PHOTO/NATS
161B, 171A

Charles Mann
76, 83A, 99B, 126A, 133A, 156, 160B, 173A, 178B, 182B, 186A, 187B, 206

Robert F. McDuffie: PHOTO/NATS
167A

Frederick McGourty
178A, 200A

Scott Millard
91B, 114A, 118B, 130B, 141A, 194B

Monrovia Nursery Co.
107A, 127B

Suzi Moore
130A, 160A

Terrence Moore
106B, 159B

Jennie Plumley: PHOTO/NATS
118A

Index

Numbers in **boldface** *type refer to pages on which color plates appear*